The Promise Keepers

The Promise Keepers

Servants, Soldiers, and Godly Men

JOHN P. BARTKOWSKI

RUTGERS UNIVERSITY PRESS
New Brunswick, New Jersey, and London

Library of Congress Cataloging-in-Publication Data

Bartkowski, John P., 1966–
    The Promise Keepers : servants, soldiers, and godly men / John P.
Bartkowski
        p. cm
    Includes bibliographical references and index.
    ISBN 0–8135–3335–X (alk. paper)—ISBN 0–8135–3336–8 (pbk. : alk.
paper)
    1. Promise Keepers (Organization) I. Title.
BV960 .B37 2003
267'.23—dc21

                                                        2003009689

British Cataloging-in-Publication data record for this book is available from
the British Library.

Portions of chapter 3 are reprinted with permission and first appeared in
John P. Bartkowski's essay "Godly Masculinities Require Gender and Power,"
Standing on the Promises: The Promise Keepers and the Revival of Manhood,
Dane S. Claussen, ed. (Cleveland: The Pilgrim Press, 1999), 121–130. Copyright © 1999 Dane S. Claussen.

Portions of chapter 3 also appeared in 2001 in John P. Bartkowski's essay
"Godly Masculinities: Gender Discourse among the Promise Keepers." *Social Thought & Research* 24 (1& 2): 53–88.

Portions of chapters 3 and 5 are reprinted with permission and first appeared in 2000 in John P. Bartkowski's essay "Breaking Walls, Raising Fences:
Masculinity, Intimacy, and Accountability among the Promise Keepers." Sociology of Religion (vol. 61, no. 1, 33–53).

*For all of us struggling
to keep our promises*

Two Errors: 1. to take everything literally, 2. to take everything spiritually.

—Pascal, Pensées

BODY PIERCING SAVED MY LIFE
—T-shirt worn by Promise Keeper
man at 1999 PK Conference

Do I contradict myself? Very well, then, I contradict myself. I am large, I contain multitudes.
—Walt Whitman, "Song of Myself"

Yahweh goes forth like a soldier, like a warrior he stirs up his fury; he cries out, he shouts aloud, he shows himself mighty against his foes. For a long time I have held my peace, I have kept still and restrained myself; now I will cry out like a woman in labor, I will gasp and pant.
—Isaiah 42:13–14

Contents

Acknowledgments

When a new book arrives in my mailbox, my first order of business is to crack open the volume to the acknowledgments section. In my view, as much can be determined about a monograph and its author from the people who are thanked in its acknowledgments as from those who appear in its bibliography. Although there is no formal record kept of debts laid bare in an acknowledgments section, the influence of those named is typically substantial. I wish to recognize my many debts here, and hope that I have not overlooked anyone's contribution.

This volume would not have been possible without the openness and candor of the Promise Keeper men whose viewpoints and experiences are the subject of this book. My heartfelt thanks go to the men who participated in this inquiry. They have sought to demonstrate the influence of faith on so much of what is vital in life, and I have learned a great deal from them. Where I analyze and, at times, disagree with their viewpoints, I strive to do so in a respectful manner. It is my hope that the stories rendered in this volume complicate academic and popular perceptions of conservative Christian men that have tended to be one-dimensional and pejorative.

I am grateful to my family, Nicci, Stephen, and Christine, all of whom exhibited patience and encouragement from the research phase of this study to its write-up in this volume. They accompanied me in research-related travel, and memories from those trips will remain with me. I could not imagine having completed this book without the love and support of my wife, Nicci. Our relationship has taught me the value of keeping promises. My thanks to my parents for teaching me the importance of education, intellectual pursuit, and so many other of life's lessons. This book is very much a product of the values they taught me. Kent and Carole McIntire, my in-laws, have shown an enduring interest in my work. Their warmth and support have been indispensable.

This study would not have been possible without funding from the Rural Health, Safety, and Security Institute, as well as the Criss Fund, Research Initiation Program, and Department of Sociology, Anthropology, & Social Work—all at Mississippi State University. The Louisville Institute provided a summer stipend to facilitate the writing of this book. James Lewis and others at the Louisville Institute's 1999 Winter Seminar provided insightful and indispensable feedback. My colleagues never failed to provide encouragement. I am especially thankful to Louis Bluhm, Arthur Cosby, Adele Crudden, Frank Howell, Matthew Lee, Martin Levin, and Karen Woodrow-Lafield, and to Xiaohe Xu. Martin Levin made my trip to the San Antonio PK conference possible with departmental support. Suzanne McClain's transcribing expertise was greatly appreciated. At the University of Texas, I am grateful to Christopher Ellison.

Within the wider academic world, my debts are manifold. Sally Gallagher and Michael Emerson both reviewed an earlier generation of this manuscript when it was a mere prospectus accompanied by a few sample chapters. Together with David Myers (then editor at Rutgers), they saved this volume from becoming an obscure investigation fraught with opaque terminology more appropriate for journal articles than for a monograph. It is quite rare that the review process works this well. Their comments (with Sally Gallagher serving twice as reader) brought about a book that needed to be written about the Promise Keepers, one quite different from the one I had initially envisioned. This book would not have come to fruition without their incisive remarks. Kristi Long took over as my editor at Rutgers while the book was being written. I pay her tribute in saying that I could not imagine a smoother editorial transition. My thanks to Kristi and to Adi Hovav at Rutgers for their energy and support.

Ongoing conversations with Nancy Ammerman and Stephen Warner about religious culture were also quite helpful. Their work on congregations and religious identity, as well as their longstanding commitment to ethnography, have been an inspiration. That influence is readily apparent here. I have benefited similarly from the work and thoughtful remarks of Meredith McGuire. Many thanks to Brad Wilcox for reviewing an earlier, more succinct draft of this work for a conference, and for pointing out the fruitfulness of examining PK boundary work. Discussions with David Yamane were especially helpful in pulling me through the home stretch of writing. David suggested the concluding chapter's title. He also provided sage advice that (as any author knows) is as truthful as it is humorous: "Just keep writing, the ideas will come." I greatly value the friendship shown by both Brad and David.

Thanks are also due to Kristin Anderson, Bob Connell, Kirsten Dellinger, Melinda Denton, Penny Edgell, Brent Elwood, Edith Elwood, Sean Everton, Roger Finke, Louis Fisher, John Hoffmann, Larry Iannaccone, William Lockhart, Dale McConkey, Daniel Rigney, Christian Smith, Anthony Stevens–Arroyo, Joseph Tamney, Charles Tolbert, Rhys Williams, Alan Wolfe, and Robert Woodberry for comments and chats—some quite brief, others more extensive—that bore meaningfully on the subjects treated here. Public lectures based on this work were delivered to the Women's Studies faculties at Mississippi State University and the University of Mississippi, among other audiences. These debts notwithstanding, I take full responsibility for the portrait rendered here.

The Promise Keepers

1 | The Rise and Fall of the Christian Men's Movement

"Remember the Promise Keepers?" So queried a summer 2000 *Boston Globe* article[1] on the evangelical men's movement that had captured America's imagination and generated intense controversy during much of the 1990s. This is indeed a valid question. From today's vantage point, the final decade of the twentieth century seems like eons ago. During the 1990s, the economy boomed. Enron and WorldCom were considered model corporations. Southwestern art broke out from New Mexico to grace fashionable homes nationwide. Then-President Bill Clinton was impeached. Homeland security and Al Qaeda were not yet part of the American vocabulary. And, all those years ago, a Christian men's movement named the Promise Keepers emerged from the obscurity of a small 1991 gathering of around four thousand men at its first conference in Colorado to fill stadiums and, a scant six years later, the National Mall in Washington, D.C. "PK," as it was commonly called, became the most popular in a long line of men's movements that had flourished during the last two decades of our nation's history. Now, just a few years past that triumphant march, this very same organization is haunted by questions of remembrance.

It is undoubtedly premature to pen an obituary for the Promise Keepers. Nevertheless, the movement has seen some phenomenal changes in its fortunes during the past few years. Many point to October 1997 as the movement's finest hour. It was then that an estimated

600,000 to 800,000 men from across the country gathered on the National Mall to offer somber prayers, sing manly hymns, and most famously, share tearful embraces. Coming two years after Louis Farrakhan's Million Man March, PK's October 1997 "Stand in the Gap: A Sacred Assembly of Men" was covered extensively by the press (see Waters 2000). And the vast majority of the coverage given to this event, and to PK in general, was quite favorable (see Claussen 1999, 2000; Waters 2000). PK was a media darling from the moment the press picked up on the group beginning in 1993. In fact, the Religion Newswriters Association dubbed the Promise Keepers' march on the National Mall the second most newsworthy story on religion in 1997 (Vara 1998). In what now seems rather an ironic twist, Stand in the Gap had been beaten out as the most newsworthy religion story by the death of one lone religious woman—Mother Teresa. Nevertheless, those were heady times for PK supporters. Many wondered—some privately, others publicly—if the movement was ushering in a sort of Third Great Awakening that would outshine religious revivals of centuries gone by.

Yet, soon thereafter, those who viewed the meteoric rise of PK as evidence of a spiritual revival among American men were shocked by a series of disappointing developments. A scant four months after Stand in the Gap, the organization laid off its entire office staff because of its dwindling finances. Armed with the catchy slogan, "Open the gates in '98!" PK had decided to drop its conference admission fee of sixty dollars at more than a dozen venues across the nation. The donation-only strategy of fundraising was designed to attract a more economically and racially diverse group of men to PK conferences. PK had long promoted reconciliation among men from different racial, socioeconomic, and denominational backgrounds under the banner, "Break Down the Walls." Yet, the most significant breaking that took place in 1998 was of the financial sort. With more than seventy percent of the organization's budget drawn from stadium conference attendance (Claussen 1999; Culver 1997) and with a dearth of strategies for alternative fund-raising options, the Promise Keepers watched their financial solvency erode. The group quickly became notorious for this gross miscalculation. The layoff was widely reported in such prominent press outlets as the *New York Times*, *Washington Post*, and *USA Today*, among others (*Baltimore Sun* 1998; Kenworthy 1998; O'Driscoll 1998; Murphy 1998; Niebuhr 1998). Many headlines and articles minced no words. One was especially pointed: "Promise Keepers Needs Cash" (*Columbus Dispatch* 1998). Even more embarrassingly, the decision to "open the gates in '98" did not produce the desired results—in 1998 or, for that matter, in 1999. Despite free admission to conferences during this two-year period, attendance flagged and the demographics of participants at these events did not seem to change significantly (Claussen 1999; Farhat 1999; Finnigan 1998; Hogan-Albach 1998; Lundskow 2002: 3).

The cancellation of its long-planned millennial march was another telltale sign of the organization's decline. Dubbed "Hope for a New Millennium: Light the Night," this event was billed as the follow-up march to Stand in the Gap, and it had been introduced to PK faithful there on the National Mall in 1997. The goal was ambitious—have PK men across America descend on capitol buildings in each of the fifty states at midnight on January 1, 2000 (Culver 1999a; McCrimmon 1999). This "Y2K" reprise to 1997's Stand in the Gap was anticipated to lend even more visibility to the movement. It was expected that the droves of men who united on the National Mall for Stand in the Gap would take the movement to the next level by fanning out in a state-by-state demonstration underscoring how global solidarity can give rise to local empowerment. Thus, Light the Night was intended to pair geographical dispersion with spiritual unity. Yet, by early April 1999, the millennial march fell prey to the Y2K bug. Discretion apparently being the better part of valor, PK leaders told men to remain home with their families to face what was expected to be a precarious transition to the new millennium (*Boston Globe* 1999; Fong 1999; *St. Louis Post-Dispatch* 1999). Although the Promise Keepers were not alone in wrongly anticipating the myriad threats to public safety that never materialized on January 1, 2000, critics were quick to point to a discernible pattern. PK showed all the signs of a movement in decline. Even to those who did not want to acknowledge as much, the evidence was mounting fast.

The organization lost much of its newsworthiness soon after laying off its staff and canceling its millennial march. In the blink of an eye, the high-profile media attention PK once enjoyed had evaporated. Gone was coverage of massive PK stadium conferences and the personal testimonials of lives changed that had graced the covers and feature stories of all the nation's top weekly news magazines. And front-page headlines captured so effectively by the group suddenly became a distant memory. Those left scratching their heads over diminished news coverage needed only a quick glance at the numbers to see the writing on the wall. The Promise Keepers' annual budget dwindled from $117 million in 1997 to $34 million in 2001, and its surviving office staff of one hundred—those rehired after the layoff—was a skeleton crew when compared with the veritable army of three hundred and fifty that it employed during its heyday (*Chattanooga Times* 2001a, 2001b; Niebuhr 2001; Rivera 2001; Tubbs 2002).

More convincing yet, the organization's stadium gate draw became a mere shadow of its former self. Once able to attract more than 50,000 men to each of around twenty football stadiums during its "conference season," the movement shifted to the more modest goal of filling convention halls and civic centers of about 15,000 (Maraghy 2001; Rivera 2001; Wall 2000; White 2000). One of the more striking examples of the drought in attendance was found in Minneapolis. PK attracted 62,000 men to the Metrodome in 1995, but could muster only 16,000 men at Minneapolis's much smaller Target Center in 2000 (Drew 2000). Similar drops in attendance occurred in other repeat venues throughout the nation, including Atlanta, Baltimore, Milwaukee, Memphis, and Jacksonville. Whereas PK conference attendance topped one million in 1996, conference season totals dropped to 300,000 in 2000 and to 207,000 in 2001 (*Chattanooga Times* 2001a; Niebuhr 2001; Tubbs 2002). Given PK's fallen stock and humbled stature, the organization's conference series was no longer being "shadowed" from one venue to the next by large groups of feminist and gay rights protesters. A lack of protesters at PK events may have been the most damning sign of all. A movement would seem to be on the ropes when even its most dogged critics abandon it as unworthy of their protest.

Resurrection? Recent Efforts to Revive PK

For their part, the Promise Keepers have not resigned themselves to being dismissed as yesterday's news. When questioned about their drastically diminished revenues and less impressive membership rolls, PK spokesman Steve Chavis glibly asserted that the group is merely letting "the soil rest" before reinitiating its harvest of men's souls (Associated Press 2000). Chavis pointed to the fact that PK had attracted nearly five million men in just over ten years of conferences, and boasted: "That's 5 million down, 95 million to go" (White 2000). Other spokesmen adopted a more forthright—even contrite—tone. One leader described the group's well-publicized financial woes and staff layoff as its "puberty era" (Maraghy 2001). Such images suggest that PK has "grown up" from a gangly revivalist movement to a more mature men's ministry. Still others have sought simply to downscale expectations. Tru Nguyen, the organization's Director of U.S.

Ministries, painted the Promise Keepers as a front-line crusade whose primary goal has always been to serve as a "starting point" for channeling converted men into local churches (Drew 2000). According to this logic, once the baton has been passed to local churches, observers should not expect to see PK tally the same numbers in fund-raising or conference attendance they had before.

Yet, this last explanation is confounded by antiestablishment tendencies that surface now and again in the group. Oftentimes, the Promise Keepers' appraisal of institutionalized religion has been less than sanguine, and its stance toward Christian churches seemingly more critical than collaborative. The terrorist attacks on September 11, 2001 prompted PK founder Bill McCartney to criticize the business-as-usual demeanor of Christian churches: "When our nation declared war [on terrorism], the church needed to do the same [by declaring a war for souls]. But my sense is that when President Bush said go back to normal, the church said, 'Oh, OK.' And churches are now in danger of not recognizing the day we live in and [are] in danger of missing the window of opportunity we have" (Clarke 2001). Still, when summing up the movement's past fortunes and anticipating its future, McCartney blended critical rhetoric with a more conciliatory tone: "In 12 years, we have held 140 stadium and arena events, reaching 4.8 million men. Yet our focus has never changed. We're still keeping promises, one man at a time" (Ritchie 2002). McCartney recently resigned from his position as president of PK to care for his ailing wife, thereby casting additional uncertainty on the group's future.

More compelling than such rhetorical maneuvering are PK's practical efforts to reinvent itself in recent years. The form and substance of PK conferences has changed in significant ways. Increasingly, two-day conferences have been replaced by more modest one-day events. And live dramatic performances, including a reenactment of Jesus Christ's cross-bearing walk to Calvary, have been used recently to breathe new life into local PK conferences. In contrast to the glitzy high-tech conferences of years past, recent events have taken on a more earthy, traditionally evangelical feel.

This is not to say that PK has suddenly become a technophobic organization. PK continues to redefine the very notion of "electronic church," a phrase sociologists first used in the 1980s to describe the phenomenal growth of Christian radio and televangelism. Information technology has come a long way since the 1980s. Never the Luddite, PK continues to use all of the latest technological media to their best advantage. PK conferences are now commonly broadcast live over the internet through the group's use of webcast technology. PK's website (*www.promisekeepers.org*) features a "myPK" link that, among its other features, can connect individual Promise Keepers with their brothers in the "PK Online Community." And, during his tenure as president, PK founder McCartney used an array of electronic media to reach American men. McCartney's popular three-minute "4th and Goal" radio broadcast, carried by nearly five hundred local radio stations at its peak, was supported by a companion website (*www.4thandgoal.org*) as well as an e-mail distribution list. The Promise Keepers even offer a filtered internet service provider, "*pkFamily.com,*" and its own "internet accountability software" called "Eye Promise"—the latter with a catchy, panoptic "eye" logo that helps men to feel as if they are under the caring yet watchful gaze of the group as they surf the web. A host of local Promise Keeper faithful have followed suit by constructing their own websites at which they pay homage to the group and its influence on their lives. At many such sites, old-time religion meets high-tech spirituality.

Alongside such efforts, the Promise Keepers have also sought to broaden their target constituency in noteworthy ways. In 2001, PK began sponsoring a youth ministry series called Passage, complete with conferences aimed at young evangelical males (*Chattanooga Times* 2001b; Mahoney 2001; Moss 2001). PK described this cohort of young evangelicals as "The Next Warriors For Christ," and provided the hip admonishment, "THIS AIN'T YOUR *DADDY'S* PK!" Passage events featured big-name Christian musical artists, such as Michael W. Smith and the Katinas, who are widely popular among evangelical youth. Not to be dismissed as out of touch with today's youth culture, Passage's supporting websites (*www.passage2001.com, www.passage2002.com*) featured pictures of teen surfers and skateboarders alongside Bible-reading adolescent boys. Passage conferences also featured young Christian athletes—a new generation of Muscular Christians, it would seem—performing extreme sports to pulsating but sanitized tunes that resembled the emergent genre of "ska music" sweeping through American teendom. The climax of every Passage conference was the pairing up of each teen boy with an adult male mentor. Like accountability partnerships that were formed in their "Daddy's PK," the expectation was that this mentor–protégé relationship would last well beyond the event itself. The Promise Keepers' new emphasis on youth ministry was presaged by the 2001 eighteen-city conference series, "Turn the

Tide: Living Out an Extreme Faith," which melded a biblical reference to promoting social change through Christian living (Romans 12:2) with the concept of "extreme sports" popular among young people today (Anderson 2001; Niebuhr 2001). Passage conferences were touted as an "in-your-face experience." Balancing their antiestablishment orientation with respect for competing forms of youth ministry, PK leaders were quick to emphasize that Passage was not aimed at supplanting more traditional church-run ministries or male youth groups such as the Boy Scouts (Moss 2001). Notably, however, PK had decided to discontinue Passage events with the resignation of founder McCartney.

The Promise Keepers have also broadened their reach beyond U.S. borders through Promise Keepers International (PKI). PKI hosts "International Summits" designed to unite evangelical Christians from around the world in brotherly prayer and worship. These summits are translated into no fewer than seven languages, are enlivened with world music (albeit from a Christian perspective), and feature "presentations from representatives of nations from every continent, including Messianic Rabbis, Pastors from Africa, Asia, Latin America and Europe" (*www.pk-intl.com/summit.htm*). By 2002, PKI had been established in nine countries, including Canada, Germany, New Zealand, South Africa, Sweden, the United Kingdom, and other European nations. And, true to form, several of these PKI chapters have their own websites.

PKI extends the group's longstanding engagement with cultural diversity. PK was criticized early on for having a disproportionately low number of racial minorities on its staff and for its failure to attract men of color despite its stated emphasis on racial reconciliation (see Allen 2001; Diamond 1998; Hawkins 2000; Jones and Lockhart 1999). Even McCartney himself, grandfather of two multiracial children, had previously acknowledged the group's failure on this front (Culver 1999b). However, in the last few years, the movement has begun to offer a more culturally diverse slate of speakers and is guided by a more genuinely multiracial cadre of leaders (Dujardin 2001; Rivera 2001). PKI is designed to take PK's multicultural brand of evangelicalism to the next level by broadening its base to include born-again Christians from outside the United States.

Polarized Perspectives: Promise Keeper Apologists and Detractors

As the Promise Keepers' popularity increased, the movement became the subject of journalistic investigations, social commentary, and scholarly analysis. Observers were unanimous in recognizing that PK was striking a chord with American men. How else could the full stadiums and rapid growth of the movement be explained? Yet, two distinct camps quickly formed over the broader interpretation of these developments—apologists in one corner, detractors in the other. Thus, religious studies scholar Randall Balmer (2000a: 1) correctly dubbed Promise Keepers "the Rorschach test of the 1990s. Analysts of every stripe—and there was no shortage of analysts—saw in this men's mass movement almost anything, or at least whatever they wanted to see" (see also Williams 2001).

The apologists struck the first blow. Many media outlets provided glowing coverage of PK as it rose to prominence. Communications scholar Dane Claussen (2000) astutely observed that media coverage of the Promise Keepers was "more like advertising" than reporting. The recipe was simple: (1) Report that a Promise Keepers' event was going to take place or had recently taken place in a local area. (2) Summarize PK's stated purpose and the substance of its message as articulated by the movement's leading spokesmen. Use colorful quotes as space permits. (3) Provide examples of the organization's effect on men who attend its events, with special attention to dramatic and touching conversion stories of lives renewed and family commitments revivified. (4) Relegate the presence and views of protesters to somewhere in the final third of the article, doing so only as space permits. As such, a great deal of media coverage bordered on promotional apologias for the movement, rather than a more evenhanded analysis of it. From a public relations standpoint, PK had far "outspun" the National Organization for Women and the gay rights groups who, respectively, protested its advocacy of male family leadership and its opposition to homosexuality (Kelley 2000; Waters 2000).

Apologists surfaced in other forums as well. The very first book published on the Promise Keepers, Ken Abraham's *Who Are the Promise Keepers? Understanding the Christian Men's Movement* (1997), is emblematic of the apologist camp. At first glance, Abraham's treatise appears to be a journalistic investigation aimed at identifying the "real story" behind the group's emergence and appeal. The promotional information on the volume's dust jacket describes Abraham as "the eyes and ears of an inquisitive person who wonders what [Promise Keepers] is all about." But readers are quick to realize that this book cannot be judged by its cover—or, for that matter, its dust jacket. To be sure, Abraham (1997: 203) shows a healthy skepticism toward the group at some points, particularly when discussing his "exasperation with the Promise Keepers hierarchy" and his frustration with the "paranoia" of PK "gate keepers" who have sought to "manage" the organization's image.

Yet, Abraham's "report" on the group is otherwise glowing. Recounting the lives transformed, the number of staff persons employed, and the budget commanded by the group in the middle of the 1990s, Abraham (1997: 7) remarks that the "sheer numbers are impressive." This group is no "religious flash in the pan," says Abraham (1997: 31). Rather, PK is a "spiritual power-saw" that cuts through today's "politically correct cultural climate" and instead "return[s] to time-honored concepts of manhood" (Abraham 1997: 15). The group is said to be fully self-disclosing about its finances and is careful to respect union guidelines when securing stadium workers to stage its events (Abraham 1997: 7–8). Perhaps most tellingly, Abraham portrays the Promise Keepers as unambiguously healthy for men in physical, psychological, and spiritual terms (1997: 1–2, 5, 14–15, 22, 47–48, 70–72, 82–84); uniformly good for families (21, 57–64, 86–87, 92, 113–114, 117) and for society at large (13–14; 78–80); inclusive of Christians of various stripes (11, 73–77, 145–150); and unflinchingly committed to racial and cultural diversity (3–4, 11–12, 19, 24, 73–77, 93, 97).

In a rather moving account, Abraham describes the point at which a PK stadium conference at Pittsburgh's Three Rivers Stadium

> drew to a close . . . with a low-key appeal for men who wanted God to change them—and make them into better husbands, fathers, and brothers—to come to the staging area to pray. The spontaneous outpouring of men flowing onto the tarp surprised even experienced Promise Keepers staff members . . . Men began to kneel on the tarp, faces to the floor, weeping and calling out to God. . . . Rather than ending in a round of "Let's go take on the world!" hype and hoopla, the Pittsburgh conference ended in a holy, reverent hush, sending the men back to their hometowns and families, ready to roll up their sleeves and make positive changes in their primary relationships and in the world. One usually sardonic reporter in the press box turned to another writer who had been skeptical of Promise Keepers at the outset and said simply, "This is God." The second man was me.

If such turns of phrase leave readers wondering about the perma-

nence of the author's changed views, visual depictions in this apologia
clarify matters. Every chapter in the volume and each of the Seven
Promises discussed in chapters 3–5 is flanked by an artistic rendering of the Christian cross. And a collection of photos situated between
pages 116 and 117 of *Who Are the Promise Keepers?* features stadium
scenes of jubilant cheering, tearful hugs, quiet reflection, racial reconciliation, and men's public pronouncements of affection for their
mates through a series of placards reading "W–E L–O–V–E R
W–I–V–E–S." Hence, it is no surprise that by the volume's end,
Abraham (1997: 204) extends the following invitation to his readers:
"Is Promise Keepers for you? I encourage you to look into it. What do
you have to lose? . . . One thing is for sure: You will not encounter
Promise Keepers and come away unaffected. I promise."

How do the characterizations of detractors compare with such sanguine portrayals? The difference, as might be expected, is like night
and day. Rhetorical volleys were traded with regularity in the popular print and electronic media. Thus, favorable news accounts and in-
sider apologias were challenged by outspoken critics who worried about
the authoritarian values and political influence of PK. At the peak of
PK's prominence, the president of the National Organization of Women
(NOW), Patricia Ireland, offered frequent critiques through press re-
leases and public pronouncements. At the same time, NOW tracked
the growth of PK's pernicious influence across America on its website
(*www.now.org*) and urged local chapters to protest at conference venues. In a characteristic statement, Ireland argued: "Promise Keepers
have created a false veneer of men taking responsibility, when they
really mean taking charge. Their targets are women, lesbians, gay men
and anyone who supports abortion rights or opposes an authoritarian,
religiously-based government" (as quoted in Hetherly 1997). Ireland
also criticized PK founder Bill McCartney as a "right-wing extremist,"
while charging that "Promise Keepers check their wives and daughters at the door like coats" to receive the group's promotion of the "submission of women" and "feel-good male supremacy" (as quoted in
Kelley 2000; see Ireland 1997).

In scholarly circles, detractors of the Promise Keepers far outnumbered apologists. No surprise here, given the scholarly penchant for
skepticism and the abundance of antireligious sentiment in academe.
But a careful reading of these critiques reveals that many of them are
as intellectually attenuated as the apologias they provoked. Communications scholar Robert Cole conducted field research at PK confer-

ences and with the movement's accountability groups. His conclusions are far from positive. Cole (2000: 123) charges that PK

> elevates or, better said, reduces masculinity to an "old boys club." PK's club is a digital affair where one either stands with or against and, foremost one is treated as either man or Other . . . one is a Christian man, understood in the evangelical, Biblical-infallibility sense, or one is Other. In PK's version of masculinity, virtually no common ground is found between Christian men and the rest of the world. Presumably, for admittance to this club one shows evidence of a Christian phallus in lieu of a membership card or secret handshake, all the while winking at the shared belief that women are dependency-spawning, feminizing agents of societal destruction against whom the club must rally. To rally men to action, PK warmongers with its own version of a religious jihad. The audience of men is mustered into an army whose commander is Jesus and whose leaders are the clergy. . . . The war to be fought is for the leadership of families and communities, where strong male influence is to be reestablished. No hint of willingness to negotiate roles is found.

Through militaristic metaphors that efface what I call here the paradoxes of promise-keeping (cultural distinction coupled with social engagement), Cole argues that PK is wholly disengaged from the most laudable values at play within contemporary American society—civility, equality, tolerance, and respect.

Karla Hackstaff offers another scholarly critique of the Promise Keepers. In her book, *Marriage in a Culture of Divorce* (1999), Hackstaff chastises PK for "being on the offensive to sustain male authority as well as marriage culture." As evidence, Hackstaff (1999: 164–165) plucks a quote—reprinted ad nauseam by PK critics—from one of the movement's most traditional authors, Tony Evans. It is noteworthy that Hackstaff cites Tony Evans's writings not firsthand, but secondhand as quoted in Michael Messner's (1997) book on men's movements. Evans's now hackneyed words are worth reprinting one more time here to provide some context. In his contribution to *Seven Promises of a Promise Keeper*, Evans tells male readers to "reclaim" their manhood: "I am not suggesting that you *ask* for your role back, I'm urging you to *take it back* . . . .There can be no compromise here. If you're going to lead, you must lead. Be sensitive. Listen. Treat the lady gently and lovingly. But *lead!*" (1994: 79–81; emphasis in original). Hackstaff is right to criticize Evans's overwhelmingly patriarchal tone. She is also correct to express concern about the way in which such language could be used to legitimate a husband's use of coercion and force in the home.

However, Hackstaff employs a number of rhetorical devices in her work that are emblematic of shortsighted criticisms of PK (and American evangelicalism in general). To begin, in using only Evans's words when discussing the Promise Keepers, she insinuates that he accurately represents "the position" of those in the movement. This rhetorical ploy begs serious questions about what social scientists call "representativeness." The issue of representativeness prompts thoughtful observers to ask: "What knowledge about a whole group can be justifiably derived from studying only one of its members?" But this is not a question that some critics of the Promise Keepers, including Hackstaff, are interested in addressing.

Even more disturbingly, the rhetorical ploy of selective quoting does not withstand empirical scrutiny. A great deal of research has shown that there is not one definitive gender ideology articulated by Promise Keeper leaders (Bartkowski 1999, 2001a, 2001b, 2002; Bloch 2001; Lockhart 2001). Indeed, had Hackstaff actually read the *Seven Promises* volume, she would have noticed more democratic, egalitarian views of family life articulated there alongside the more traditional position advocated by Evans. PK author Gary Smalley (1993: 108) asserts that successful families are beholden not to a patriarchal hierarchy but to consensus governance in which each member "agrees, preferably in writing, on a menu of options for quality life and relationships" (see also Bartkowski 2001a for review). Thus, some of PK's most dogmatic critics make the same mistake as apologists—they tell only part of the story, leaving out those aspects of the Promise Keepers that do not fit their argument. The implication drawn by the uninformed reader of such scathing indictments? Given such seemingly uniform patriarchal rhetoric, the foot soldiers in this movement must be thoroughly bent on reclaiming the dominance that they have recently seen erode. End of story.

Finally, there is the problem of representation (which is quite distinct from representativeness). Detractors of PK commonly portray the Promise Keepers as reactionary by eliminating the nuance of Promise Keeper discourse through the use of ellipses. Three strategically placed dots (". . .") can be a crucial ally in rendering the portrait a scholar wishes to paint about a person or group. To wit, the portion of Tony

Evans's words that Hackstaff (and Messner) eliminate through the uses of ellipses lend nuance to his otherwise blunt words. In the excised portion of his essay, Evans anticipates—perhaps correctly—that the wife of a delinquent husband will be reluctant to trust her male mate with child care and bill-paying responsibilities, as well as participation in other household tasks, after her years of putting in a "second shift" at home. Thus, after telling men to "take back" their leadership role with "no compromise," Evans suddenly doubles back to adopt a somewhat more compromising tone. Interlaced with his admonitions for women to "give back" family leadership to their men, he concedes that wives might justifiably protect themselves by "handing the reins back slowly" and taking this transition "one step at a time." Such nuance, it seems, makes matters too complicated for the movement's most vocal critics.

PK detractors also jettison other nuance in favor of sensationalism. A careful reading of Evans's work demonstrates that he rejects some aspects of traditional masculinity even as he clearly accepts others. Hegemonic masculinity is defined in part by commanding a sizable wage and parlaying those resources into conspicuous consumption. Yet, Evans admonishes men not to sacrifice their family life in the pursuit of careerist ambition and consumerism (1994: 76–77). And, in contrast to the stoicism of hegemonic masculinity, Evans tells men to display "compassion," "tender feelings," and sensitivity toward "those weaker or less fortunate than themselves" (1994: 78). Regarding marital relationships, he asserts that couples must honor their "commitment to each other"—which, in the singular form, implies that a marriage is defined by a shared commitment rather than divergent roles (1994: 80). Yet, these egalitarian interjections are deftly elided by critics who want to reprint sensationalistic quotes. It is understandable that the overtly patriarchal language of some PK leaders raises red flags for advocates of progressive gender relations. As someone who cares deeply about women's social opportunities and gender equity, I share this concern. Nevertheless, this does not justify scholars' efforts to reduce the messy, complicated perspectives of PK leaders into sensationalist sound bites.

Like other staunch critics of PK, Hackstaff does not stop at misreading popular texts in the movement. Her preconceptions reduce the movement's objectives to the religious reassertion of "male dominance." Although none of the men she interviewed in her otherwise intriguing qualitative study of married couples is actually affiliated with the Promise Keepers, Hackstaff (1999: 178–179) uses the particulars of what she calls a "traditionalist '70's couple" to warn about the danger of religious men's movements like PK:

> When the Promise Keepers urge men to take back their leadership, such gendered patterns are not obscured; they clearly aim to bolster men's manifest power in marriage. . . . Yet, when Promise Keepers urge men to keep commitments—a seemingly benign and de-gendered proposal—they may obscure how latent and invisible power can be maintained through these calls. . . . Latent power means wives . . . must anticipate their husbands' needs ("Yes, dear, anything you want, I understand, it's for your career"). Invisible power is the power hidden in taken-for-granted assumptions about the nature of reality . . . the "natural order." Promise keeping represents power keeping—whether male dominance is explicit or implicit—because marital commitment has historically been on male terms.

Despite the fact that she has no empirical evidence about the actual marriages of Promise Keepers, she accuses the group of consolidating men's power—through both overt and covert means. Such portrayals are as passionate and artful as PK apologias. Yet neither is credible.

Other detractors of the Promise Keepers have painted the movement as the third generation of the "religious right"—a homogenizing term that demands closer inspection. As this criticism goes, the Promise Keepers promote the same reactionary political agenda—in an even more stealthy and insidious form—as the Moral Majority, Eagle Forum, or Concerned Women for America (CWA) during the early 1980s and the Christian Coalition during the early 1990s. Jean Hardisty (1999: 94), a political scientist whose work "monitors anti-democratic movements and trends," describes the Promise Keepers as "a popular and effective addition to the right's infrastructure . . . guided by a literal reading of the Bible." Hardisty (1999: ix) is disturbed by what she calls the "extremism of the religious right." She concedes that "the Christian Right's political agenda is not explicitly promoted at PK rallies" (Hardisty 1999: 94). However, she seems to think that the same insidious form of religious manipulation is at work here. She concludes that "the Promise Keepers serves much the same role as Concerned Women for America in providing a massive pool of recruits to that agenda. But PK uses none of the spiteful rhetoric of CWA. It is a softer, kinder version of Christian Right recruitment" (Hardisty 1999: 94). But it is "recruitment" nonetheless. PK is apparently backward and conservative enough to merit mention in the title of Hardisty's book, *Mobilizing Resentment: Conservative Resurgence from the John Birch Society to the Promise Keepers.* For what a title is worth, the implication is clear: the Promise Keepers can be likened to a modern-day John Birch Society. In some bizarre twist of history, then, *The New American* of Bircher fame has evolved into the *New Man* of PK. (If this pun escapes the uninitiated reader, *The New American* is the John Birch Society's bimonthly periodical while the *New Man* served for a time as the Promise Keepers' official monthly magazine.)

What evidence is there to support the view that the Promise Keepers are merely the most recent vehicle commandeered by the religious Right? It is indeed true that the backbone of the Promise Keepers is evangelical religion. And, to be sure, born-again Christians were at the center of the Moral Majority and the Christian Coalition. Where this criticism goes wrong, however, is in assuming that American evangelicalism is wholly conservative in its political outlook and uniformly reactionary in its cultural orientation (see Bartkowski 2001a; Gallagher 2003; Gallagher and Smith 1999; Quicke and Robinson 2000; Smith 2000 for critiques of this assumption). The Promise Keepers, a revival-style movement, is governed by a loose organizational form rather than a top-down autocratic structure. Moreover, PK is guided by an open-ended set of religious convictions—the Seven Promises—rather than a set of codified theological principles or a body of religious dogma. (As I will argue in this volume's conclusion, these factors likely contributed to the group's rapid demise.) The point is that the Promise Keepers defy tidy typifications that portray them as yet another manifestation of the "religious Right."[2]

Debates about the Promise Keepers themselves have largely receded. But discussions about the overall impact of the group and its place in American evangelicalism are likely to continue for some time. Critics will undoubtedly continue to celebrate any signs of the movement's decline. Apologists will point to the organization's still-popular men's ministries in local congregations, as well as its new efforts to bolster godly manhood among the young and those abroad. Thus, there are those who will charge that rumors of PK's demise have been greatly exaggerated. Such debates and speculation aside, one thing is clear. PK is a religious movement attempting to redefine itself in light of—and, it would seem, in spite of—a glorious past. Today, that past casts a large shadow indeed.

Why This Book? Analyzing American Religion and Culture through the Prism of PK

With PK's glorious past now just a hazy outline in the short American memory, a pressing question surfaces. Why write a book—much less purchase and read a monograph—about a religious movement whose pinnacle of prominence seems to have passed it by? What's more, why is yet another book needed on the Promise Keepers? Two monographs, both initially written as dissertations, have appeared on the movement. Other books on PK were planned and then abandoned—perhaps a tacit acknowledgment of PK's passage into the historical dustbin of American social movements.

Among those books that did come to fruition, Bryan Brickner's (1999) volume, *The Promise Keepers: Politics and Promises*, examines PK largely through the lens of political theory. Bricker construes PK as an organization through which evangelical men cultivate social capital, and he explores the group's influence on men's gender identities. George Lundskow's (2002) *Awakening to an Uncertain Future*, another volume on PK, is centered on explaining the seemingly overwhelming appeal of the Promise Keepers. By his own admission, Lundskow (2002: xi) seeks to address the question: "Why are the Promise Keepers so popular?" More recently, L. Dean Allen (2002) compares PK with a historical predecessor, the Men and Religion Forward movement of the early twentieth century.

All of these volumes provide important insight into men's motivations for joining the Promise Keepers and shed light on a movement at the zenith of its popularity. Yet, all are incomplete in important ways. As noted, the fortunes of the Promise Keepers have changed dramatically in recent years. This turnabout requires serious consideration. To put perhaps too fine a point on it, the obvious rejoinder to Lundskow's impetus for studying the popularity of PK is: "Why *aren't* the Promise Keepers popular any more? What factors have contributed to their demise? What broader insights can be gleaned from the rise and the apparent fall of the movement?"

Given the time at which they entered the publication stream, virtually all previous works on the Promise Keepers have been long on theoretical analyses and interview quotes but quite short on conclusions about the movement and its broader implications. Two of the aforementioned volumes feature concluding chapters that are, well, strikingly inconclusive. Brickner's two-page conclusion, "Mere Thoughts," and

Lundskow's four-page conclusion, "Final Thoughts," share not only a striking similarity in title but also a remarkable brevity. Thus, these monographs add a great deal to our understanding of why men join PK, and how the movement caught on so quickly. But there are several important issues that have yet to be addressed, and broader implications that require scholarly interrogation.

Perhaps most unfortunate in the lack of sustained reflection on the Promise Keepers is the missed opportunity to address the changing place of evangelical men in American society. A wealth of recent studies has illuminated the inner lives and social experiences of evangelical women (Brasher 1998; Griffith 1997; Ingersoll 1995; Manning 1999; Pevey, Williams, and Ellison 1996; Rose 1987; Smith 2000; Stacey 1990; Stacey and Gerard 1990). Taken together, this body of scholarship reveals evangelical women to be thoughtful, articulate, and quite adept at negotiating gender within conservative religious communities. Evangelical women are hardly the victims of "false consciousness." Antireligious academics can no longer claim that women who join conservative religious groups are unwitting accomplices in their own oppression. Yet, despite the consciousness-raising that has taken place in the academy concerning conservative religious women, evangelical men remain largely overlooked. This oversight is likely animated by the unfortunate—and, I argue here, inaccurate—assumption that evangelical men are the arbiters of patriarchy in conservative Protestantism. Highlighting the tactics of resistance employed by the oppressed is more in vogue than studying the strategies of domination used by alleged oppressors. I try to correct that oversight here.

Hence, this volume is concerned not only with understanding the appeal of the Promise Keepers but also with exploring the reasons for its recent decline. With the dust having settled quite a bit since the movement's heyday, I seek to provide a broader and more up-to-date portrait of the movement while evaluating its impact on the landscape of American religion. In this respect, my study is an analysis of organizational growth and decline—and attempted reemergence in the wake of such decline.

Second, this volume aims to provide a more balanced evaluation of the Promise Keepers than those written by the movement's own apologists and its most ardent critics. A balanced appraisal of apologias and critiques is more possible now that the cacophony of voices supporting and opposed to what was once a wildly popular movement have died down to a whisper. By using the word "balance," I do not mean to suggest that my account is disinterested, dispassionate, or objective. I do not believe for a minute that social scientists can treat their subject matter like an "object" (as the term "objectivity" implies). Social scientific research cannot be likened to a geologist analyzing a rock or a biologist a simple organism. I seek to render a balanced appraisal inasmuch as I strive to *balance* two countervailing imperatives of interpretive social research. On the one hand, I provide a sympathetic rendering of PK men's actions, viewpoints, and experiences. In this sense, I take men at their word. Because I treat the men with whom I interacted as knowledgeable agents, I am interested in understanding how they interpret the world, how they describe who they are, and how they explain their motivations. Yet, on the other hand, sociological analysis entails placing these firsthand accounts in a broader cultural context and examining the social forces that bear down upon men. Hence, I do not reduce PK men's views or experiences to isolated, individualized "choices." Men's agency—and, in a broader sense, the collective accomplishment of sport, gender, religion, and race through PK—occurs within a field of structural forces. These forces, which include historical flow, cultural milieu, and life circumstance, are conferred and negotiated rather than simply chosen.

Aside from hoping to make these contributions, I am motivated by an even broader and more ambitious goal. Throughout this volume, I argue that there are many insights to be gained about the changing contours of American religion, culture, and social life by carefully examining the Promise Keepers from their inception to the present day. In this respect, I treat the Promise Keepers as a prism through which an array of social forms—evangelicalism, gender, family, therapeutic culture, sport, and multiculturalism—can be carefully scrutinized. At the same time, I take pains not to ignore structural factors such as economic changes and racial inequality that intersect with new developments in American culture. The prism metaphor is limited inasmuch as the goal here is not to examine these cultural forms as "refracted beams" of social life in isolation from one another. Instead, I hope to explore the intersections, tensions, and dynamic relationships between them as manifested in the movement. A prism can help observers see things anew, and I have no less a goal in mind here. New insights can be gained about religion, culture, and social change in the contemporary United States by carefully examining the character and contagious appeal of the Promise Keepers, as well as its recently flagging fortunes and ongoing efforts at self-reinvention.

Layout of the Volume

Some skeptical readers might question the assertion that new insight into American religion and culture can be gained by examining a single men's movement. Chapter 2 offers a justification for doing so by situating the Promise Keepers in a broader historical and cultural context. The chapter begins by drawing historical parallels between the "age of fraternity" that emerged in the early twentieth century and the men's movements of the present day. I argue that a careful reading of history reveals a series of early twentieth-century forerunners to the Promise Keepers, including men's fraternal organizations and Muscular Christianity. This historical rendering demonstrates that the Promise Keepers are situated in a social milieu that, very much like that of the early twentieth century, is undergoing a dizzying array of changes—what some gender scholars have termed "gender vertigo" (Connell 1995; Risman 1998). Thus, there are many striking parallels to be drawn between men's movements that surfaced at the beginning of the twentieth century and at its end. Yet, despite such parallels, history is not merely repeating itself through the Promise Keepers.

The second portion of chapter 2 reveals that, far from being a historically backward movement or a sign of cultural retrenchment, the Promise Keepers forge new forms of social engagement. Drawing on Christian Smith's subcultural identity theory (Smith et al. 1998; Smith 2000), I show how the Promise Keepers utilize the cultural repertoire of conservative Protestantism—a commitment to biblical authority, Jesus Christ's divinity, and personal conversion—to maintain a relationship of "distinctive engagement" with mainstream American culture. Here, I analyze PK's Seven Promises and reveal how the movement embraces some dimensions of contemporary culture while keeping other aspects of it at arm's length. In many respects, the Promise Keepers move well beyond the tactics employed by their historical predecessors. As a sort of nouveau Muscular Christianity, PK uses such cultural objects as football stadiums and extreme sports to spread the gospel. And, in adopting a paradenominational and multicultural approach to evangelism, PK strikes a nice harmony with many of the defining elements of contemporary American culture—diversity, inclusiveness, and equality. Furthermore, while religion is a master status around which Promise Keepers rally, PK is not solely a religious movement. Taking a cue from Michèle Lamont (1992, 2000; Lamont and Fournier 1992), I reveal how PK engages in other forms of boundary work by renegotiating cultural differences related to race, class, gender, and sexuality. The Promise Keepers also reconfigure the relationship between spirit and body. Drawing on the work of Pitirim Sorokin (1957), I argue that the Promise Keepers deftly weave together sensate and ideational aspects of religious culture. Within PK, and increasingly in evangelical churches throughout America, the lines between spirit and flesh are blurred. This pattern is emblematic of American religion, which chapter 2 reveals has long been as concerned with corporeality and embodiment (the promotion of physical fitness, the bridling of bodily appetites) as with spirituality.

The terms of the Promise Keepers' engagement with mainstream American culture are in many respects laid out by the movement's slate of speakers, many of whom have written tracts on the subject of godly masculinity. In an effort to gain new insight into elite constructions of godly manhood within the movement, chapter 3 examines a select group of advice manuals written by leading Promise Keepers. As it turns out, there is no singular definition of masculinity within PK. Instead, leading authors advance competing archetypes of the godly man. The Rational Patriarch archetype advanced by traditionalist Promise Keepers predates the rise of PK. Yet, by making room for this traditionalist archetype within the movement, the Promise Keepers remain loosely connected with old-guard evangelicals. The Rational Patriarch archetype posits a radical notion of gender difference and advocates a patriarchal family structure, while expressing vocal opposition to feminism and gay rights. Each of the other godly man archetypes evidenced in the writings of leading Promise Keepers reflects the movement's strategic rejoinders to the panoply of men's movements that have sprung up within the past two decades. These post-traditional archetypes (Expressive Egalitarian, Tender Warrior, and Multicultural Man) give the movement a more contemporary flair. The Expressive Egalitarian archetype of godly manhood is the Promise Keeper's counterpart to the men's liberation movement. This liberationist discourse advances a more androgynous conceptualization of gender and champions marital egalitarianism. With a nod toward the mythopoetic men's movement, PK's Tender Warrior archetype aims to sate evangelical men who prefer poeticized visions of the godly man. Works in this genre deploy rich symbolism and complex spiritual metaphors to explore the twin essences of the godly man who is at once strong and sensitive. Finally, the Multicultural Man archetype prominent among a number of PK authors and speakers is centered on the motif of racial reconciliation. This discourse moves away from universalizing archetypes of the godly man and explores the particularities of men's identities and experiences. By offering these multiple depictions of godly manhood and expanding these archetypes beyond a singular focus on gender, elite Promise Keepers seek to provide an elastic portrait of godly manhood capable of appealing to men in diverse life circumstances.

The stadium conference, PK's signature event and the movement's primary means of evangelism, is the focus of chapter 4. There, I provide an inside look at these events and identify the social sources of their transformative power. Part rock concert, part sports event, and part crusade-style religious revival, PK conferences are best understood as syncretic spectacles of godly masculinity.[3] The loud music and raucous cheering at such events is complemented by sustained periods of quiet reflection, tender exchanges between men, and manifestations of masculine gentility. PK conferences create an environment of rowdy respectability in which men can drop their guard and embrace their brotherhood, as well as their brothers. Here, then, is spirit made flesh. Hand-holding, hugging, and altar calls at such events entail flesh-pressing that is reminiscent of victory celebrations in the sports world. Yet, in this venue, victory is defined as winning men for Christ. Where gender issues and family responsibilities are concerned, PK conferences "bargain with patriarchy." Conference rhetoric and activities affirm some aspects of hegemonic masculinity while undermining others. Finally, chapter 4 examines evangelical outreach to the unchurched nonbeliever ("seeker") at these events. To gain a broad following among men from such diverse religious and social backgrounds, PK conferences utilize an array of evangelizing strategies and portray heartfelt conversion as something other than "organized religion." If even those efforts do not suffice, spirituality is made more palatable for men through the adroit mixing of revivalistic sentiment (radical, spontaneous spiritual conversion) with rational deliberation (intentionally chosen religious conviction) at conferences.

Following the exploration of PK cultural production in elite circles and mass events in the two preceding chapters, chapter 5 interrogates the negotiation of godly manhood in the movement's trenches—namely, grassroots accountability groups.[4] Local PK men's encounters are informed by the application of three distinctive tools from the movement's cultural repertoire—accountability, brotherhood, and confession. Within local PK gatherings, these cultural resources are used to negotiate social boundaries and sustain religious conviction. Boundary work within accountability groups enables men to scrutinize their own practices, and those of their fellows, in light of agreed-upon moral standards (accountability); allows men to forge compassionate and companionate ties within other Promise Keepers (brotherhood); and produces a therapeutic culture that gives rise to cathartic emotional exchanges in PK small groups (confession).

One of the most distinctive features of the Promise Keepers has been its emphasis on the formation of these grassroots groups among its members. Accountability groups are intended to complement, channel, and sustain the collective effervescence produced at Promise Keeper stadium conferences. By defining godliness through the twin notions of accountability and integrity, PK men appraise one another's "walk with the Lord" and open themselves up to such scrutiny as well. The edge is taken off such man-to-man monitoring by the PK principle of brotherhood. Fraternal boundaries facilitate a sense of compassion and equality among brothers who, in terms of this imagery, are family. Inasmuch as brotherhood creates manly camaraderie and underscores shared faith convictions, gender identity and religious affiliation emerge as these men's master statuses—often trumping their differences in race, education, occupation, and personal life circumstances. Accountability and brotherhood create a foundation from which these small groups can generate a confessional ethos. PK's confessional culture is characterized by interactions that, while free-flowing, generally conform to a sequence of admission, contrition, and absolution. In this way, accountability groups give new meaning to the Protestant notion of the "priesthood of all believers."

The substantive portion of the volume concludes by examining the ways in which the Promise Keepers address the vexing issue of cultural diversity—particularly, racial difference.[5] Chapter 6 begins by sketching out the complicated relationship between evangelicalism and cultural pluralism. Although evangelicals are actually quite tolerant of cultural and religious diversity (Smith 2000), there remains a color line within this religious subculture (see Emerson and Smith 2000). The evangelical color line is influenced by broader racial divisions in America, as well as by the particular repository of resources within this religious subculture's tool kit. This chapter, then, examines the Promise Keepers' efforts to create a multiracial and, more broadly, multicultural evangelical movement for men. Despite the fact that PK conferences have been overwhelmingly attended by white men, the movement deploys a great deal of multiracial symbolism at these events. I explore these symbolic representations of race and examine conference activities designed to promote racial reconciliation. Then, I recount how PK has caused men to think of race differently in light of their involvement in the movement. In the end, PK's efforts toward racial reconciliation are limited by a reluctance to recognize the structural character of racism in America. The Promise Keepers emphasize racial reconciliation among individuals in hopes of eradicating racism "one soul at a time." Defining racism as a product of personal sinfulness gives men a sense of moral urgency about this problem and encourages them to cultivate meaningful interracial friendships. Yet, at the same time, this individualistic approach to eradicating racism forestalls the pursuit of longer-term structural solutions that might expand social opportunities for marginalized groups in what some call America's "post–Civil Rights era."

The volume's conclusion examines the Promise Keepers' unique contributions to evangelical Protestantism and the religious landscape in the United States. It also returns to reflect on the dramatic changes in American culture that gave rise to the shooting star—burning brightly, then quickly fading—that was the Christian men's movement. To be sure, Promise Keepers was not the first movement of its kind to weave together antinomies in the domains of religion, race, and gender or to reconfigure the relationship between spirit and flesh. But, as evidenced in several of its organizing principles (the Seven Promises) and distinctive social forums (stadium conferences, accountability groups), the Promise Keepers were able to produce a unique and appealing blend of these cultural forms. Ironically, then, this same factor has likely contributed to the organization's demise. The paradoxical goal of eradicating racism and denominationalism "one soul at a time," combined with the unwieldy mix of ideational and sensate cultural forms, contributed not only to PK's meteoric rise but to its equally rapid fragmentation.

2 Situating the Promise Keepers

History, Culture, and Religious Identity

Before diving headlong into the particulars of promise-keeping, some attention must be given to the historical and cultural context from which PK emerged. This chapter begins with a brief historical treatment of social changes that have taken place during the last century, paying special attention to the dramatic transformation of American manhood in the last few decades. Because the overall focus of this volume is contemporary rather than historical, these considerations are treated synoptically here. Thereafter, I distill several important points of connection between the Promise Keepers and contemporary American culture. I argue that PK enlists key tools from American culture, transposing them in a way that supports the evangelical worldview. Finally, I presage the empirical motifs that run through the remaining chapters by outlining the theoretical approach to which this account is beholden. My goal on this front is to advance the emerging literature on religious culture and identity while justifying the claim that the Promise Keepers are a prism through which to investigate broader changes in American religion and culture.

From Century's Beginning to Millennium's End: Manhood in Twentieth-Century America

Even the most cursory glance at historical developments reveals that the Promise Keepers are not a wholly unique phenomenon. In fact, America has seen many forms of men's groups emerge and recede during the course of the twentieth century. A spate of men's movements not unlike those of today erupted at the turn of the twentieth century in the form of fraternal orders, young men's organizations, and Muscular Christianity. The historical context in which these movements emerged was marked by dramatic changes in the social order and by men's collective confusion about their place in society. In short, Americans of the early twentieth century found themselves living in circumstances much like our own.

For much of the nineteenth century, the ideology—and, indeed, the practice—of separate spheres dominated American life. The public sphere, including the workplace, politics, and sport, was seen as the exclusive domain of men while the private sphere of marriage, family, and parenting were consigned to women. Religious institutions, like many other voluntary associations, occupied a nebulous middle ground between the public and private realms in Victorian America (Bartkowski 2001a). Victorian gender norms were brought down by their own ideological contradictions, as well as by the structural changes and social activism that surfaced in the early twentieth century (Evans 1997; Kimmel 1996; Rotundo 1993).

For the better part of the nineteenth century, the dominant masculine archetype was that of the Self-Made Man (Kimmel 1996). This archetype, though always more of an ideal than a reality among Victorian men, was ushered in by the industrial revolution of the early nineteenth century. As Americans moved from the countryside and small towns to new factories in urban areas, the Self-Made Man replaced earlier visions of masculine character rooted in landownership (the Genteel Patriarch) or, alternatively, small-scale craftsmanship and trade (the Heroic Artisan). With urban households beginning to outnumber families living on the farm, frontier, and small township, American men jockeyed for jobs and sought sizable wages to prove their worth. Sociologist Michael Kimmel astutely writes about the dramatic transformation that accompanied the advent of industrialization in nineteenth-century America. The Self-Made Man, Kimmel says, emerged as "American men began to link their sense of themselves as men to their position in the volatile marketplace, to their economic success—a far less stable yet far more exciting and potentially rewarding peg upon which to hang one's identity " (Kimmel 1996: 9). Given the shaky foundation on which masculine identity was situated under wage-labor capitalism, testing one's manhood and proving one's mettle became a necessity:

The Self-Made Man of American mythology was born anxious and insecure, uncoupled from the more stable anchors of land-ownership or workplace autonomy. [Suddenly] manhood has to be proved. . . . The Self-Made Man [was] ambitious and anxious, creatively resourceful and chronically restive, the builder of culture and among the casualties of his own handiwork, a man who is, as Alexis de Tocqueville wrote in 1832, "restless in the midst of abundance." (Kimmel 1996: 9)

Flashing forward to the late nineteenth century, we see this archetype begin to unravel. A second wave of industrialization—namely, corporate capitalism—called into question the very idea of man's self-making among those not fortunate enough to be born into the Carnegie or Rockefeller households. Men, once primed for capitalist competition but now mere cogs in the corporate wheel, were increasingly becoming subject to orders handed down to them in the workplace.

Contradictions abounded in American homes as well. The father was expected to stand in authority over his family as its patriarch. However, male providership required a full workday and its attendant commutes. Turn-of-the-century capitalism removed men from the home for the better part of the day. Thus, households that could survive solely on the husband's wage relied on the quotidian authority and decision-making of women—wives, mothers, and sometimes nannies—to get through the day. Man, already little more than an order-taker at work, was too absent from the domestic scene to be anything more than a nominal rule-maker in the home. Short on both workplace autonomy and domestic authority, the Self-Made Man was fast being revealed as a sham in both public and private life.

This subtle form of structural displacement was only one challenge faced by the Self-Made Man. In addition to falling prey to these structural transformations, the Self-Made Man faced an explicit challenge from post-Victorian women's movements (Evans 1997). Through collective action and social protest, first-wave feminists sought to change the economic status of women in early twentieth-century America while expanding their sphere of influence beyond the confines of the home. The early twentieth-century "New Woman," as she was then called, rode the tide of first-wave feminism to overthrow wifely domesticity and pursue new career opportunities. To be sure, the lion's share of these new opportunities were found in performing "women's work" for pay (weaving and sewing in textile mills) or in establishing a career among one of the nascent "women's professions" (elementary education, social work, and librarianship) (Williams 1995). Nevertheless, wage-earning gave the New Woman freedoms that her more dependent forebears could hardly have imagined. When combined with access to new contraceptive technologies and the youthful sensuality of the flapper generation, marriage became more a choice than a necessity for the New Woman.

The Self-Made Man was dealt another serious blow with the expanding political clout of women at the turn of the nineteenth century to the twentieth. In prior generations, the Victorian notion of Republican Motherhood had defined women's political participation and patriotism in terms of their domestic role (Evans 1997: 57). In raising good citizens, it was widely accepted, women could exercise an indirect yet significant influence over the affairs of the state. However, by the early twentieth century, the effete hands that rocked the cradle were no longer content to rule the world solely through their children's patriotism and citizenship. In their effort to expand women's sphere of influence, suffragists such as those in the National Woman Suffrage Association contrasted the rhetoric of equality in the nation's Constitution with the practice of a political double standard. They also argued for the right to vote on less noble grounds—fear of growing political influence among the "immigrant hordes" that threatened "civilized" governance by well-bred, native-born citizens. Regardless of the tactics employed, these claims were heard. Support for women's suffrage grew, eventually leading to the ratification of the Nineteenth Amendment by thirty-six states in 1920.

Left with nowhere else to turn, the Self-Made Man sought refuge in sport (Burstyn 1999; Kimmel 1996). Even here there was little relief. The post-Victorian New Woman's breakthroughs into the public sphere soon filtered into the realm of sport through the emergence of competitive women's athletics (Cahn 1994). Here the change was quite striking. In late Victorian America, physical education for women was accepted, but was restricted to "tonic" activities that would not strain their fragile constitutions. The first generation of women's physical educators permitted their collegiate pupils to engage in appropriately "feminine" forms of exercise. But with the passing of Victorian mores, women's sports soon broke with such constraints and gained a solid foothold. A scant two decades into the twentieth century, competitive women's athletics were flourishing in the form of swimming, track, field hockey, and basketball—the last of these played on a full court, no less. Women's basketball, which took root through "industrial leagues" formed in working-class urban neighborhoods, became particularly competitive. Not long after, women's sport federations formed in the United States and abroad.

Despite these affronts, the Self-Made Man would not shrink from the challenges laid before him. He was by definition, after all, master of his fate and captain of his ship. Consequently, it was on the heels of these developments that men formed an array of homosocial (that is to say, male-only) organizations in which to valorize and recapture the "true" masculine character. Religious institutions were more than happy to oblige in this pursuit. Clearly, one of the best ways for men to recapture their manhood was to define its essence and transmit it to the next generation. With the aid of religious institutions, various organizations cropped up to liberate boys from the soft maternalism to which they were increasingly exposed at home and through primary education. "Boy's lib" organizations abounded—the Boys Brigades, the Boone and Crockett Club, Knights of King Arthur, and Men of Tomorrow (Kimmel 1996: 168). The last two of these boys-only organizations were founded by William Forbush, a minister who advocated the development of "savage virtues" through all-boy summer camps.

The Boy Scouts of America, clearly the most influential of such organizations, was administered by leaders of religious congregations throughout the United States. Like related organizations, the Boy Scouts were founded in light of mounting concerns about the erosion and softening of masculine character in urban, industrialized America (Kimmel 1996: 168–171). For the early Boy Scouts, the key to restoring the masculine character was found in removing boys and adult males from the "civilized" and indolent urban environment and placing them instead in the "wild" outdoors. It was here that erstwhile "primitive" virtues could be developed as boys traded the persona of the civilized sissy for a peculiar mix of the bold frontiersman and the earthy Indian tribesman. In fact, symbolic representations of primitive masculinity were integrated into the Boy Scouts' catechism through the use of "traditional" Native American rituals. "Headdress feathers became merit badges, symbolizing exemplary activity; Indian names or animal totems became symbolic representations of the troop" (Kimmel 1996: 169).

Despite these retrograde features of early scouting organizations, it would be wrong to see the Boy Scouts as a wholly reactionary movement looking to restore the dominance of the Self-Made Man arche-type through the socialization of young males. In fact, the early Boy Scouts "placed a heavy emphasis on subordination of the boy to his larger group"—that is, the troop and pack to which the youngster be-longed (Rotundo 1993: 238). Thus, many Boy Scout activities simul-taneously glorified individual achievement and reinforced dependence on one's fellows. As such, the Boy Scouts selectively appropriated some elements of the Self-Made Man archetype while rejecting others. They valorized qualities of hard work and achievement that were ostensi-bly found in such abundance among self-made men. Yet they rejected the radical independence of the Self-Made Man by promoting group cooperation, dependence on one's fellow scouts, and subordination of self-interest to the collective good of the troop.

Organizations for adult men also blossomed at this time. Frater-nal orders, lodges, men's clubs, and young men's fraternities sprang up everywhere, prompting one commentator to dub the turn of the century "the Golden Age of Fraternity" (see Kimmel 1996: 171; see also Rich and de los Reyes 2000). Often organized to cater to particu-lar classes or races of men, more than three hundred different frater-nal orders claimed the allegiance of nearly six million American men in the early twentieth century. From Freemasons to Oddfellows, from Red Men to Knights of Pythias, men met weekly at one or more of an estimated 70,000 fraternal lodges (Kimmel 1996: 171–172). In part, these organizations flourished because economic means of achieve-ment were not readily available. Kimmel (1996: 172) remarks that "at a time of economic stagnation and thwarted economic mobility, fra-ternal orders provided an arena in which men were moving up the ladder. At virtually every meeting, someone was being initiated into the next, highest level of the order. . . . [Therefore, if] they couldn't make it in the economic sphere, here in the comfort of the lodge, Ameri-can men experienced the mobility the nation had promised but not delivered." Fraternal orders thus enabled men to "reinvent themselves as men, to experience the pleasures and comforts of each other's com-pany and of cultural and domestic life without feeling feminized." Given the avocational pursuits, mystical initiation rites, and warm fel-lowship that were fostered in such fraternal organizations, "the lodge was alternately the artisanal guild, the church, or the home—or all three simultaneously" (Kimmel 1996: 172).

Here again, the archetype of the Self-Made Man was integrated only selectively into such gatherings. On the one hand, fraternal orders sought to avoid the feminizing influence of the "gentler sex." "Cluck-ing mother hens" and even "effete ministers" had no place in this male bastion (Kimmel 1996: 173). Yet on the other hand, the absence of femi-nine influence at the lodge enabled men to let down their guard and develop profound emotional attachments to one another. To be sure, manly affection was to be expressed through the "proper" mode of fra-ternalism. Nonetheless, the very notion of brotherhood undermined one of the core precepts upon which the Self-Made Man was founded—namely, the idea that a man could be wholly autonomous, indepen-dent, and emotionally detached. Working-class fraternal organizations took the notion of brotherly fellowship beyond mere emotional sup-port. Much like craft guilds that were by then defunct, they offered mutual aid to members facing misfortune and disadvantage (Bartkowski and Regis 2003).

With work life no longer providing the tools for man's self-mak-ing, efforts to reassert order in gender relations were also evident in the realm of sport (Burstyn 1999; Cahn 1994; Kimmel 1996: 137–141; Rotundo 1993: 239–246). Thus, it is not surprising that as women's athletics gained legitimacy during the early twentieth century, men's sport was transmogrified to underscore the differences between it and its feminine counterpart. "Proper women" returned to playing the half-court variety of basketball that made women "glow" rather than sweat (Dworkin and Messner 1999). And, oddly, the rise of women's athlet-ics led men's sport to become both more rational and more passion-ate (Burstyn 1999). The rational elements of men's sport were most clearly manifested in the nascent fixation on statistical measurement and record-keeping. Instrumental means of gauging athletic perfor-mance showed clear evidence of men's physical superiority, particu-larly in those sports where women—as well as immigrants and people of color—had made recent inroads. At the same time, the passionate elements of men's sport were evoked through fans' mythic identifica-tion with male sports figures. The emotional charge of men's sport was further bolstered by the quasi-religious worship of sports stars and the homage paid to the athletic event as the quintessential display of men's physical prowess.

Thus, early in the twentieth century, sport became a key site for proving superiority in the form of race, class, nationality, and now gen-der. Given this uneasy mix of rationality and emotion, men's sport made it possible for "civilized virtue" and "primitive instinct" to be viewed as the two key components of a "balanced" masculine character (Burstyn 1999: 91). Here too, religious communities were an integral part of this transformation. Men's sport had long been promoted by American churches. Hard manual labor was believed to promote sexual restraint and proper discipline—both of which were imbued with religious significance—by effectively "taming" the "masculine beast" (Burstyn 1999: 92–93). Salvation could not be attained by spiritual means alone; it required physical exertion that bridled bodily passions.

The connection between religion and sport was most boldly evidenced in Muscular Christianity, a movement that arose at the turn of the century (Kimmel 1996: 175–181; Ladd and Mathisen 1999; Rotundo 1993: 224). Notable advocates of Muscular Christianity included such visible figures as professional-baseball-star-turned-fundamentalist Billy Sunday, as well as the inventor of basketball, James Naismith. To be sure, Muscular Christians sometimes disagreed about the extent to which the movement should sanction indulgent elements of secular sporting culture such as drinking, gambling, and bodily display. However, they were united in using sport as a tool to masculinize evangelical Christianity and disseminate the gospel to nonbelievers. Christian men could be fiercely competitive in their athletic pursuits but equally passionate in their love for Jesus Christ. And what a man Christ was! Historian Anthony Rotundo (1993: 224) writes:

> Using metaphors of fitness and body-building, Christian thinkers imagined a strong, forceful Jesus with a religion to match. . . . This hardy Jesus with rippling muscles was no "prince of peace-at-any-price." He was an enforcer who "turned again and again on the snarling pack of his pious enemies and made them slink away." The key to Muscular Christianity was not the idea of the spirit made flesh, but of the flesh made spirit. . . . [Muscular Christians proclaimed] that the condition of character follows from the condition of the body.

Thus, Muscular Christians jettisoned the image of Jesus as a "thin, reedy man with long, bony fingers and a lean face with soft, doelike eyes and a beatific countenance—a man . . . gazing dreamily heavenward"; rather, Billy Sunday argued, Jesus was "the greatest scrapper who ever lived" (as quoted in Kimmel 1996: 176–177). The notion of Jesus as a "man's man" made intuitive sense to Sunday, who traded his lucrative professional baseball career for itinerant evangelical ministry.

Sunday was said to have "brought bleacher-crazy, frenzied aggression to religion" (see Kimmel 1996: 179).

Like many conservative religious movements in early twentieth-century America, Muscular Christianity focused on the basics—recapturing the "fundamentals" of Christian belief while stripping away lofty theological doctrines that had obscured them. Thus, the movements' advocates argued for a "vigorous, robust, muscular Christianity . . . devoid of all the etcetera of creed" (as quoted in Rotundo 1993: 224). In his effort to masculinize evangelical conviction, Billy Sunday was commonly known to offer scathing critiques of organized religion and the church establishment. As Kimmel (1996: 179–180) reveals, Sunday decried biblical scholars as "anemic rank skeptics," dismissed intellectuals as "fudge-eating mollycoddles," and derided Protestant ministers as "pretentious, pliable mental perverts." Sunday's most fervent prayer was telling: "Lord save us from off-handed, flabby cheeked, brittle boned, weak-kneed, thin-skinned, pliable, plastic, spineless, effeminate, ossified, three karat Christianity!"

If these early twentieth-century developments sound vaguely familiar, it is because they largely mirror those of the last two decades of that same century. In fact, the primary difference between the beginning and the end of the twentieth century may be described succinctly in one sentence. Changes that were initiated in the early twentieth century—the expansion of women's workforce participation and political clout, the emergence of women's sport, the decline of marriage, and economic threats to men's provider status—had all reached their full flowering by the century's end. At both points in time, women's workforce participation and political clout expanded. In fact, women's once precarious foothold in public settings such as the workplace and politics had become rock-solid by century's end. Historic highs in women's labor force participation rates in the late twentieth century show no signs of reversing themselves, and civic-minded women now hold political office themselves rather than offering their support for candidates only as voters.

Add to this the emergence of women's sport in the early twentieth century and its parallel resurgence some sixty years later. The vitality of competitive women's sport, whether played in industrial basketball leagues for working-class women of the 1920s or in the more handsomely rewarded Women's National Basketball Association in the 1990s, is one more sign that the Self-Made Man's days are numbered.

Finally, during both the early and the late twentieth century, upheavals occurred in the domestic realm. Both points in time witnessed the emergence of serious challenges to male authority in the home. Prior to the twentieth century, patriarchy had meant protection of one's family from physical harm and provision for its economic needs. Yet, with the new century's displacement of frontier threats by a combination of workplace drudgery and an increasingly deficient male wage, the Self-Made Man seemed to be gasping his last.

Thus, while our forebears began fashioning the tombstone and grave of the Self-Made Man in the early twentieth century, we appear committed to nailing shut his coffin and lowering him into his final resting place. Of course, there are many noteworthy twentieth-century developments that are left out of this selective historical account. Two world wars. A Great Depression. The pro-family 1950s. The turbulent 1960s. Yet one thing is unmistakably clear. The chaos and confusion faced by men in the early twentieth century paralleled that confronting men at the century's end. The key difference is that the hazy etchings begun in the early twentieth century have been deeply and clearly engraved as an epitaph three generations later: Self-Made Man, Rest in Peace.

It was from this context that the men's movements of the 1980s and 1990s emerged. Chapter 3 charts these developments in more detail by locating the Promise Keepers within the field of late twentieth-century men's movements. The remainder of the present chapter introduces the Promise Keepers by surveying its organizing principles and teasing out its connections to recent developments in American religion and culture.

American Religion and Culture through the Prism of PK

The account of the Promise Keepers rendered in this volume draws together key insights from cultural sociology and the sociology of religion. Studying everything from food, music, and festivals to religion, gender, and embodiment, cultural sociologists are a diverse lot (see, for example, P. Smith 1998; Spillman 2001). Still, they are generally averse to reducing complex social phenomena to singular causes and they typically avoid rendering universal explanations when studying what Charles Lemert (2002) has termed "social things." In what follows, I discuss the sociological perspectives in culture and religion that bear most directly on the interpretations I offer here.

Rules and Tools: Religion, Structure, and Culture

In a now classic contribution to cultural sociology, Ann Swidler (1986) likens culture to a "tool kit" (see also Swidler 2001). This metaphor is critical to my investigation. Just as physical tools like a hammer or screwdriver help a craftsperson to accomplish an array of tasks during the workday, cultural tools help people accomplish their work as social beings—constructing a meaningful identity, forming significant relationships with others, and navigating their way through labyrinthine social worlds. Symbols, meaningful objects in our social environment, are one type of cultural tool. Symbols include ideologies and worldviews (whether Christianity or Islam, feminism or patriarchy), as well as the inanimate material things that are meaningful to people (religious scripture, a rosary, a wedding dress). Symbols also include representations of people (a priest or imam, a mother or father, a best friend or lover) and other sentient creatures (God among theists, a dove for a spirit of peace). It is important, however, not to reduce culture merely to symbols. To do so neglects the way in which culture is produced through social practices.

Strategies, a second dimension of culture, provide the means for organizing action through time (Swidler 1986). Strategies are practices through which we craft our personhood (identity) and navigate encounters with others (sociality). Social practices are diverse—speaking and singing, praying and meditating, eating and drinking, laughing and crying; commuting from home to work and back again; doing the laundry or negotiating an exchange at the local supermarket. The term "strategy" implies that actions have an intent by which they are motivated—sharing a meal to create a sense of fellowship and community, using humor to lighten the mood, performing housework to "help out" a loved one. Though actions are strategic in this way, they often give rise to unintended consequences and sometimes reveal unconscious motives. In the realm of humor, jokes may fall flat, failing to elicit laughter. Or a good-natured jest might unintentionally incite anger.

Despite their many points of distinction, symbols and strategies often blend together in everyday life. Many religions, for example, typically compile their sacred writings in a holy book—the Jewish Torah, the Muslim Qu'ran, the Christian Bible. Within the cultural repertoire of each of these religious traditions, scripture is a valuable symbolic resource. Yet, from a sociological perspective, the sacred meaning of scripture does not reside statically in the text. Rather, the text becomes sacralized through ritual practices and everyday habits that are themselves strategies of action. Such action strategies may entail delivering a public sermon about select scriptural passages during weekly worship, or the daily study of scripture alone or in small groups. These strategies—and the scriptural interpretations to which they give rise—vary considerably by social location (Bartkowski 1996, 1997, 2001a). Religious elites, for example, are often formally trained in the hermeneutic practice of "exegesis"—a strategy of interpretation, typically incorporated into a sermon during Christian worship, that involves building an argument via a circular, "parts-whole" movement through the text. The interpretive strategies of laypeople, by contrast, often entail reading sacred text in light of the problems of their everyday lives rather than abstruse theological concepts. Passages that bear on private troubles—economic woes, relationship difficulties—are imbued with particular significance, and the text becomes a template for overcoming personal dilemmas (Smilde 2003).

The symbolic forms and strategies of action in religious communities vary greatly. Consider a persuasive sermon, a touching eulogy, or an inspiring hymn. These religious artifacts are all made possible by bringing seemingly "static" symbols (words) to life through the strategies of rhetoric, oratory, and musical composition. And these strategies do not simply reproduce existing symbols. They also set new meanings in motion. Sermonizing, eulogizing, and singing give rise to new symbolic forms, as audiences collectively evaluate the persuasiveness of the minister's argument, discuss the eulogist's representation of the deceased's character at a post-funeral gathering, or judge the singer's rendering of a classic hymn. And, of course, these nascent meanings themselves often feed into new strategies of action—a somber "amen" at the sermon's end, a mass rush forward after an altar call, a teary eye in response to a touching hymn or moving eulogy.

Beyond the everyday blending of these two cultural forms, symbols and strategies vary over time and across social contexts. Radical reinterpretations of scripture and unconventional styles of worship often arise in prophetic movements situated at the sectarian margins of a religious tradition. Yet, as such schismatic movements grow and become better established over time, their scriptural interpretations and worship styles commonly become more "priestly" and ritualistic (which is to say, less radical and more conservative) (Weber 1947, [1922] 1963). In short, cultural tools lend themselves to an array of uses. They are not social givens. At the same time, their particular uses are strongly influenced by the social positions their craftspeople occupy and the milieus in which they are utilized.

Recent scholarship has shed light on the cultural repertoire of American evangelicals while exploring how conservative Protestants use their cultural tools to craft a distinct collective identity (Bartkowski 2001a; Gallagher 2003; C. Smith 1998, 2000). Three key tools are particularly prominent within the cultural repertoire of American evangelicals. First, evangelicals hold the Bible in very high regard, contending alternately that it is inerrant, infallible, or authoritative. Biblical inerrancy is the belief that the Bible is without error (though some evangelicals charge that this is the case only for the Bible's "original autographs"). Infallibilism is the conviction that careful study of the Bible in the proper spiritual mindset will not lead Christian adherents astray. Biblical authority is more a commitment to the belief that the scriptures are the superior source of knowledge on the subjects to which they speak. Regardless of the particular position taken, evangelicals view the scriptures as a critical resource in the pursuit of godly living.

Jesus Christ is a second tool in the evangelical cultural repertoire. For conservative Protestants, Jesus Christ is not a fictional character but a real historical personage. For that matter, most evangelicals believe that Adam, Eve, Moses, Paul of Tarsus, and others discussed in the Bible were actual people and are generally represented accurately in the biblical text. Evangelicals believe that Jesus lived a life of ministry, service, and self-sacrifice. They further charge that he died by crucifixion and was resurrected from the dead just as the Bible says. From an evangelical standpoint, Jesus Christ is the only son of God and the savior of the human race—the single path to salvation. While this singular commitment to the Bible and Jesus Christ as the only means to salvation does lead some conservative Protestants to condemn other Christian traditions (Catholicism, mainline Protestantism, Mormonism) and look askance at non-Christian religions, many evangelicals mix a strong commitment to their own faith with a tolerance and respect for the religious convictions of others (Smith 2000).

Finally, evangelicals evince a strong commitment to a born-again conversion experience. Those who have been converted are "saved" and those who have not are described alternatively as "unsaved" or "nonbelievers." In the parlance of evangelicalism, getting "saved" amounts to an individual "accepting Christ" as his or her "personal savior." Though evangelicals disagree about the precise role of "works" (that is, personal behaviors) in one's salvation, most believers would readily agree that salvation is influenced by an individual's turning away from "sin" while striving to live in accord with Christian teachings as specified in the Bible. This process of life transformation is commonly described as one's "walk with the Lord." When a believer accepts Christ, he or she is thought to receive the Holy Spirit that Christ is said to have promised his followers. Though disagreement exists about "fruits of the Holy Spirit" manifested in the individual, this person of the Godhead is generally believed to inform the conscience of believers, helping them to discern between right and wrong in their "walk with Christ."

Despite conservative Protestants' strong emphasis on personal conversion, the evangelical cultural repertoire is characterized by a mix of individualism and collectivism. Evangelicals foster collective bonds —affectionately dubbed "fellowship" by the faithful—through an array of social networks: church worship activities; congregational ministry programs for men, women, married couples, youth, and whole families; small-group Bible studies; outreach service programs to the poor, elderly, and imprisoned; and, of course, para-church organizations such as Focus on the Family, Campus Crusade for Christ, Women of Faith, the Promise Keepers, and countless others.

The strength of social bonds among believers is buttressed by the longtime evangelical tradition of revival. Revivals are periodic renewals of the faith community's collective commitment to Christ through extended sessions of communal worship, preaching, praise, and fellowship activities. Revivals can take place within congregations; or, as is the case with the Promise Keepers, they may take the form of a parachurch ministry. Such forms of connectedness are further promoted through evangelicals' collective commitment to missionary work—that is, spreading the Christian gospel to unbelievers in accordance with the Great Commission. Thus, while salvation remains defined largely as a personal choice—a private matter "of the heart"—among evangelical Protestants, this individualistic orientation intersects with powerful bonds of connectedness among the faithful. It is together that evangelicals pursue "godly living." And it is as fellow Christians that evangelicals confront the challenges posed by secular culture.

These basic insights about culture bear directly on the investigation of the Promise Keepers presented in this volume. PK seizes on an array of symbolic tools and action strategies from the cultural repertoire of American evangelicalism. The Bible and Jesus Christ are at the core of the Promise Keepers' mission. The first of PK's "Seven Promises"—the movement's organizing principles—says as much. Through it, men affirm their commitment "to honoring Jesus Christ through worship, prayer, and obedience to God's Word [the Bible] in the power of the Holy Spirit." Likewise, the Fourth Promise identifies "biblical values" as critical to promoting healthy family relationships and the Sixth Promise champions "biblical unity" among Christians of different denominational stripes.

Other evangelical symbols and strategies are present in the movement as well. Whether in the form of small weekly "accountability groups" or full-blown stadium conferences, Promise Keeper events are centered around the goal of personal conversion—bringing men to Christ "one man at a time." But this classic evangelical emphasis on individualism is melded with collectivist symbols and practices. Altar calls at PK conferences promote mass conversion, as men collectively rush the stage to "accept Christ" and have their brothers pray over them through the laying on of hands. PK events are also intended to strengthen social bonds among the faithful through spiritual revival. The Second Promise underscores the importance of "pursuing vital relationships with a few other men, understanding that he needs brothers to help him keep his promises," while the Fifth Promise obligates the Promise Keeper to support his local church and honor its pastor.

At the same time, PK's noninstitutionalized, antiestablishment strategies of conversion and revival lead the movement to utilize some evangelical tools in innovative (prophetic rather than priestly) ways. PK promotes prophetic scriptural interpretations targeted at overcoming racism, classism, and denominational divisions among believers. And PK signature styles of worship—raised hands, swaying bodies, and raucous cheering—would be considered unconventional by many conservative Protestants (for example, traditional Southern Baptists) situated outside the subculture's Pentecostal and charismatic wings.

Evangelical Identity and Boundary Work

To what ends do religious communities use cultural tools? Among their many functions, cultural symbols and strategies are essential for the crafting of religious identities (Ammerman 2004). Among scholars studying American evangelicalism, Christian Smith's (1998, 2000) subcultural identity theory is particularly noteworthy. Smith argues that the key to the vitality of evangelical Protestantism is its ability to sustain a relationship of "distinctive engagement" with American culture. Evangelicals are socially engaged to the extent that they define their identity and articulate their views using key aspects of American culture. The definition of conversion as a product of personal volition, popular among evangelicals and Promise Keepers alike, dovetails quite nicely with the ideology of American individualism. Evangelical movements like the Promise Keepers also use quintessential elements of American culture in their effort to remain current with emerging social trends. The Promise Keepers enlist a diverse array of communication technologies such as radio, film, and (even more recently) webcasting, internet chat rooms, e-mail distribution lists, and online communities to spread the Christian gospel. And despite the fact that they reject efforts to describe PK as a "self-help group," the Promise Keepers import many elements of therapeutic culture into their men's ministry programs. PK does so through the formation of accountability groups in which men mentor one another, and with the aid of various media (books, audiotapes, and videotapes) that are all tied together around the motif of self-improvement, albeit with the help of God. And, of course, the Promise Keepers draw on cultural repertoires of war and sport to fill football stadiums with "Christian soldiers" who are locked in strenuous combat with Satan and who collectively worship Jesus by doing "the wave" in his honor. In all these ways, PK warmly embraces core elements of American social life and deftly uses these cultural forms to pursue its subcultural agenda of evangelization.

At the same time, evangelicals take pains to distinguish themselves from the cultural mainstream. The Promise Keepers are openly critical of moral relativism, which they see as breeding unethical conduct anathema to foundational "biblical values." They mince no words in decrying the "sins" associated with the sexual revolution, particularly as manifested in what they allege to be Americans' increasing tolerance for pornography, homosexuality, and sex outside of marriage. The third of the Seven Promises underscores PK's cultural distinctiveness by holding men to a "higher" standard—namely, "spiritual, moral, ethical, and sexual purity." Many of the organization's leaders also reject "radical feminist" advocacy of sexual equality and "gender blending" despite the increasing acceptance of such ideas and practices among the population at large. In these and other ways, PK distances itself from mainstream American culture.

Thus, evangelical groups like the Promise Keepers are engaged in what might be best described as a collective "approach-avoidance dance" with mainstream American culture (cf. Rubin 1983). Highly engaged with those aspects of contemporary social life that support their evangelical convictions, Promise Keepers criticize other popular trends that run counter to their values. The tensions inherent in a melding of social engagement with cultural distinctiveness are clearly apparent in several of the Seven Promises. In describing the husband's relationship to his family, the Fourth Promise melds language that hearkens back to a nineteenth-century institutionalized marriage (husbandly protection) with the twentieth-century ideal of companionate marriage (husband-wife love). And the last of the Seven Promises reflects the delicate balancing act of "being in, but not of, the world" faced by evangelical Christians at large. The Seventh Promise reads: "A Promise Keeper is committed to influencing his world, being obedient to the Great Commandment (see Mark 12: 30–31) and the Great Commission (see Matthew 28: 19–20)." The Great Commandment instructs Christians to love God above all else and to love their neighbors as themselves. And the Great Commission entails using every opportunity to spread the gospel to those outside the fold. But simultaneously loving God and one's neighbors—particularly if one's neighbors are ungodly nonbelievers—can be a most difficult proposition. This twin imperative makes Christians vulnerable to the corrupt culture through which they must travel in their efforts to evangelize the unsaved.

Although subcultural identity theory sheds new light on evangelicals' relationship to mainstream American culture, it runs the risk of oversimplifying the process of identity negotiation. The negotiation of a religious identity—evangelical or otherwise—is not just a matter of managing one's theological beliefs and religious practices vis-à-vis mainstream culture. Religious identities are inflected by an array of social cleavages and cultural differences that extend well beyond the realm of faith and spirituality (Ammerman 2004). Thus, the most adequate understanding of religious identity negotiation entails analyzing the broader array of social boundaries that intersect with that identity. Michèle Lamont's (1992, 2000) perspective on boundary work provides an analytical approach for examining the "intersectional" character of identities.

Lamont astutely observes that all of us occupy an intersecting array of statuses by nature of our race, gender, class, sexuality, nationality, and religion—though the last is given short shrift in her work. Two key insights of this perspective are particularly noteworthy. First, the forging of a subcultural identity often entails the simultaneous negotiation of several different boundaries. In many circumstances, religion may be a "master status" for evangelicals. Yet, like their non-Christian counterparts, American evangelicals find themselves inhabiting a world in which cultural diversity manifests itself in various forms—not only as religious pluralism, but also through differences in race, class, nationality, sexuality, and so forth.

And, given the manifold social boundaries that actors negotiate in their everyday lives, the effects of such boundary work are hardly predictable. Boundary work can serve orthodox ends by reifying extant cultural differences, such as those that highlight the seemingly inherent distinctions between masculine aggression and feminine docility (Bartkowski 2001a), or the divergent linguistic expressions commonly used by blacks and whites (Ferguson 2000). Alternatively, boundary work can serve progressive ends by challenging and even subverting such cultural distinctions. This form of boundary work may entail either emphasizing the similar characteristics among different groups or lauding characteristics that have been socially devalued. Liberal feminists have long argued for equal opportunity by emphasizing the basic similarities in social ability between women and men. By contrast, radical feminists embrace "traditional" notions of essential gender difference, such as women's penchant for empathy and compassion, while seeking to revalue these otherwise denigrated attributes. Whatever form it takes, boundary work is rarely wholly orthodox or progressive in its social effects. Paradoxically, any one form of boundary work in a religious community can simultaneously reinforce and subvert notions of cultural difference (see Warner 1997).

Thus, as the Promise Keepers undertake what I have called their approach-avoidance dance with mainstream American culture, much more than religion alone is at stake. Where boundary work is concerned, religion, gender, race, sexuality, and other forms of social difference intersect. Nowhere is this more apparent than in the Promise Keepers' efforts to eradicate denominational divisions and racial cleavages among evangelical Christians. The sixth of the Seven Promises is telling in precisely this way: "A Promise Keeper is committed to reaching beyond any racial and denominational barriers to demonstrate the power of biblical unity." In a similar fashion, the Promise Keepers' goal in waiving conference admission fees in 1998 and 1999 was to "open the gates" to men whose meager economic resources would not permit them to attend such events. Yet, alongside PK's attempts to subvert the invidious boundaries of denomination, race, and class, other forms of cultural difference are reinforced. Conference speakers sometimes reify cultural difference by seizing upon elements of local culture—for example, Tejano culture in San Antonio—and integrating them into PK conferences. The result is at once a "coloring" of evangelicalism, now capable of reaching across racial barriers, and the reinforcement of homogenizing racial identities ("Mexican machismo," "black Americans"). Boundary work, then, attunes scholars to the "intersectional" nature of identities (Glenn 1999; Ammerman 2004) while demonstrating how the negotiation of cultural difference is marked by both orthodox and progressive tendencies (Bartkowski and Regis 2003).

Embodied Evangelicalism: The Sensate Dimensions of Religious Experience

It is indeed remarkable that many of the reigning theories in the study of American religion fail to recognize that the body is a key tool in the production of religious culture and a significant site for the negotiation of religious identity.[1] Yet, as seasoned ethnographers readily acknowledge, religious identity and religious culture are not simply negotiated through rational abstractions or linguistic turns of phrase. They are rendered through the bodily practices of actual believers (Bartkowski 2001b).

Thus, it is necessary to account for what might best be described as the "sensate" dimensions of religious experience. Pitirim Sorokin's (1957) distinction between sensate and ideational forms of culture is instructive here. As Sorokin's term of choice suggests, sensate culture seizes on corporeality and is rendered through embodied practices. Where religion is concerned, sensate culture entails "ecstatic" forms of worship such as call-and-response sermonizing, speaking in tongues, and being "slain in the spirit" as well as more mundane forms of embodied worship—singing hymns, partaking of communion, or conferring a blessing through the laying on of hands. Ideational culture, which Sorokin counterposes to the sensate, is generated through more ethereal forms of engagement with the world. Ideational culture also abounds in religious communities. Logically argued, didactic sermons—whether rooted in scriptural rationales or theological propositions—are one of the most pervasive forms of ideational culture in Christian religious denominations; others are private prayers and somber meditation.

Sensate culture, as I define it here, entails recognizing the cen-

trality of embodiment to religious experience. The literal bodies of believers, in all their physicality, are not epiphenomenal to the experience of religious awakening, conviction, and fellowship. Quite the
contrary, bodies are both agents and objects of cultural production in
any religious community (cf. Bartkowski 2001b; Connell 1995). Insurgent bodily practices such as speaking in tongues and ecstatic worship can give rise to uncharted faith experiences, yield new theological
meanings, and destabilize established religious hierarchies. And yet,
as objects of religious practice, the bodies of the faithful do not stand
apart from pressures brought to bear upon them by religious culture
and structure. In many faith traditions, the bodily activities of religious adherents are structured by theological edicts that prescribe ritual
posture and public comportment (prayer styles, forms of religious
dress), consumption habits (ritual fasting, abstinence from proscribed
substances, the ingestion of sacred foods), and sexual practices (moral
frameworks specifying the appropriate conditions for physical intimacy). Hence, religious groups of many stripes are organized around
a disciplining of the body—one that is both productive (yielding new
social forms and cultural meanings) and prohibitive (restricting the
avenues for social engagement and cultural expression). The point not
to be lost here is that bodies are bound up in both the production and
the consumption of religious culture. Embodied religious practices
(what I call here "sensate religion") enlist existing social structures
such as gender, race, and sexuality while also recreating those structures—often doing so simultaneously.

Three caveats are in order concerning the character of sensate religion. First, for Sorokin, the sensate and the ideational could be fit-
ted quite neatly on opposite ends of a cultural continuum. Ideational
culture edifies the mind and enriches the soul, whereas sensate culture incites the body and stimulates the senses. The ideational touches
upon our higher faculties (compassion, love, altruism), while the sensate caters to our base instincts (intolerance, selfishness, war). (Sorokin
saw idealistic culture as the midway point between these two poles.)
In an even broader sense, ideational culture is often seen as evidence
of sophistication, cultural refinement, and "good taste," while sensate
culture is portrayed as base, unrefined, and "low-brow." In calling attention to sensate dimensions of religious experience, I reject such distinctions and the pernicious hierarchies they imply. As the following
account reveals, the Promise Keepers show themselves to be quite facile
in complicating such categories and boundaries.

Second, my effort to highlight the sensate aspects of religious experience does not imply that they can be readily divorced from the ideational elements of religion.[2] The actual production of religious culture and the quotidian negotiation of religious identities defy such tidy distinctions. The chapters that follow provide ample evidence of how sensate religion among the Promise Keepers is often blended together seamlessly with ideational elements of evangelicalism. For example, the Bible's New Testament contains multiple Pauline references to the "body of Christ" (e.g., 1 Corinthians 12:13, 24–26; Ephesians 2:13–16). In conference addresses, Promise Keepers seize on this ideational representation to reconfigure the actual relationships between embodied believers.[3] Conference speakers cite this metaphor and the image of "biblical unity" found in the sixth of the Seven Promises to promote physical closeness—tearful embraces, hands-clasped prayers— among men across racial lines. In practice, then, clear-cut distinctions between sensate and ideational forms of religious experience often give way to a messy simultaneity.

Finally, a word is necessary concerning the analytical approach adopted in many of the chapters that follow. My desire to revalue the sensate dimensions of religious belonging (and, more broadly, the action strategies of promise-keeping) entails rendering a volume that is replete with on-the-ground ethnographic accounts of interactions as they unfold. Where appropriate, I use interview data to enrich the ethnographic portraits presented here and to explore their meaning, especially in chapters 5 and 6. However, writing a book about a revivalistic movement requires a writing style that itself has verve and liveliness. With these caveats in mind, I now turn my attention to the particularities of promise-keeping. Chapter 3 situates the Promise Keepers within the broader field of American men's movements that began in the early 1980s while examining how PK elites define godly manhood.

3

Godly
Masculinities
Archetypes of
Christian Manhood

At the peak of its prominence, Promise Keepers had attracted criticism from many quarters for its valorization of what many interpreted as gender traditionalism. In this chapter, I analyze a select sample of best-selling men's advice manuals written by elite Promise Keepers. These manuals are part of a broader pastoral literature that aims to provide PK members with advice on a range of topics—the essence of godly manhood, the importance of Christian men's fellowship with one another, the pursuit of a godly marriage, and strategies for effective fathering. Such manuals are sold though stadium conferences, the Promise Keepers' official web site, local Christian bookstores, and other venues.

My comparative analysis of these advice manuals reveals that leading Promise Keepers do not advance a singular, coherent notion of godly manhood. Rather, PK elites promulgate a diverse array of godly masculinities. These competing gender ideologies have given rise to four distinct discourses of Christian advice manuals for evangelical men, each of which is oriented around a particular archetype of the godly man: the Rational Patriarch (traditional masculinity), the Expressive Egalitarian (men's liberationism), the Tender Warrior (poeticized manhood), and the Multicultural Man (interracial masculinity).[1] In sketching the contours of these gender discourses, I explore how PK luminaries utilize two rhetorical devices—discursive tacking and gendered metaphors—to manage the tensions and contradictions that surface within and among them. These archetypes enable the Promise Keepers to define themselves with reference to other new social movements and changing definitions of gender in American society.

The Rational Patriarch:
Reaffirming Traditional Masculinity

It would be difficult to find a more enthusiastic purveyor of traditional masculinity than Edwin Louis Cole. Cole's *Maximized Manhood: A Guide to Family Survival* (1982), initially written in the heyday of the New Christian Right, is in its eighteenth printing and boasts nearly one million copies in print. (The book was revised, though only slightly, and republished under the same title in 2001. The modesty of the revisions in the new edition, which is essentially the same book with about twenty-five new pages added at the end of it, speaks to the volume's enduring quality. I use the original edition of the book because that one was available during the Promise Keepers' rise to prominence, and because the original edition clearly illustrates connections between conservative evangelicalism during the 1980s and its more recent emergence in the form of the Promise Keepers.) This book remains a best seller and is considered a "classic" by many within the movement. Its status as a "classic" in the movement is telling. The discourse of traditional masculinity predates the Promise Keepers, but is imported into the movement by the likes of Cole. Traditional masculinity is therefore a proto-PK discourse with which the movement remains conversant, but beyond which it has moved in defining itself. PK traditionalists like Cole therefore serve as a bridge between the Promise Keepers and bygone forms of conservative Protestant political mobilization.

The discourse of traditional masculinity invoked by Cole is predicated on a notion of radical gender difference that links manhood to rational thinking while naturalizing patriarchal authority. The traditional discourse is unabashedly antifeminist and decries the devaluation of traditional masculinity in contemporary American society. PK discourses of traditionalist masculinity are founded on an ideology of strict essentialism—the notion that men and women are innately, categorically, and immutably different from one another (cf. Bartkowski 1997; Schwalbe 1996). According to this ideology, manhood is characterized by rationality and strength. Men, naturally adept at long-range vision and preoccupied with instrumental achievement, are initiators. By contrast, PK traditionalists connect womanhood to fragility, intuition, emotional attunement, and relational attachment. Women are portrayed as responders.

For his part, Cole (1982: 72) frequently remarks on the significance of dichotomous gender differences: "It is possible to get spirituality from women, but strength always comes from men. A church, a family, a nation is only as strong as its men. Men you are accountable. There is no sleek escape chute. God requires manhood of all men." Cole's treatise is replete with totalizing statements about masculine-feminine difference: "Men and women are different. Really different. For example—Men are head-liners, women are fine-print people" (1982: 147). Men's ostensible penchant for rational thinking and long-range vision is contrasted with women's apparent attunement to nuance and detail. Cole (1982: 78–79, 82) is unabashed in articulating his support for strict essentialism, the ideology that gender characteristics are dichotomous and immutable: "Every woman needs to be unique in her own eyes. . . . Every woman craves the intimacy of some man. She was made that way. When she is denied that intimacy with her husband, her nature is to seek out an alternative source. . . . Every woman needs to know she is unique to her man." References to women's "intuition" are common in Cole's manual. After discussing his own wife's penchant for intuition, Cole (1982: 96) concludes tersely: "You know how women are."

The clear implication emanating from this strict essentialist ideology is that men's and women's divergent, divinely ordained natures predispose them to occupy different social roles. Women's "fine-print" nature makes them more capable caregivers for young children, a point Cole conveys via a narrative recollection of a visit he and his wife paid to their new granddaughter:

> I flew across the continent and then drove for hours to see my brand-new granddaughter in the hospital. When I saw her, I checked her out thoroughly. There she was—arms, legs, eyes, nose, mouth—all the parts were there, everything was okay. That was sufficient for me. I was ready to leave. Not my wife and daughter. Half an hour later, they were still examining the length of the eyelashes, the shape of the fingernails, the texture of the skin, as if the nursery window were a magnifying glass. Fine print, fine print. (Cole 1982: 147)

Cole's (1982: 82, 102) vision of traditional masculinity also leads him to defend a patriarchal family structure in which the husband is the undisputed leader—in his terms, the "priest" or "head"—of the family. Married women are said to desire male leadership within the home (Cole 1982: 77). In case readers might question the veracity of such claims, Cole (1982: 81) quotes the Bible's 1 Peter 3:1–2, a portion of which reads: "You married women, be submissive to your husbands— and adapt yourselves to them . . . [show] reverence for your husband . . . which includes, respect, deference, honor, esteem, admiration, praise, devotion, deep love, and enjoyment."

Traditionalists contend that household authority could not be legitimately allocated in any other fashion. Cole (1982: 68, 108, 109) argues that one of the essential characteristics of manhood is courage, and concludes: "Courage has always been a requirement of leadership . . . God has planned for someone to take charge. Men—it is you" (Cole 1982: 107, 111). Reasserting the connection between masculinity, patriarchy, and rationality, he argues: "*The Kingdom of God is based on truth, not human sentiment. Decisions must be made the same way. Decision-making is one of the marks of a man. Every man I know that is a success is decisive*" (Cole 1982: 66, emphasis in original).

Masculine initiation and feminine submission would seem to be endemic to virtually all aspects of male-female interaction, including sexual relations. Deploying a gendered metaphor that melds together biological sex, sexual intercourse, and submission, Cole characterizes the act of intercourse itself as an encounter in which an emotionally tender woman "submits" herself to the sexual drive of her aggressive male lover. He argues: "even women who are promiscuous feel a measure of guilt in having sexual relations without any love. So, prior to submitting to a man's love-making, they ask the age-old question, 'Do you love me?'" (Cole 1982: 82).

Underlying this strict essentialist view of gender is a belief in the divinely ordained appropriateness of heterosexuality as well as an explicit critique of homosexuality and any attempts at perceived "gender blending" (e.g., feminism, gay-rights advocacy). Cole's advice manual even draws connections between sin, apocalyptic imagery, and gender blending. Heaven is a heterosexual haven for Cole, who describes the end times as a point when "the 'problem person' plunges into a Christless eternity . . . and homosexual 'problems' will be no more" (Cole 1982: 34; see also 126–127). Shifting deftly from such apocalyptic imagery to a more upbeat gendered metaphor based on sports, Cole (1982: 34) expresses his hope that "sins" and "perversion" such as homosexuality can be eradicated in this lifetime if males "begin to tackle sin like men." The alternative to God's plan for patriarchal leadership—what Cole (1982: 108) calls the emerging "matriarchal society" —is a development he finds most disturbing.

Why all of the concern about homosexuality, feminism, matriarchy, and gender blending? Purveyors of strict essentialism engage in such boundary work because they are anxious about a cultural devaluation of masculinity within the contemporary United States (Cole 1982: 107–108). Such authors are especially troubled by the willingness of contemporary "feminized" men to relinquish leadership to women. Deploying feminized terms such as "tippy toe," "tulips," and "pussyfooting," Cole (1982: 35) defines masculinity in opposition to the traditional woman who exudes softness in her bodily comportment, her emotional sensitivity, and her supple sexuality: "I like real men. . . . I don't like the pussyfooting pipsqueaks who tippy toe through the tulips. . . . I like men to be men."

The Expressive Egalitarian:
Men's Liberation in PK

The Rational Patriarch is only one of several different images of godly manhood promulgated by leading Promise Keeper authors. The Promise Keepers have been wise to incorporate gender traditionalism into their movement without letting themselves be defined solely by this orthodox viewpoint—lest PK risk being dismissed as backward, reactionary, and out of touch with current developments in gender politics. A very different image of godly masculinity—that of the Expressive Egalitarian—emerges from a rival gender discourse in the movement. The emotionally expressive, liberated Christian man depicted in this discourse is most readily championed by Promise Keeper Gary Oliver. Oliver's *Real Men Have Feelings Too* (1993) is one of many advice manuals sold through the Promise Keepers organization and is heartily endorsed by its founder, Bill McCartney. Like Ed Cole, Gary Oliver is a frequent contributor to Promise Keeper anthologies written by an array of the organization's leading spokesmen. Through this archetype, PK negotiates several boundaries simultaneously—at once distancing itself from the stodgy traditionalism of old-guard evangelicalism (the New Christian Right) and placing itself alongside another popular men's movement (men's liberationism).

Oliver articulates a discourse of godly manhood rooted largely in androgynous conceptualizations of gender. Androgyny begins with the assumption that gender differences are artificial and pernicious. The concept of androgyny, championed initially by liberal feminists and more recently by men's liberationists (Messner 1997: chap. 3), enjoins both men and women to cultivate admirable "human" qualities beyond the narrow limits imposed by stereotypical gender roles. In stark contrast to the traditional Rational Patriarch, Promise Keeper writers who subscribe to the Expressive Egalitarian model encourage men to get "in touch" with their own emotions and to exhibit compassion and sensitivity toward the feelings of others. Within this liberationist discourse, the more rational elements of manhood (e.g., logical thought, decisive judgment) are viewed as oppressive straitjackets for the men charged with typecasting themselves so narrowly.

Largely consistent with the ideology of androgyny, Oliver (1993: 23–32) argues that traits commonly associated with being male (e.g., bravery, strength, stoicism, an insatiable sex drive, a preoccupation with achievement) are not really masculine at all. Moreover, he contends that characteristics typically associated with being a woman (e.g., gentleness, compassion, tenderness, meekness, sensitivity) are not really the property of an essential feminine temperament (1993: 19–20). Instead, Oliver contends that personality characteristics often linked with womanliness are actually "human" traits clearly exemplified by Jesus Christ:

> Here's what for many is the shocker. All of those words [e.g., compassion, tenderness, sensitivity] are descriptors of our Lord Jesus Christ. *And that's the problem*! Those words don't describe a woman. They aren't feminine, they're human! They describe emotions and actions of healthy males and females. But sin has so damaged and distorted our culture that what God designed to characterize healthy people now characterizes only women. That's tragic! (Oliver 1993: 20, emphasis in original; see also 61–62, 65–66)

The PK discourse of men's liberation, then, has an agenda that differs dramatically from that which guides its traditional counterpart. Rather than have men "maximize" the rational aspects of their manhood, Oliver (1993: 19) argues for a more sensitized masculinity—one in which men can learn "how to be human, how to feel, how to love, how to be better husbands, fathers, and friends." While he does not single out evangelical traditionalists for criticism by name, Oliver is quite critical of radical views of gender difference. He says that such "myths of masculinity" have "produced a generation of men who define themselves by the negative. Whatever women are, whatever strengths or attributes they have, whatever characteristics they possess, positive or negative, men aren't. And if women are emotional, then real men aren't. And any attempt to say they could be or should be is [erroneously viewed as] an attempt to 'feminize' men" (Oliver 1993: 37).

In a striking departure from PK authors who equate masculinity with rationality and stoicism, Oliver (1993: 46–49, 68, 70–72) encourages men to explore, trust, and express their emotions rather than place the "mind over emotions"; to recognize that the free expression of emotions is supported by a careful reading of the Bible; and to acknowledge the benefits of this expressive masculinity—namely, the physical, psychological, and relational benefits of open emotional expression. In articulating this discourse of expressive masculinity, Oliver (1993: 20, 22–32) pays sustained attention to a series of emotional issues with which men in general are believed to wrestle, due to human sinfulness and its pernicious counterpart, gender stereotyping. Oliver provides chapter-length discussions detailing the steps by which his male readers can learn to process a wide range of otherwise unwieldy emotions, including fear (chap. 4), anger (chaps. 5–7), loneliness (chap. 8), love (chap. 9), worry and depression (chaps. 10 and 11), grief (chap. 13), and—for the somber, overly serious Christian man—joy (chap. 14). From this standpoint, the stress and anxiety produced by the traditional masculine stereotype has exacted a toll not only on men's psyches but on their bodies as well—through, for example, higher rates of life-threatening physical illnesses and an average lifespan shorter than that of women.

Evangelical advocates of expressive masculinity articulate support for marital egalitarianism by invoking the principle of mutual submission (see Bartkowski 2001a). PK critics of gender traditionalism argue that a patriarchal family model places an unfair burden on husbands and fathers, who are alone charged with decision-making responsibility in the home. This patriarchal family structure is viewed as similarly oppressive for wives who are enjoined to submit to their husbands' capricious domestic authority.

Oliver (1993: chap. 12) directs Promise Keepers to implement a model of conflict resolution very different from that implied by the

Rational Patriarch archetype. Whereas the Rational Patriarch holds fast to the reins of husband-headship and expects wifely submission from his mate, Oliver makes a case for marital egalitarianism. He does so by mixing popular psychological rhetoric with biblical references. Using a married couple as an example of this process, Oliver outlines five different "conflict styles" couples often employ. He then assesses each conflict style with regard to meeting one's "personal needs" and the couple's "relationship needs." Finally, he provides seven steps couples can follow to achieve genuine "resolution"—which is the conflict style he recommends above all others.

Rather than advocate a patriarchal chain of command for familial decision-making, Oliver (1993: 230) argues that achieving an authentic "resolution" to marital disagreements requires that couples "discuss and decide on a mutually acceptable solution." So, whereas PK traditionalists are dismayed by men's relinquishing of family leadership, Promise Keepers adhering to the Expressive Egalitarian archetype of godly manhood lament that men are often reluctant to find a mutually acceptable solution to family problems. Oliver recognizes that authoritarian tendencies are likely to be entrenched among some of his male readers. Undeterred, he chides them with biblical passages that equate Christlike love with selflessness and other-centeredness:

> Deciding on a mutually acceptable solution can sound easy. Over time it can become easy, but in the early stages of changing your conflict patterns it may be difficult. Be sure to set aside ample time for discussion and prayer. . . . Remember that you are choosing to bargain some of your personal needs for some of your relationship needs. Read 1 Corinthians 13 out loud. [1 Corinthians 13 contains the oft-quoted biblical passages describing love as "patient," "kind," "not proud," "not self-seeking" etc.] . . . At this point in workshops men have raised their hands and asked, "But what if we can't agree on a mutually acceptable solution?" After a brief pause I usually smile and respond by saying, "Well, if you can't agree on a solution, reach into your pocket, pull out a coin, ask the other person if they want heads or tails, and flip it." This usually brings a lot of laughter. "I'm serious," I quickly add. "If you can't decide, it's better to try something that might work than something that is a proven failure." (Oliver 1993: 230–231)

Tacking toward the Center: Constructive Contradictions in Traditionalist and Egalitarian PK Discourse

Given the strikingly different views of godly manhood advanced by PK authors (Rational Patriarch here, Expressive Egalitarian there), how can this religious movement have successfully captured the souls of nearly five million American men since its genesis? Would not even a cursory reading of PK manuals—or, for that matter, a weekend visit to a PK stadium conference where such authors address thousands of men—highlight the gross contradictions contained in elite Promise Keeper rhetoric? How do elite Promise Keepers write and speak on the topic of godly manhood without recognizing the dramatic disjunctures between their perspectives on this subject?

Elite Promise Keepers who embrace traditionalist and liberationist versions of godly manhood manage ideological contradictions by employing a rhetorical device that can be best described as "discursive tacking." I draw the term "tacking" from sailing parlance. Docking a sailboat against an offshore wind requires the boater to employ a "tacking" strategy—oscillating the boat left, then right, then left again repeatedly—until the boat reaches shore. Experienced boaters know that they cannot dock their boat by sailing directly into an offshore wind. In a remarkably similar fashion, the gender discourse in traditionalist and egalitarian PK advice manuals does not move in a singular direction against the headwinds of secular American culture. Indeed, the quick rise to prominence of the Promise Keepers was likely connected to the way in which its traditionalist and egalitarian leaders established a godly man archetype (whether Rational Patriarch or Expressive Egalitarian) only to depart from and return to that archetype repeatedly through each of their manuals. By employing this tacking strategy, PK authors such as Ed Cole and Gary Oliver built dexterity into their respective archetypes. In the end, these archetypes seem to overlap rather than overtly contradict one another.

Traditionalist Tacking

Despite his unabashed advocacy of domestic patriarchy, Ed Cole periodically expresses concern that his endorsement of husband headship may be misinterpreted by men who wish to act in a callous, cavalier, or abusive fashion toward their family members. Thus, while Cole unflinchingly crowns the husband and father as the "leader," "priest," and patriarch of the family, he is expressly critical of men who would use their domestic authority in a heavy-handed fashion. Cole (1982: 52) decries such abuses of power as "dictatorial authoritarianism." He argues that patriarchal leadership does not rule out "equality" with one's wife, who is scripturally described as the husband's "joint heir" (1 Peter 3:7) within the home (Cole 1982: 61, 89–90, 93). Cole does not elaborate on this latter contradiction. His readers are thus left to sort through a rhetorical paradox commonly deployed by traditionalist evangelical authors—an advocacy of strict essentialism and domestic patriarchy set alongside caveats about the purported "equality" of the husband and wife in God's eyes (Bartkowski 2001a). Nevertheless, this form of tacking enables the traditionalist Cole to sound—at times—remarkably similar to men's liberationists like Gary Oliver.

Cole tacks away from—and then returns to—traditionalist notions of masculinity on other subjects as well. He offers various warnings designed to discourage men from indulging in the perceived excesses of the very manliness he champions. Cole and other strict essentialists often paint men's sexual appetite as far eclipsing that of their female counterparts (Bartkowski 2001a). However, within particular portions of *Maximized Manhood*, Cole expresses concern that some male readers will misinterpret statements about men's hypersexuality as a license to engage in promiscuous sex. Cole (1982: chap. 3) identifies this issue as the "playboy problem." To circumvent a misinterpretation of his position, Cole reasserts the importance of male rationality and discipline. He argues that the "playboy" is not genuinely manly (i.e., "tough") because such sexually undisciplined men are enslaved by their own prurient appetites: "Affections, desires, appetites, all must be dealt with in discipline. Even love must be disciplined, or what we love will kill us. Discipline requires toughness."

"Toughness" itself is a concept Cole utilizes to navigate—that is to say, tack—deftly between a thoroughgoing male insensitivity and the liberated man's emotional hypersensitivity. Cole (1982: 61) attempts to cast his advocacy of "masculine toughness" as a reasonable middle path between some men's use of excessive force (decried as "roughness") on the one hand, and other men's capitulation to a feminized contemporary American culture (derided as "softness") on the other. Consequently, in apparent contradiction to his definition of manhood as "ruthless courage" not prone to "sentimentalizing" (1982: 68), Cole (1982: chap. 6) peppers such assertions with periodic admonitions that men must balance "tenderness" with "toughness."

Yet Cole himself is unable to sustain his rhetorical commitment to the middle path he charts between the "tough" and the "tender." In the end, Cole situates himself clearly on the side of the "tough" man rather than his "tender" counterpart: "Perhaps years ago, as a general rule, parents, educators, and political leaders may have erred on the side of toughness—but today it is the softness that is killing us. We must learn to be ruthless with ourselves at times" (1982: 61–62).

If this rhetoric fails to carry force with his male readership, Cole (1982: 62) points to the person he considers the paragon of toughness, albeit balanced with a minimal amount of tenderness—Jesus Christ: "Jesus was a perfect balance of the tender and tough." In the end, though, Cole (1982: 62) betrays his preference for toughness over tenderness by relegating Jesus' alleged tenderness to one concise sentence in his manual: "[Jesus] revealed His tenderness in His messages of love, His actions of healing and comforting, His death on the cross." Immediately after conceding this point, Cole lingers over Jesus' apparent toughness in considerably more detail. Make no mistake—Jesus was not a soft, liberated, feminized man:

> The same Jesus who swept little children up into His arms gripped that scourge of cords and drove the money-changers out of the temple. Some "sissified" paintings of Jesus come nowhere near showing the real character of Him who was both Son of Man and Son of God. Jesus was a fearless leader, defeating Satan, casting out demons, commanding nature, rebuking hypocrites. He had a nobility of character and a full complement of virtues which can be reproduced in us today— by the same Holy Spirit that dwelt in Him. God wants to reproduce this manhood in all men. What kind of manhood? *Christlikeness! Christlikeness and manhood are synonymous.* . . . Since to be like Jesus—Christlike—requires a certain ruthlessness, manhood does also. (Cole 1982: 62–63, emphasis in original)

Egalitarian Tacking

The discourse of liberated masculinity articulated by Gary Oliver is also layered with discursive contradictions. Here again, such contradictions move egalitarian PK manuals toward a "sensible center" that overlaps with the commentary of more traditionalist luminaries. Despite the overridingly egalitarian tone of his *Real Men Have Feelings Too*, Oliver tacks away from the Expressive Egalitarian archetype by strategically weaving gender difference rhetoric into his broader commitment to androgyny and by expressing a sense of ambivalence toward feminism. As noted above, the vast majority of Oliver's book is dedicated to debunking the six "myths of masculinity"— including "Myth 6: Men Are the Opposite of Women" (1993: 31). Yet, woven into Oliver's strong dismissal of radical gender difference is a strategic strand of suspicion for what he calls "radical" feminist notions of gender sameness.

In a scant but significant four pages of his nearly three-hundred-page tome on expressive masculinity, Oliver (1993: 33–36) blasts the "lunacy" and "ridiculous assumption[s]" of those who have "jumped on the gender-same bandwagon." Yet, paradoxically, even this four-page nod toward gender difference is layered with doublespeak that, in the end, returns to Oliver's (1993: 36ff) overarching argument *against* gender stereotyping: "It's true that men and women differ in the physiology of their brains. They are different. However, there is an unfortunate tendency to attribute many differences in individuals to sex/gender rather than numerous other factors that contribute to and shape our development."

Like Cole, then, Oliver (1993: 31–35) is interested in portraying his position as a sensible middle course between two discursive "extremes"—strict essentialism on the one hand and radical feminism on the other: "The feminist movement has been correct in emphasizing that men and women are of equal value and equal worth. Unfortunately some of the more radical feminists have failed to emphasize important ways in which men and women are different. They have interpreted equal to mean same. The two are *not* synonymous" (Oliver 1993: 35, emphasis in original). Like the discourse of traditional masculinity, Promise Keepers manuals beholden to an Expressive Egalitarian archetype of godly manhood are replete with discursive contradictions that mix and meld apparently competing gender ideologies. In the end, traditionalist and egalitarian discourses of godly manhood overlap and complement one another because authors in these divergent discourses adopt a tacking strategy—embracing and then distancing themselves from their respective archetypes.

Expanding the PK Repertoire:
Poeticized and Racialized (Re)Visions
of Godly Manhood

If feminism were the only social current against which Promise Keepers defined itself, the traditionalist and egalitarian discourses of evangelical masculinity surveyed above would exhaust the cultural tools necessary to build a grassroots constituency of godly men. Yet, social debates over gender in contemporary America are hardly so simple. The last two decades have witnessed the explosion of various men's movements—from mythopoetic men's gatherings and "wild man" retreats to the mobilization of African American men culminating in the Million-Man March (Messner 1997). Given these diverse forms of masculine mobilization, Promise Keepers must define itself not only against the women's movement, but against other men's movements as well. To compete effectively in the social field of men's identity movements, Promise Keepers has been wise to poeticize and racialize its notion of godly manhood.

Poetics of Promise-Keeping:
The Tender Warrior

The poetics of godly manhood—a PK rejoinder to the mythopoetic men's movement—is best evidenced in the popular advice manuals of Stu Weber (1993, 1997). PK men with a taste for poetic depictions of godly manhood are likely to find themselves sated by Weber's *Tender Warrior* (1993) and its follow-up volume, *Four Pillars of a Man's Heart* (1997).[2] As implied in the title of the former volume, Weber likens the godly man to a fearless warrior for the Lord. At the same time, Christian men are called to cultivate their "tender" side. Together, these complementary dimensions of godly manhood yield the Tender Warrior archetype. Given the persistence of gender traditionalism within evangelical circles, Weber (1993: 71) is quick to explain that being "tender" is not the same as being "soft"—the latter of which he assigns characteristics such as "mild, effeminate, [and] easily yielding to physical pressure."

Directly quoting the popular work of mythopoetic guru Robert Bly, Weber takes great pains to distinguish tenderness from softness. Indeed, Weber adroitly brings together the emotionally expressive language of fellow Promise Keeper Gary Oliver, the rationalistic rhetoric of compatriot Ed Cole, and the mythopoetic imagery popularized by Bly. Weber contends:

Underneath a warrior's breastplate beats a tender center. In every man there is the tender side. The side that connects to another. The thirst for relationship. The desire to touch and be touched. To hug. To link. To be with. A real man has feelings and isn't afraid to express them. . . . Now don't get me wrong. There is a difference between "tender" and *soft*. That's why they're two different words. I'm not at all advocating what Robert Bly calls the "soft male" of the 1970s. [Weber provides Bly's quote in which the "soft male" is described as "not happy," "lack[ing] in energy," and "not exactly life-giving."] We want Tender Warriors . . . not "soft males." . . . Masculine sensitivity never will and never *should* match its feminine counterpart. . . . It's a long way from macho to soft. Come down somewhere in between. (Weber 1993: 69–71, emphasis in original)

If such mixing of metaphors seems strikingly similar to the tacking discourse of Promise Keepers Ed Cole and Gary Oliver, precisely what do the likes of Stu Weber add to the PK cultural repertoire? The discourse of poeticized masculinity expands PK gender discourse through its richly symbolic and deeply metaphorical visions of the godly man. Indeed, Tender Warriors are complex creatures—reducible to neither logical reasoning (the Rational Patriarch) nor emotional release (the Expressive Egalitarian). Whereas advice manuals in the traditionalist and egalitarian discourses are didactic in tone and cerebral in their analysis of contemporary men's gender predicament, poeticized PK manuals invoke deep symbolic imagery to evoke mythic conceptualizations of godly manhood. The qualitative difference between these discourses is striking—analogous to the difference between reading an instruction booklet (the traditionalist and liberationist genres) and curling up with a richly crafted novel (the poeticized genre). Poeticized PK advice manuals are clearly aimed at men who prefer richly symbolic, metaphorical explorations of godly manhood to more detached, seminar-style treatments of Christian masculinity.

The Tender Warrior archetype is predicated on what Weber (1993, 1997) calls the Four Pillars of manhood, which themselves cover a composite of characteristics:

- the King Pillar—symbolizing men's vision and character;
- the Warrior Pillar—representing the strength and power of masculinity;

■ the Mentor Pillar—celebrating men's faith and wisdom; and

■ the Friend Pillar—depicting men's heart and their capacity for love.

These pillars are likened to other fourfold schema that appear in nature (e.g., four points on the compass, four seasons in the year). This rhetorical allusion becomes a gendered metaphor inasmuch as the Four Pillars of masculinity are perceived to be as "natural"—for which read "essential and formidable"—as the four seasons of the year or the four quadrants of the earth. And like center posts that work together to support a building, these Pillars are defined by their complementarity and, ultimately, by their combined strength. In Weber's own words, these Four Pillars work together to "stand against the elements" of the world and "hold one small civilization [the family] intact" (Weber 1997: 13).

Where marriage is concerned, Tender Warriors are neither status-conscious patriarchs nor full-fledged egalitarians. Rather, Tender Warrior husbands are "servant-leaders" who "color [their] headship in soft shades of the tender side . . . rather than in the harsh tones of the warrior side" (Weber 1993: 96–97). Nevertheless, the "steel strands" that form the "cable-like spine" of a Tender Warrior's masculinity are characterized foremost by "initiation," for "among the ancient Hebrew words for man is one meaning 'piercer.' Its feminine counterpart is 'pierced one.' . . . At his core a man is an initiator—a piercer, one who penetrates, moves forward, advances toward the horizon, leads" (1993: 45).

Consistent with the poetic imagery strewn throughout this discourse, Tender Warriors do not simply raise children—they "release arrows" into the next generation (Weber 1993: chap. 11). On the topic of fatherhood, Weber invokes complicated—but nonetheless gendered—metaphors of active subjects (archer, hunter), passive objects (target, prey), and the relations of interconnectedness (arrows, the hunt) between these otherwise disparate categories.

Weber's exploration of fatherhood begins with him plucking a poetic passage on parenting from the Bible's Psalm 127 (verses 3–4): "Behold, children are a gift of the Lord; the fruit of the womb is a reward. Like arrows in the hand of a warrior, so are the children of one's youth. How blessed is the man whose quiver is full of them; they shall not be ashamed, when they speak with their enemies at the gate." True to his mythopoetic style, Weber's parenting exegesis does not didactically list the "do's" and "don't's" of fatherhood. Instead, he probes the symbolic significance of the archetypal Tender Warrior father who is at once a disciplined archer with arrows in his quiver and a fearless hunter of bull elk:

> As I write these words, I'm looking at three arrows on my desk. . . . I'm turning one in my hand, now. Feeling the heft and balance of its shaft. Looking down its length to the round edges of its blunt head. It's a target arrow, and a good one. I wouldn't waste my time with anything less. . . . As I write these words, I'm looking at a picture on my desk. It's a picture of my three sons—Kent, Blake, and Ryan. . . . Each was crafted by the Lord God in the secret place of his mother's womb. And each was fashioned, balanced, and readied for flight within the four walls of our home. My three arrows were all designed to leap from the bow and split the air. I enjoy bow hunting, and I intend to *use* these arrows—whether on a cedar bale target or on a bull elk stamping on some back-country ridge on a frosty morning. These arrows aren't for show. They were never intended to stay in a quiver. . . . They were made to fly. They were made to pierce a target. So it is with my sons. . . . When the moment comes . . . young men—and young women—were made to experience flight. Flight to target, flight for maximum impact on that target. . . . Yet parents—and fathers in particular—are also accountable before God. Tender warriors are responsible for releasing those few precious arrows with all the sureness of eye and strength of arm that we can borrow from our God and Father. (Weber 1993: 155–157, emphasis in original)

Like the traditional and egalitarian PK discourse, poetic archetypes of the godly man enlist representations of men's bodies to construct essential masculinity. The archer-father must have a "sureness of eye" and "strength of arm." Such overt references are complemented by more subtle yet profound forms of masculine (even phallic) symbolism— the "arrow," with its "long shaft" and "blunt head," "splits the air" and "pierces its target." Yet, poeticized PK discourse rejects two-dimensional, either/or dichotomies that pit the Rational Patriarch against the Expressive Egalitarian. Instead, the Tender Warrior is defined by his complexity, holism, and polysemy.

The Tender Warrior archetype, then, engages in a form of discursive tacking that is subtle, sensitive, and (true to form) tender. By balancing reason with emotion and strength with tenderness, these tender tacking movements highlight the semi-porous boundary between "the masculine" and "the feminine." Indeed, Weber's archetype is defined by movement rather than stasis. In a metaphorical sense, Tender Warriors are engaged in a dance that synthesizes extremes and integrates disparate elements. The subtlety and fluidity of gender evidenced by the Tender Warrior archetype is complemented by a more contingent answer to the question of gender difference. As noted above, the Rational Patriarch archetype privileges strict essentialism by emphasizing the singularity and immutability of men's thoughts, feelings, and actions. From a strict essentialist standpoint, manhood is evidenced through reason and headship, while womanhood is manifested through their opposites—namely, emotional expression and gracious submission. By contrast, loose essentialism posits predispositional differences between men and women while portraying these differences as malleable and unfolding. Loose essentialism, an ideology prevalent in the mythopoetic men's movement (Schwalbe 1996), gives men license to change over the life course and to find points of overlap with women— such that men are capable of discovering their "feminine side." Whether they are mythopoetic disciples of Robert Bly or poeticized Promise Keepers in the mold of Stu Weber, these men would generally agree that the well-balanced man has come to terms with both his "inner man" and his "inner woman."

Multicultural Man:
Racial Reconciliation as Godly Masculinity

Each of the foregoing PK archetypes is predicated— from start to finish—on the notion of men's sharing a singular "essence." As Rational Patriarchs and Tender Warriors, all men are thought to possess a core set of divinely ordained characteristics—strength, vision, discipline—needed to lead their families and the nation. If men have abdicated those responsibilities, it is only because the sinfulness of human nature has corrupted God's design. According to the Expressive Egalitarian archetype, all men have been exposed to pernicious "myths of masculinity" and must reclaim the emotionally alienated aspect of their core masculine identity to become complete human beings.

A fourth discourse found in the Promise Keeper self-help literature turns away from notions of men's unity to instead wrestle with the question of men's diversity. Recall that the sixth of the Seven Promises that serve as the PK mission statement encourages each

individual Promise Keeper to "reach beyond any racial and denominational barriers to demonstrate the power of biblical unity." Racialized
PK discourses of godly manhood therefore depart from the theme of
men's singularity to address the vexing issue of racial difference. PK
engagement with the question of cultural difference leads some authors to champion an archetype—what I call the Multicultural Man—
quite distinctive from those featured above. By integrating the principle
of racial reconciliation into the PK mission statement, the Promise
Keepers further expand their cultural repertoire to engage with multiculturalism and racialized men's movements such as the Million-Man
March, with whom the Promise Keepers shared the National Mall just
two years apart, in October 1995 and October 1997, respectively.

In his contribution to *Seven Promises of a Promise Keeper*, "A Call
to Unity" (1994), PK founder Bill McCartney directly addresses the
"sin of racism" and advocates "biblical unity" through "racial reconciliation." Weaving together the antinomies of diversity and unity,
McCartney predicates interracial reconciliation on the presumption of
intraracial homogeneity. McCartney discusses how his eyes were initially opened—and were moved to profuse weeping—concerning racial injustice through his attendance at the funeral of a local black man
who played football for the University of Colorado prior to McCartney's
tenure with the team. While attending this funeral simply as an official representative of the current University of Colorado football program, McCartney was surprised to find himself "deeply affected" by
"the mournful singing of the mostly black congregation [as they] expressed a level of pain I hadn't seen or felt before. . . . This wasn't
just a funeral; it was also a gathering of wounded, long-suffering believers." Later, as McCartney (1994: 158) began to relate his church-
going experience to close African American friends and confidants, he
was "amazed . . . that despite the wide differences in their ages and
the places where they had grown up, they all identified directly with
the pain I had felt in the church that day." Experiences such as these
ultimately led McCartney (1994: 158) to "come in touch, for the first
time, with the pain, struggle, despair, and anguish of the black people."

PK diagnoses of racial injustice bring a distinctively evangelical
sin-and-redemption narrative to bear on the vexing problem of racism. In PK parlance, racism is a "sin" and "redemption" from such
sinfulness requires "racial reconciliation" in which "seeking forgiveness" and "establishing trust" figure prominently. To be sure, such spiri-
tualized and personalized imagery is more likely to resonate with the

individualistic sensibilities of an evangelical constituency than would global and generic appeals to "equal opportunity" or "social justice" (cf. Emerson and Smith 2000; Emerson, Smith, and Sikkink 1999; Smith 2000).

In the PK genre of racial reconciliation, the practice of discursive tacking takes the same hither-and-thither form as manifested in other genres while focusing on a different content—the sources of and possible solutions to racial inequality. PK writings on racial reconciliation regularly edge toward but then back away from a critical analysis of institutionalized racism. On the one hand, some terse statements by McCartney suggest a willingness to define racism as an institutionalized feature of social life in America. McCartney mentions the lack of head coaching opportunities for one of his black assistant coaches at the University of Colorado—"if he were white, he would have been a head coach somewhere years ago" (McCartney 1994: 159).

Yet, on the other hand, the evangelical penchant for defining sin as an individual transgression and reconciliation as a God-inspired personal conversion means that institutions recede into the background where PK solutions to American racism are concerned. Promise Keeper solutions to racism fall largely within the private realm. Drawing on the image of the warrior-like godly man whose personal prayers eclipse all social efforts to eradicate racism, McCartney urges: "Godly men must be impassioned with righteous determination to make amends [concerning racism]. Society tries in vain. Government efforts are losing ground. . . . May our prayer warriors work overtime. Let the pulse of the Body of Christ quicken and not rest until we see change. And let it begin with you and me" (1994: 165). He continues: "As one missionary said, 'I don't know how to love the poor except one at a time.' We can embrace that same wisdom in overcoming hostility and division in the body of Christ—one relationship at a time" (1994: 166).

While Christians in other times and places have urged unity under the "body of Christ" banner, McCartney's reinterpretation of this metaphor as a manifesto for American racial reconciliation—albeit one relationship at a time—represents a distinctly evangelical application of this cultural tool. McCartney (1994: 164) thus challenges each of his PK brothers to reconcile himself personally with some*one* of another race, saying that believers must:

- "enlarge our circle of understanding so we can appreciate another's history and experiences";

- "become good listeners and share the pain of those who have been hurt by past domination"; and
- "endure confrontations and crises until we establish trust in one another."

Strikingly, McCartney's vision of racial justice invokes metaphorical notions of "poverty" and "riches" that efface the practical, material dimensions of economic need: "This kind of love means that we come together in our *common poverty*, weaknesses, and sins to receive *God's riches*, strength, and grace—together" (McCartney 1994: 164–165, emphasis added).

How are Christian believers to get there ("racial reconciliation," "God's riches") from here ("the sin of racism")? True to Promise Keeper form, McCartney utilizes a metaphor of the body—in this case, the ultimate male body—to chart the path to racial reconciliation. Citing 1 Corinthians 12:24–26, McCartney's (1994: 166–167) essay ends with a plea for unity and love to be demonstrated among Christian "brethren" who are all members of the "body of Christ." From this vantage point, then, the unifying forces of men's shared gender ("brethren") and a common faith (membership in "the body of Christ") can trump racial divisions that would otherwise keep men separated from one another.[3]

Conclusion

Each of the PK gender discourses analyzed in this chapter is organized around a particular archetype that defines the "essence" of the godly man. In the traditional discourse of Promise Keeper advice, the godly man is depicted as a Rational Patriarch. This discourse, which predated the rise of the Promise Keepers but is incorporated into the movement through its most traditionalist spokesmen, is critical of feminism and gay rights. This traditionalist ideology charges godly men to embrace their divinely ordained status as disciplined patriarchs who unflinchingly lead their families with masculine logic. The PK masculine liberation discourse, which is more conciliatory toward feminism, defines the godly man as an Expressive Egalitarian. This evangelized ideology of male liberation subscribes to androgyny while championing men's open emotional expression and marital egalitarianism as the true marks of the godly man.

Borrowing a page from the mythopoetic men's movement, the PK discourse of poeticized manhood depicts the godly man as a Tender

Warrior. This archetypal image brings together a uniquely masculine blend of strength, sensitivity, and servant-leadership. Finally, the Promise Keepers discourse of racialized masculinity invokes an archetype of the Multicultural Man. This discourse recognizes differences and divisions among men; however, in the end, the PK discourse of racialized masculinity urges men to unite under the banner of Christian brotherhood.

I have identified two key rhetorical devices that PK writers use to construct their competing visions of godly manhood—the practice of discursive tacking and the deployment of gendered metaphors. Where thematic contradictions arise within and across these self-help literatures, Promise Keeper writers turn inconsistency into complementarity through discursive tacking. Like a sailboat that must "tack" by repeatedly redirecting itself to dock safely against an offshore wind, PK writers invoke—and then periodically distance themselves from—masculine archetypes such as the Rational Patriarch and the Expressive Egalitarian. Tacking is accomplished in a much more subtle fashion where the Tender Warrior and Multicultural Man archetypes are concerned. The practice of tacking enables Promise Keeper writers to construct discursive bridges over the chasms that would otherwise place these ideologies at odds. Discursive tacking enables PK writers to produce flexible visions of godly manhood that appear "holistic" and "well-rounded."

Leading Promise Keepers are linked by another rhetorical device they commonly deploy—gendered metaphors. PK luminaries frequently use men's "maleness"—actually, symbolic representations of the male body—as the means for "fleshing out" their masculine archetypes. Writers in the traditional and poeticized PK discourses emphasize the strength and hardness of men's bodies—often through a combination of overt and subtle sexual or phallic references. Liberationist authors highlight the cathartic effects—both physically and psychologically—that can result from men's emotional release and a more egalitarian approach to social relationships. The racialized PK discourse uses differences in men's bodies—black/white skin color—to engage issues of men's diversity and inequality; however, this discourse ultimately invokes the biblical metaphor of integrative embodiment—the church as a singular "body of Christ"—in an effort to privilege themes of Christian unity and oneness in the face of racial and denominational diversity.

This loose melange of gender discourses is likely one reason for the Promise Keepers' quick rise to prominence during the 1990s. Given the diversity and flexibility of these gender ideologies, PK was able to appeal to men with a wide variety of gender sensibilities. However, flexible ties are not those that bind. As I argue in the conclusion to this volume, the ideological diffuseness of the Promise Keepers probably contributed to the movement's equally fast decline.

4 Reforming American Culture

Sport, Gender, and Religion at Stadium Conferences

Having examined the ideological resources elite Promise Keepers provide for the movement, in this chapter I consider the group's signature event—stadium conferences. In rendering this portrait, I rely largely on fieldwork[1] conducted at the 1999 Choose This Day conference held in the San Antonio Alamodome. I also draw selectively on interview accounts of PK men's conference-going experiences. Conferences, the most distinctive and successful evangelizing tool utilized by the Promise Keepers, are a radical departure from men's everyday worlds. During these events, conference-goers engage in an array of practices that both reinforce and undermine conventional forms of American culture. This chapter analyzes the series of cultural paradoxes that characterize the relationship between PK conferences on the one hand and sport, gender, and religion on the other.

Conference activities enable men to renegotiate cultural boundaries that conventionally demarcate rowdy celebration from somber reflection, masculine reason from feminine emotion, and staid religion from insurgent revivalism. In renegotiating these boundaries, PK conferences generate intense feelings of cohesion and liberation among the men who attend them. PK conferences are not, however, characterized by a thoroughgoing erasure of social boundaries. Even as men dramatically subvert some elements of sport, gender, and religion at conferences, they reinforce other conventional aspects of these cultural phenomena. By appropriating selective elements from the repertoires of sport, gender, and religion—and then evangelizing these cultural borrowings—PK conferences create an environment in which men can safely experiment with novel ways of understanding themselves, relating to their fellows, and interpreting the world in which they live.

Rowdy Yet Respectable: Evangelizing Sport and Leisure

Given the legions of men streaming into the San Antonio Alamodome and the loud music emanating from its outermost doors, it is easy to assume that the crowd's collective sojourn to this southwest Texas sports mecca is motivated by a desire to see the world champion San Antonio Spurs basketball team crush National Basketball Association opponents with its "twin towers" of David Robinson (now retired) and Tim Duncan. But that is not the case. Nor will it involve watching the Dallas Cowboys or their famously underdressed cheerleaders hold training camp as they do each preseason here. The dome is also the home of a long list of other noteworthy events—high school football's all-star All American Bowl and college football's Alamo Bowl, boat and auto shows, monster truck extravaganzas, rock concerts, and the Tejano Music Awards. Yet, none of these is on the bill during this sultry summer night in San Antonio. Tonight men are beckoned to the dome not by competitive sports but by spiritual pilgrimage.

At the heart of any Promise Keepers conference is the melding together of rowdiness and respectability. Here, conviviality and abandonment meet gentility and restraint. The rowdiness of PK conferences—which, quite tellingly, begin on Friday evenings—is fostered by the cultural residue of sport that is found in stadiums and arenas across America. The raucous spirit of sport haunts these spaces even when other types of events, including PK conferences, take place in them.

As the contemporary heir to Muscular Christianity, the Promise Keepers appropriate and evangelize sport rituals at their conferences. Chanting, cheering, and screaming erupt during each break period between conference speakers' addresses. At several points during the San Antonio conference, men were challenged to cheer for Jesus at the top of their lungs by men on stage. "Come on! That's not loud enough," boomed someone up front with his hand cupped behind his ear. "I can't hear you! Jesus can't hear you!"

The sense of abandon at PK conferences is further heightened by men on stage who urge the dome's all-male audience to clap, stomp their feet, and cheer—at times, in noise-making contests that pit one faction of conference-goers against another. Drawing on the competitiveness of sport, Mike Silva (the first speaker at Choose This Day-San Antonio) divided the arena full of men down the center aisle. During his talk, he periodically engaged these rival factions of conference-goers in a call-and-response competition. At each high point in his talk, he would turn toward the men situated in one half of the arena and yell into the microphone, "Get it?"—to which the men would scream instantaneously (after some rehearsing), "Got it!" If men on either side of the arena responded weakly, they were chided by Silva, who would shrug his shoulders at the competing faction of men on the other side of the arena. Nevertheless, such competitiveness is done in a playful and good-natured fashion. And, consistent with motifs of mercy and forgiveness that are emphasized throughout PK conferences, Silva was always careful to give each half of the dome an opportunity to redeem itself for paltry responses. Even so, such rituals produce a rowdy atmosphere of abandonment in which men seek to outdo one another as friendly adversaries in contests of physical (in this case, vocal) strength.

At conferences, the frivolity of noisemaking is complemented by a range of gestures and chants transposed from the world of sport. Between speakers, music blares and "the wave" breaks out, traveling through the circular dome like a whirlpool. As men cheer for Jesus and offer raucous rounds of applause for speakers, spontaneous chants often erupt from among the crowd. Again, such chanting pits brother against brother not in physical conflict but more in sanguine verbal contests. Adapting an old sports favorite, cadres of men yell in unison, "We love Jesus, yes we do! We love Jesus, how 'bout you?," with each successive group trying to outshout the one that preceded it.

Despite these cultural transpositions from the world of sport, Promise Keeper conferences are also replete with signature gestures that are uniquely "PK." Some of these require a kinetic fluency (cf. Mazer 1998)—that is to say, a mastery of bodily movement and physical coordination on the part of the men who perform them. During prayerful songs, many men stand with both of their arms raised toward the heavens for lengthy periods of time. When undertaken in the upper deck of the Alamodome's steeply banked seats, standing "no hands on the edge" is dizzying and, in a sense, physically liberating—akin to riding a roller coaster "no hands" over its steepest hill. Beach balls bounce around the audience between speakers, creating a festive

atmosphere and keeping men alert. From time to time, large paper air-
planes glide through the air. The crowd watches and cheers, eager to
see whose craft will stay aloft longest before careening into the crowd.
To be sure, the physical skills needed to perform such playful acts are
not on a par with Michael Jordan slam-dunking a basketball, Brett Favre
throwing a touchdown pass to a fellow Green Bay Packer, or Tiger
Woods driving a golf ball off the eighteenth tee. Yet, these convivial
practices connect PK conferences to the world of sport and leisure,
thereby creating an atmosphere in which men can "let go."

During speakers' talks, references to sport, local teams, and star
athletes abound. The National Basketball Association's San Antonio
Spurs reigned as world champions during 1999, when Choose This
Day-San Antonio was held. Consequently, speakers frequently mentioned the Spurs and their most prominent stars—center David
Robinson and forward-center Tim Duncan. Each of these men stretch
the tape at over seven feet tall, and the mere mention of their names
elicited raucous cheers from conference attenders. When one speaker
mentioned that he was from New York City, he was met with a low-
pitched but good-natured chorus of boos. To win the 1999 NBA cham-
pionship, the Spurs had to defeat the league's most physical team, the
New York Knicks.

Immersion in the sensate culture of sport at PK conferences quickly
leads to other forms of conviviality. Conferences feature a great deal
of loud music and festive singing. Given the broad repertoire of PK's
Maranatha! Promise Band, conferences feature both traditional hymns
like "A Mighty Fortress is Our God" and upbeat contemporary Christian anthems such as "Lord I Lift Your Name on High." Thus, ear-splitting sounds are complemented by heart-stirring songs. As one of the
more popular PK T-shirts reads, "REAL MEN SING REAL LOUD." PK
men spend a great deal of time singing together throughout conferences, and much of the Friday night "warm-up" entails long bouts of
singing one song after another. The songs chosen for these events are
noteworthy for their low, rich tones and baritone keys—thereby emphasizing the deep pitch in men's voices.

Men who attended Choose This Day in San Antonio received a
"special treat," as it was described to them by Isaac, the Latino emcee of the affair. After lunch on Saturday, the San Antonio conference
included a concert by The Katinas. This band of five brothers has been
adopted by many in southwestern Texas, where they have throngs of
adoring fans. During the concert, a large cadre of young conference-

goers cheered, danced, and paraded in front of the stage. The Katinas concert left no doubt about this band of brothers' incredible musicianship and relentless energy.

Lest this event be mistaken for a regular (secular) concert, the high-decibel songs played by The Katinas are designed to penetrate not only the ears, but the hearts and souls of men at the conference. The beats are vibrant and the tunes are catchy, even as the lyrics are replete with spiritual references. Despite their engagement with popular music, The Katinas have never "sold out." As it was explained to us, the group turned down a lucrative contract with a major record label when producers at the label told them they would need to adopt more "mainstream" (that is to say, nonreligious) lyrics.

Whether conference anthems are offered by The Katinas, the Maranatha! Promise Band, Michael W. Smith, or other popular Christian musical artists, the objective is always the same: getting men to cut loose. PK conferences jettison the dry, auditory act of "listening" to music for what might be best described as rhapsodic rapture. Here, melodies are felt, experienced, and imbibed rather than merely heard. Like rock and hip-hop concerts, deep bass riffs and powerfully amplified drums engulf, stimulate, and caress the senses of conference-goers. Convivial music creates an atmosphere of abandonment, frivolity, and unapologetic emotional expression.

As is often the case with sports events and musical concerts, PK conferences blur the line between performer and audience. The raucousness of the crowd at the Alamodome was enhanced by large overhead television monitors. Between conference talks, these overhead monitors broadcast live footage of festive men from an array of "audience cams" panning the floor-level seats and mezzanine areas. As audience cams scan through the Alamodome, men wait in anticipation to see if they and their comrades will be featured on the overhead monitors. If successful in their efforts to appear onscreen,[2] they cheer, raise their hands, and sing more loudly than ever, their rowdy antics broadcast for all fifty thousand conference-going spectators to see. During periods of extended singing, video images on the overhead monitors prominently display the smiling faces and swaying bodies of close-knit godly men. While men sing, these monitors also feature the scrolling words to songs along the bottom of the screen. In this way the screens level the playing field between those unfamiliar with the words to the songs (such as PK newcomers and unsaved "seekers") and those who know the lyrics by heart (veteran churchgoers, longtime evangelicals). Rowdy festivals in all these respects, PK conferences evoke powerful feelings through their sustained assault on men's ears, eyes, hands, voices—and hearts.

While the rowdiness of PK conferences is inspired by the world of sport, the standards of respectability that emerge at such events keep the excesses of the athletic world at bay. In this way, godly manhood is characterized not solely by abandon and conviviality, but also by restraint and soberness. In fact, PK conferences encourage soberness both literally and figuratively. Despite the sense of frivolity associated with PK conferences, a de facto sobriety is ensured by prohibitions against the sale of alcohol in stadiums during these events. This prohibition creates an atmosphere in which men can "let go" and "be themselves" without the recklessness, boorishness, and violent outbursts that often accompany the use of alcohol at sporting events, concerts, and mass gatherings of the secular variety. Thus, while the stadium itself provides an ethos of sport in which men can "get rowdy" and "let go," the prohibition against alcohol at PK conferences channels this effervescence in a positive direction. Here, rowdiness is tempered by sobriety, and playfulness never devolves into petulance.

Masculine respectability is also fostered at PK conferences through a soberness that is more metaphorical in character. PK conferences are not all fun and games. They are also a time for sober reflection about things that "matter most" in men's lives—faith, family, friendship, and each brother's relationship with his God. Conference speakers exhort men to remain committed to the "daily disciplines" of Christian living—meeting frequently with God in prayer, reading the Bible regularly, attending church with their families, and sharing the gospel with unsaved friends. In this context, "discipline" has a distinct meaning. These daily disciplines underscore men's moral responsibilities to their loved ones in the home, their colleagues in the workplace, and fellow citizens in their local communities. Respectability, in this sense, entails responsibility—for one's life and relationships with others.

At several key points during conferences, men are asked to "break out" into small groups and form prayer circles with their brothers. As men form breakout groups and prepare for small-group prayer, they discuss their standing before God with other men at the conference. Trading names, telephone numbers, and email addresses after a time, they also vow to hold one another accountable for meeting the moral standards articulated in the Seven Promises—each of which is discussed at the conference. Accountability entails encouraging a PK brother's continued adherence to the Seven Promises, and more broadly to the daily disciplines of prayer, scripture study, church attendance, and family-centered living. These breakout groups and prayer circles often give rise to intense expressions of emotion, as some seekers "accept Christ" for the first time and those who have lived unrighteously seek reconciliation before God and recommit their lives to Jesus Christ with their brothers' support. Within prayer circles, supplication is commonly sought in close quarters by men who are holding hands or joined together with arms around one another. Prayer here is a tactile, sensual experience, as the wide berth of physical space that typically characterizes man-to-man interactions gives way to a closeness that is at once physical and emotional.

Somber reflection is fostered further by speakers who raise issues that underscore men's common concerns and shared sense of vulnerability. Gary Rosberg, a conference speaker whose regular job is as a Christian therapist, related the moving story of a man who had recently discovered that his wife was having an affair. Rummaging through the couple's closet in search of a mundane household item, this man had stumbled on a letter written to his wife by her lover. The poignancy of this story was evidenced by the utter silence that fell upon every one of the fifty thousand men in the dome as it was told. As sullen expressions surfaced on the faces of men throughout the Alamodome, Rosberg invited each married man at the conference to consider the feelings that such a discovery would evoke in him if the letter had been addressed to his own wife. After bringing conference-goers down into this valley of despair, Rosberg ushered hope back in by discussing this husband's evolving recognition of his own culpability—through his emotional insensitivity—for his wife's affair. Frowns broke into smiles among conference-goers as Rosberg recounted how this man went about winning back the affections of the woman he loved and sought to repair their broken relationship.

Given the feelings of shared vulnerability and empathy generated at PK conferences, trust runs deep among the men who attend these events. Indeed, they refer to one another as "brother." During my fieldwork, several Promise Keepers told me that conferences were the only events that they have ever attended in a stadium or arena where they felt that they could trust each and every one of the thousands of men there. Some even went so far as to say that if they ever lost their wallet at a PK conference, they were sure that it would be returned to them with the money and credit cards intact.

Given the stadium venues at which PK conferences are held, an ethic of respectability is manifested in some ways that may seem mundane at first blush but are rather startling upon reflection. At all conferences, Promise Keepers are told that they must not leave litter of any kind—cups, cans, plates, paper—in the aisles or under their seats. At the Choose This Day conference in San Antonio, the emcee Isaac exhorted men to "leave the dome cleaner than we found it." In pursuit of this objective, organizers come prepared with garbage bags that they pass out after lunch and near the end of the program. These garbage bags make their way around the dome by being passed from one man to the next. Palpable norms of collective responsibility prod men sitting near aisles to venture out in small groups from their seats to pick up items that clutter walkways. While American sports fans are notorious for a slovenliness that leaves heavily littered stadiums in their wake, standards of respectability at PK conferences leave host stadiums and arenas in immaculate condition.

Bargaining with Patriarchy: Gender and Family at PK Conferences

Apart from selectively appropriating social elements from the world of sport, PK conferences also speak to the domains of gender and family. At the peak of PK's prominence, critics charged that the movement essentially sought to reassert the legitimacy of male privilege and men's authority in the home (what gender scholars call hegemonic masculinity). This charge deserves some scrutiny, and requires a brief foray away from the goings-on of PK conferences into the realm of gender theory. Hegemonic masculinity, a term first coined by R. W. Connell (1987), refers to the most widely held beliefs about manhood in a society at any given time. Regardless of the beliefs that constitute it, hegemonic masculinity is always defined in opposition to emphasized femininity. Emphasized femininity is the constellation of ideas believed to constitute the "essence" of womanhood. Despite their wide acceptance, the characteristics that constitute emphasized femininity are invariably devalued relative to hegemonic masculine traits. In its contemporary form, hegemonic masculinity naturalizes men's penchant for aggression, social dominance, and rational thinking by distinguishing these qualities from their devalued feminine counterparts—meekness, submissiveness, and emotional sensitivity. A great deal of work in the sociology of gender has revealed that these ideologies are real in their social consequences. Hegemonic masculinity has led to a cultural valorization of the work performed in social arenas traditionally dominated by men (the economy, male-dominated occupations, and the political sphere) while stigmatizing "women's work" (predominantly female occupations, housework, and child care).

In addition to marginalizing feminine qualities, hegemonic masculinity also subordinates rival definitions of manhood. Despite some significant changes in social attitudes toward gays, hegemonic masculinity remains a staunchly heterosexual ideology. Social practices that stigmatize or marginalize gay men often do so by feminizing them. Moreover, these practices are legitimated on the grounds that same-sex relationships are "against nature." Among the elite discourses of godly masculinity featured in chapter 3 of this volume, the Rational Patriarch archetype—defined by its commitment to essentialism (innate gender difference) and patriarchy (husband-headship) and by its vocal condemnation of homosexuality—is most closely aligned with these aspects of hegemonic masculinity.

Hegemonic masculinity, however, has recently undergone some significant changes. Within the last several decades, feminism has called into question many of the privileges that American men have long enjoyed in both public and private spheres. At the same time, arguments for gender egalitarianism in the home and workplace have found fertile soil in the American consciousness. Such cultural changes have gone hand in glove with dramatic structural transformations, such as skyrocketing rates of labor force participation among women and the economic independence wives and mothers reap from wage-earning. Given these developments, Connell (1995: 77) himself has been careful to call attention to the adaptability of hegemonic masculinity, which he describes in more recent work as a "historically mobile relation" with "ebb and flow." Confronted with threats to its legitimacy, hegemonic masculinity has changed. Sexism is no longer acceptable behavior, and wife-battering is considered a major social problem.

Noteworthy changes in gender and family ideologies have been evident not only in mainstream American culture, but also within the subculture of evangelical Protestantism. Contrary to damning portrayals that paint religious conservatives as a culturally backward monolithic bloc, evangelical Protestant luminaries and laity do not agree on questions of gender difference, the exercise of authority in the home, or the household division of labor (Bartkowski 2001a; Smith 2000). Such ideological fissures are certainly evident within the Promise Keepers, where traditionalist advocates of the Rational Patriarch archetype can easily be seen as an anachronism when compared with their more contemporary counterparts—the Expressive Egalitarian, Tender Warrior, and Multicultural Man (see chapter 3).

To cut to the chase and bring this brief conference intermission to a close, several questions surface. Given recent challenges to hegemonic masculinity and the diversity of godly man archetypes within PK, to what extent do Promise Keeper conferences amount to a gender backlash designed to reassert male privilege and reinvigorate patriarchal dominance? If critics of the movement are to be believed, it is no surprise that men would flock to all-male gatherings at football stadiums in an effort to recapture lost ground or salve the wounds inflicted by their diminished social status. But are such accounts credible?

A careful examination of Promise Keeper conferences reveals important nuances and contradictions concerning gender and family relations that are missed by reductionistic explanations such as "backlash" and "protest." In truth, PK conferences mix elements of gender orthodoxy and family traditionalism with progressive visions of godly manhood. In short, PK conferences provide men with strategies for "bargaining with patriarchy" (cf. Kandyoti 1988). As was the case with the world of sport, such bargaining entails a selective appropriation that mixes the old with the new and blurs the lines that demarcate taken-for-granted social categories like "masculinity" and "male family leadership."

Among the aspects of hegemonic masculinity affirmed at Promise Keeper conferences are traditional ideas that distinguish masculinity from its feminine counterpart, as well as those that draw lines between heterosexuality and homosexuality. Conference speakers, and many of the conference-going men to whom I spoke, were quick to define qualities like strength, bravery, and leadership as part of the natural masculine character. Conference talks regularly honor male scriptural characters who are believed to personify these distinctly masculine qualities. Military warriors discussed in the Bible, such as Joshua and Naaman, are described by speakers with such adjectives as "strong," "self-sufficient," and "a man's man." At the Alamodome conference, Joshua was valorized as a "patriarch" on more than one occasion. Thus, when the word "patriarch" is used at conferences to describe men in the Bible, it is not a disparaging term (as it would be among feminists and gender egalitarians). Within PK, to be called a "patriarch" is to be given high praise, as this compliment underscores the manly exercise of household leadership—one that couples the strength of masculine authority in the home with the responsible man's protection of his family.

Consistent with the Rational Patriarch archetype, conference speakers sometimes interpret scriptural verses in a way that uphold hegemonic masculinity. The scriptural passage upon which the Choose This Day conference series was based is Joshua 24:15—"Choose this day whom you will serve, whether the gods your fathers served in the region beyond the River, or the gods of the Amorites in whose land you dwell; but as for me and my house, we will serve the Lord." This passage emphasizes the importance of masculine strength and leadership evidenced by Joshua on behalf of a displaced people. Among people who have been banished from their home and thrust into an evil land (as have all God's children), men who "take charge" are to be revered. Isaac, the emcee of Choose This Day-San Antonio, called men's attention to this passage at the conference's opening session. He explained that Joshua earned the title of "great patriarch" in his family. Joshua did not shrink from the mantle of authority God had placed upon him—and neither should men today. Raising his voice until it boomed through the Alamodome's public address system, Isaac shouted: "It is a man's responsibility to choose for his household whom they will serve! And as long as you live under this roof, honey, we will serve the Lord in this family!"

During talks and small-group interactions, speakers and conference-goers often liken masculinity to "iron," drawing on a key passage from the Bible's Book of Proverbs (27:17) as they do so: "As iron sharpens iron, one man sharpens another." As many Promise Keepers interpret this passage, the hard "iron" masculinity of one man is needed to sharpen the equally tough character of his brother. Anything softer and weaker than this durable metal-masculinity will be incapable of molding God's sons into the men they are intended to become. At times, this metaphor gives way to the telling of stories about men in the Bible who exhibited "wills of iron." At Choose This Day, one speaker depicted Shadrach, Meshach, and Abednego in just this way. As described in the Bible's Book of Daniel (chapter 3), these three men were confronted with the choice of worshiping a gold idol or being burned to death in a fiery furnace by the wicked King Nebuchadnezzar. Upon their refusing to bow down to the idol, the king became furious and had his henchmen make the furnace seven times hotter. After being bound up, Shadrach, Meshach, and Abednego were summarily thrown into the furnace. The furnace was said to have been so hot that it killed even the henchmen who brought the three toward the fire. Once Shadrach, Meshach, and Abednego were thrown in the furnace, King Nebuchadnezzar was astonished to see the three men walking about unbound in the fire with a fourth figure, described cryptically in the biblical account (Daniel 3:24–29) as follows:

> Then King Nebuchadnezzar leaped to his feet in amazement and asked his advisers, "Weren't there three men that we tied up and threw into the fire?"
>
> They replied, "Certainly, O king."
>
> He said, "Look! I see four men walking around in the fire, unbound and unharmed, and the fourth looks like a son of the gods."
>
> Nebuchadnezzar then approached the opening of the blazing furnace and shouted, "Shadrach, Meshach and Abednego, servants of the Most High God, come out! Come here!" So Shadrach, Meshach and Abednego came out of the fire, and the satraps, prefects, governors and royal advisers crowded around them. They saw that the fire had not harmed their bodies, nor was a hair of their heads singed; their robes were not scorched, and there was no smell of fire on them.
>
> Then Nebuchadnezzar said, "Praise be to the God of Shadrach, Meshach and Abednego, who has sent his angel and rescued his servants! They trusted in him and defied the king's command and were willing to give up their lives rather than serve or worship any god except their own God. Therefore I decree that the people of any nation or language who say anything against the God of Shadrach, Meshach and Abednego be cut into pieces and their houses be turned into piles of rubble, for no other god can save in this way."

Stories like this, of course, underscore the thoroughgoing nature of spiritual conversion. The evil Nebuchadnezzar is transformed into the most ardent defender of Shadrach, Meshach and Abednego and their god. In the context of PK's all-male conferences, these three biblical heroes underscore the tenacity of faith exhibited by godly men and the protection God provides to those sons who show an unrelenting commitment to him.

Traditional masculine ideals are also reinforced by the very space in which PK conferences take place—football stadiums. It is no mere coincidence that PK was founded by a highly successful collegiate football coach, Bill McCartney. While he coached the University of Colorado Buffaloes (tellingly nicknamed the "Buffs"), McCartney led a team that was regularly ranked among the best in the nation, was feared by its conference rivals, and convincingly won the national title near the end of his coaching tenure. Molded by his years as a coach of one of the elite teams in collegiate football, "Coach Mac" typically serves as the headline speaker at PK conferences and delivers rousing talks befitting his title.

By drawing so heavily on the masculinized sport of football, PK reveals itself as the leading incarnation of modern-day Muscular Christianity (Ladd and Mathisen 1999). Despite the recent inroads that women have made into various sectors of the public sphere—including women's sport—football continues to be a domain in which unrelenting determination and physical prowess are embodied by the male "warriors" that play the game (cf. Burstyn 1999; Dworkin and Messner 1999). The military model that has long pervaded men's sport reaches its apex on the football "gridiron"—one of the few remaining sanctuaries in the world of sport that has not been invaded by female athletes.

Given the masculinized character of American football, stadiums are veritable temples in which faithful fans ritually worship the superior skills of male athletes and the bloodthirstiness of top coaches. Virtually all of the Promise Keepers that I interviewed remarked on the importance of holding conferences in stadiums. Several mentioned that they felt "at home" or "comfortable" in such venues. And because many had played football as young boys or attended football games at the very stadium in which they later attended a PK conference, football stadiums are quite literally "familiar turf."

Beyond the symbolic meanings or subjective memories associated with these masculinity-saturated spaces, the physical architecture of football stadiums (and arenas in general) lends itself to rituals that blur the line between sport and spirituality while shoring up masculine identity. One pastor recounted the "shivers" that went up his spine when a conference speaker invited every minister in attendance to take the stage for a show of gratitude from the men who depend on them to live a godly life. As these pastors began parading toward the stage located in one end zone of this football stadium, they were greeted with a gradual escalation of cheering and foot-stomping provided courtesy of the sixty thousand men in attendance. Once the ministers were all on stage, the conference speaker provided some additional chiding for the conference attenders to show their thankfulness to pastors who sacrifice so much for the good of men and their families. With that, the whole stadium erupted in a deafening roar that didn't let up for several minutes. Pastors stood on the stage, at once visibly startled and deeply moved by the men's boisterous show of support. Typically not one to be at a loss of words, the pastor who recounted this experience to me during an interview struggled to convey the significance of the experience. Clearly affected by this memorable moment and searching for the words to articulate it, he finally explained that he now understands "the rush" that members of the Dallas Cowboys and Texas Rangers get as they are cheered on by throngs of rabidly devoted fans.

Finally, the Promise Keepers organization reinforces hegemonic masculinity through an explicitly stated opposition to homosexuality. Early on in the movement, leaders attracted the ire of gay rights supporters by posting a position paper on their website that defined homosexuality as "sexual sin." (For that matter, the PK leadership define any sexual contact outside of marriage as sinful.) What's more, Ed Cole, the PK author featured in chapter 3, is not alone in condemning homosexuality. PK founder Bill McCartney actively campaigned against gay rights when Colorado's Amendment 2 stimulated political controversy across the nation in 1992 with its proposed prohibition of the extension of protected class status to gays and bisexuals. Although Promise Keeper speakers are careful not to condemn gay persons—"hate the sin, love the sinner" is the common phrase—this form of boundary work is consonant with hegemonic masculinity.

Despite these points of congruence with hegemonic masculinity, PK conferences are also a site for subverting gender and family traditionalism. In fact, if the accounts of PK conference-goers are to be believed, the transformative power of these events is rooted less in their reinforcement of hegemonic masculinity than in their subversion of it. Hence, just as it is inaccurate to pigeonhole elite Promise Keepers as a monolithic bloc of stuffy sentimentalists who wax nostalgic for the "good old days" when "men were men," it is erroneous to reduce PK conferences to a collective reinforcement of hegemonic masculinity. How, then, do PK conferences undermine hegemonic masculinity?

One of the most striking features of conferences involves the physical and emotional closeness exhibited by men who attend them. Promise Keepers are an emotionally expressive lot, and nowhere is this more clear than at conferences. PK speakers talk extensively about getting men emotionally connected with their "brothers." Hence, a primary goal of PK conferences is the cultivation of intimacy—or, as one speaker cleverly put it, "into me see"—between men. PK conferences feature many opportunities for emotional expression and social support, including admissions of past transgressions and forgiveness conferred by one's brothers. Often such experiences are heart-wrenching for the man seeking spiritual renewal and are quite moving to observe. Small-group sessions that take place at several points during the program provide men with the opportunity—or rather the imperative—for entering into soulful exchanges with their brothers. During these small-group exchanges, men reveal their darkest secrets and share their deepest fears with one another, including struggles with sexual temptation, feelings of racial prejudice, and seemingly intractable problems with their wives and children. As men express their anxieties and struggles on issues of common concern, tears well up in some men's eyes and hunched over bodies indicate the emotional brokenness of others. Inevitably, these men are consoled with warm hugs from other men in their group or outstretched hands on their shoulders. Typically, such gestures of affirmation give way to close-knit prayer circles in which men, linked arm-in-arm, offer supplication for hurting brothers within their group.

Dramatic departures from hegemonic masculinity take other forms at PK conferences as well. Although words like "patriarch" and "male leadership" are common fare at these venues, the meaning of these terms is complicated by efforts to distinguish men's benevolent family leadership from domestic domination. A speaker who urged men to "take leadership" in their homes said that he defines leadership in terms of servanthood. In fact, terms like "servant-leadership" are now quite common within the evangelical subculture and among grassroots Promise Keepers, to the point that the more hierarchical notion of "headship" has been gradually supplanted by softer neopatriarchal language. Men who enlist terms like "servant-leadership" to describe male authority within the home are, of course, borrowing a page from the Tender Warrior archetype of godly manhood.

Interestingly, the standard by which many in the movement judge their leadership in the home is their service to other family members. Several married men explicitly say that the goal of the Promise Keeper is to "outserve" his wife. How? By doing more to serve his wife than she does in return on any given day. A husband's effort to "outserve" his wife is an odd mix of progressive and traditional domestic relations. On the one hand, the husband in this relationship is charged with being self-sacrificing and with proactively ascertaining and then meeting the needs of his wife. Yet, on the other hand, the notion of "outserving" someone else is traditional in the sense that husbands are competing with their wives to see who can perform more acts of selfless service for the other in the course of any given day.[3]

Many of the men I interviewed take such principles quite seriously and strive to become better husbands by holding themselves to standards in which leadership actually entails sensitivity and service. Jamon, an African American Promise Keeper in his mid-thirties, suggested that his involvement in PK has helped him to overcome "a lot of marital problems over the years" that he and his wife have had. While not all men reported having problems with their wives prior to becoming involved in PK, Jamon's response is typical in the sense that it portrays PK as a valuable resource for becoming a more sensitive husband. When asked how his involvement in PK has affected his marriage, he replies:

> I understand that it is my calling to serve her and to love her. What the Promise Keepers have helped me initially to realize [is] that I have to love her, even beyond my own ability. . . . There's only one resource that will take me there—that is Christ. [PK] has been helpful to me. The literature that I've read about honoring your wife, about keeping promises, about being men of integrity, about realizing God does not want us to divorce, about dying to our wives. I read a book. I still haven't finished it, I'm about half way through, called *Disciplines of a Godly Man*. The second chapter . . . talked about *sanctifying* your wife, *suffering* for your wife. I forget what the other "S" is—*supporting*, something like that. I realize how I don't do that and I need to do that.
>
> *[Bartkowski:] How could you do that . . . in a practical sense?*
>
> To forgive her when she makes mistakes, when she sins, when she's angry. To reach out to her. And the Bible calls us to understand our wives. I'm still not [pause]. I don't understand my wife, but I know I need to. I know there are hurts

and issues in her that are just totally foreign to me and I need to understand those if I'm going to be a godly husband to her. So, in some ways, when she says, "I want to paint the bathroom," I'm [usually] like, "Yeah, yeah, we should do that." But what am I really saying? [Am I saying,] "I heard you, but I really don't want to do anything about it?" instead of saying, "Okay, [if] you want to paint the bathroom, [then] I'm going to look at the money and the budget and I'm going to see what day we need to do this and try to get it done." Hearing her, not just doing lip service.

At conferences, leanings toward gender progressivism are often counterbalanced by elements of gender traditionalism. Thus, conferences create an environment in which men's identities are at once anchored and open to experimentation. In fact, it is likely that the Promise Keeper leadership's stated disapproval of homosexuality facilitates this process. Once questions of homosexuality are off the table, men can feel free to weep together, hug one another, hold hands, and engage in other public displays of man-to-man affection that might be difficult if questions about homosexual desire loomed over them.

Traditionalist counterbalances to gender subversion are strategically deployed in some conference rhetoric. These antinomies suggest that the further men get from the boundaries of hegemonic masculinity, the more shoring up their gender identities require. Soon after the Friday night call to faith (altar call), in which many hundreds of weeping men stepped forward to accept Christ, Isaac (the conference emcee) peered down from the stage and dubbed these courageous men "hombres for Christ." Yet this hegemonic image was soon complicated by Isaac's critique of masculine independence. As the men who had accepted Christ filed back to their seats, Isaac underscored the importance of a long-term commitment to godly living through participation in local accountability groups. Isaac explained that each man must accept his dependence on his brothers if he is to continue his walk with the Lord. In critiquing hegemonic mandates for masculine self-reliance, Isaac created an anti-model out of perhaps the most popular icon of masculine independence. "Accountability groups are vital," he told us. "You can't be a Lone Ranger." By invoking the image of the Lone Ranger in this way, PK leaders make men aware of their dependency on one another. Thus, the scriptural passage, "As iron sharpens iron, one man sharpens another," both reinforces and subverts hegemonic masculinity. Iron is a mighty metal, but it quickly becomes dull and useless without an equally strong substance against which it can be honed.

In a similar vein, one of the speakers who described the biblical character Naaman in exceedingly masculine terms during his talk was quick to add that, upon contracting leprosy, this "valiant warrior" had to learn humility. As the biblical account goes, Naaman first contacted the king of Israel for direction after he learned he had contracted this fatal disease. Blinded by his high social standing, Naaman did not realize that spiritual instruction, rather than political status, was the only avenue by which he could be cured. Aware of this fact, the king of Israel told Naaman to contact Elisha, Israel's prophet. Through a messenger, Elisha communicated to Naaman that he should wash himself seven times in the River Jordan to be cured of his leprosy. Given his stature and fame, Naaman was offended that Elisha did not personally meet with him. He also believed that a warrior as great as himself was due a more spectacular miracle than being healed through merely bathing in a river. Finally overcoming his stubbornness, Naaman submitted to the prophet's instruction and was healed. The message conveyed through this story is that men need to set aside their egos, relinquish the pursuit of social status, and "walk humbly with the Lord." Through such complicated narratives, PK conferences feature a deft weaving together of orthodox and progressive gender sensibilities.

In their most subversive moments, conferences radically redefine the very bounds of godly manhood and open up new avenues of thought and conduct for the men who attend them. Nowhere are these gender contradictions more apparent than during the "call to faith." The PK call to faith is similar to the altar calls commonly used at evangelical churches. Originally developed during religious revivals and utilized to this day, an altar call is a public invitation for each person who has been touched by the spirit during a worship service to step forward and "receive Christ" as his or her personal Lord and Savior. This moment of conversion is typically called being "born again."

In revivalistic movements like the Promise Keepers, of course, there is no formal service. Instead, there are a series of addresses that precede the call to faith. What's more, there is no actual altar at a PK conference. Instead, there is a stage area on the floor of the stadium or arena from which addresses are given. Stages at such events are bedecked with a huge color banner that serves as a backdrop and features the conference's theme and logo. To lend a natural touch, PK stages also typically have a few potted plants positioned tastefully but inconspicuously on them. Despite the fact that conferences are bereft of the trappings of organized religion, the PK call to faith and an evangelical church's altar call are quite similar in form.

At the Choose This Day conference, Mike Silva issued the Friday night call to faith. After recounting the story of Shadrach, Meshach, and Abednego, he took on a more informal tone. "How many in the audience have ever stolen something in their lives? How many have ever lied?" Silva asked. With most men raising their hands, Silva turned to the conference emcee and said: "See? I'm talking to a stadium full of liars and thieves." Evoking laughter from the crowd, he said, "We're all sinners. The Bible leaves no doubt about it." He then began to discuss quite frankly many of the most serious sins commonly committed by men—who he subtly likened to baboons by way of a story. Using the primitive masculine metaphor of baboon manhood, Silva spoke of the love baboons have for salt. To obtain a block of salt, Silva explained, the baboon will risk life and limb. And once he has obtained the object of his desire, a male baboon will fight ferociously to keep it. The baboon's obsession with salt is not unlike the human male's obsession with life's "salty" pleasures—women, status, wealth, and such. Much like salt, these pursuits seem to provide life with zest and spice. But, ultimately, a man's craving for these worldly pleasures leaves him broken and bitter. Like the baboon who would rather risk his life than give up his salt, men are most attracted to those things that will ultimately bring about their destruction. Life can be different, Silva explained, adopting a soft and somber tone. Men can learn to let go. After a pregnant pause, Silva's voice became louder and louder, until finally he was shouting into the microphone—"Let go! Let go!"—urging conference-goers to release their saltiest obsessions. With that, he issued the night's "call to faith," inviting those who wanted to accept Christ to step forward and commit their life to him.

Suddenly, men with teary eyes and determined looks began streaming forth to the front of the stage area, throwing themselves down on their knees and showing their readiness to accept Christ. As this group grew in number, another cadre of men made their way from the side of the stage to the front area, laid their hands on the heads of these new converts, and began praying over their prostrate brethren. Music burst forth, and Silva highlighted the gendered significance of these men's conversion: "God the Father loves nothing more than welcoming back one of his sons." As the number responding to the altar call grew, men's bodies became increasingly crushed together in front of the stage. After a period of time, the call to faith reached its denouement, and men began filing back to their seats. With that, the conference emcee, Isaac, stepped forward and underscored the emotional nature of the conversion experience: "It doesn't matter if you cry. It doesn't make you any less of a man." With the event returning to normal, Isaac turned to more procedural matters. He reminded men that there was much more to come in the nighttime program. He instructed men to stay put for the remainder of the evening's events and to commit to returning the next day for the full slate of scheduled activities lasting until six on Saturday evening. Promise Keepers are "not sissies," he said. "They go the distance."

Such is the nature of bargaining with patriarchy. The Promise Keeper weeps, but he is not a sissy. Each of these "hombres for Christ" is doggedly committed to his god; yet, ever dependent on the support of his godly brothers, the Promise Keeper must never be a Lone Ranger. Marked by strength and sensitivity, toughness and tenderness, the gender identity of the Promise Keeper is a paradox indeed.

Faith Meets Reason at PK Conferences: Insurgent Revivalism versus Organized Religion

Just as Promise Keepers' relationship to sport and gender is marked by paradox, so too is its orientation toward religion. A statement of this nature begs several seemingly obvious questions: Aren't the Promise Keepers an explicitly religious organization? Isn't the most distinctive aspect of this men's movement its Christian emphasis? To be sure, the Promise Keepers are religious in character. Yet, beyond this prima facie point lie several nuances. Technically, the Promise Keepers are more aptly described as a revivalistic movement than as a religious organization. This is not a matter of splitting hairs. There are important differences between revivalism and religion. The staid character of organized religion stands in bold contrast to the untamed spirit of revivalism. Organized religion smacks of establishment, whereas revivalism is defiantly anti-establishment. Organized religion is characterized by institutionalized structures that include a church, an altar, liturgy, symbols such as the cross, and formal distinctions such as pastor/congregant and member/nonmember.

Revivalism, by contrast, rejects the traditional trappings of organized religion and its dichotomies. In its place, revivalistic movements promote "spiritual renewal," free-flowing worship, and direct contact with the sacred unmediated by any human institution. This is not to say that revivalistic movements are anti-religious. They are not. Rather, the relationship between revivalism and religion is characterized by tension and contradiction. Hence, the Promise Keepers are both quite critical of organized religion and remarkably supportive of it. This paradox is quite evident at PK conferences.

The critical stance the Promise Keepers adopt toward organized religion is given force through revivalistic rhetoric and practices at conferences. It is noteworthy that, among PK insiders, altar calls at conferences are in fact referred to as "calls to faith." The name given to this portion of the event is no accident. As already noted, PK conferences are altar-free affairs. When PK conferences are held in football stadiums, there is no formal altar in the end zone. There is simply a stage. The placement of a formal altar flanked by traditional religious symbols at a PK conference would smack of religious establishment. As such, it would undermine the sense of insurgent spirituality that is the hallmark of revivalism. In churches, an altar organizes social space and social relationships in a way that centralizes religious authority (altar versus pew, pastor versus congregant) and reinforces the status of the church as a mediating institution (God-church-believer).[4] In stark contrast to the staid and institutionalized character of organized religion, PK aims to provide the believer with raw, unmediated contact with the sacred. In so doing, Promise Keeper conferences are designed to bring about a dramatic spiritual rebirth within the person. Thus, during the call to faith, seekers undergoing the process of conversion are described as being "born again." These new believers are said to have "welcomed Jesus into their heart."

PK's disavowal of organized religion does not end at altar-free worship and is not confined to the mere renaming of the traditional altar call. As a cultural practice, these calls to faith are anti-establishment and have a revivalistic flavor. Prior to issuing the Friday night call to faith at Choose This Day, evangelist Mike Silva drew clear distinctions between church-going and genuine godliness: "Maybe you've been close to church but far from God." As he moved into issuing the call to faith and men began pouring forth toward the stage, he bellowed through the microphone: "We're not talking about religion here. We're not talking about playing church. Rather, we are talking about having a satisfying personal relationship with Christ." Thus, the act of stepping forward and "accepting Christ" is not an empty religious ritual. It is a palpably transformative spiritual act. Other speakers also drew distinctions between "the church" and godliness, with one arguing during the climax of his talk that "the morality of the church is not what it ought to be." Upon hearing this, many conference-goers stood up in a call-and-response fashion with shouts of "That's right!" and "Preach it, brother, preach it!"

Why would PK disavow organized religion in this way? To begin, evangelical religion has long had a gendered cast to it (see Bartkowski 1998, 2001a: chap. 2). Defined as a "religion of the heart," evangelicalism has always been seen as inherently "feminine." Consequently, evangelical churches typically attract more women than men. In a culture where the bodily metaphor for womanhood is the heart (emotion, feeling) and that for manhood is the head (reason, logic), the feminized faith of evangelicalism is often unappealing to men. What's more, from the evangelical standpoint, both the experience of conversion and the pursuit of a godly life entail submission to God. In American culture, submission has long been seen as something that "comes naturally" to women while running directly counter to men's proclivity for leadership and dominance.

Here, then, is one of the keys to the Promise Keepers' success (however short-lived). The Promise Keepers' disavowal of institutionalized religion can be seen as a gender strategy. Revivalism makes religion attractive to men by portraying it as something other than religion—spirituality, faith, direct contact with the divine. Thus, holding conferences in football stadiums is doubly effective. First, as noted above, because football stadiums are bastions of masculinity, they create a safe space for men to experience and express deeply felt emotions. If Emmit Smith, then Dallas Cowboys running back, can cry in front of 60,000 fans when breaking the National Football League's all-time rushing record, then the Promise Keeper can follow suit when in Texas Stadium as well.

Second, the stadium is not a church or traditional religious edifice. Despite the secular hero worship that may take place within them, football stadiums are not places in which one would expect to receive religious instruction. Of course, part of what makes outdoor stadiums appealing as a site for staging a revival (as Billy Graham well knows) is the "natural" feel that can be achieved through worshiping God in an outdoor environ. Worship performed outdoors situates the believer closer to nature. Worship outdoors in "God's country" places believers and seekers closer to their creator than a formal service confined by four walls, a floor, and a roof. Thus, the feelings men experience at PK conferences can be seen as more "natural" and "genuine" spiritual promptings than those that could be "manufactured" by organized religion. In both of these ways, the PK call to faith is certainly not about "playing church."

Given the feminized character of evangelicalism as "heart religion," the Promise Keepers are also wise to play up the rational (read "masculine") elements of religious conversion. PK, like evangelicalism in general, views religious conversion not as something that is conferred or bequeathed. From an evangelical perspective, there are no "chosen people." God does not choose who he will save; rather, the evangelical believer chooses God. He does so by welcoming Jesus into his life. As it was explained to me by several Promise Keepers, Jesus is a "gentleman." The implication here is that a gentleman does not intrude but waits until he is asked to enter. Thus, Jesus will not force himself upon someone who does not first invite him into his heart.

From an evangelical standpoint, the born-again experience is both emotional (a turning of the heart) and rational (a product of reasoned deliberation). Concerning the latter, the glossy program for the Choose This Day conference series describes conversion as "THE MOST IMPORTANT *DECISION* YOU'LL EVER MAKE" (emphasis added). The very title of the 1999 conference series, "*Choose* This Day," further underscores the deliberative nature of conversion. At PK conferences, the conversion process is completed when the man responding to the call to faith signs his own "PK decision card." As indicated by the document's name, the decision card underscores the voluntary nature of religion conversion. In two senses, the PK decision card reflects utilitarian rationalism. First, it symbolizes the new convert's conscious intention (his rational choice) to commit himself to Christ. The individual, as an autonomous agent, has accepted Christ and now must strive to live in a way that honors this decision. This deliberative approach to religious conversion is quite different from the Jewish concept of a "chosen people" and departs significantly from the Catholic practice of infant baptism.

Second, the decision card serves the ends of organizational utility. Having collected these cards, staff at the Promise Keepers headquarters can strategically expand its mailing list through the extraction of contact information from its growing constituency. As an incentive to sign the decision card and a means by which the organization can remain active in the convert's newfound faith after the conference, the opportunity is offered for conference-goers to exchange this card for a free copy of the *Man of His Word New Testament.* This New Testament Bible is available in a tent set aside specifically for this (utilitarian) transaction. In short, PK conferences weave together revivalistic sentiment and rational conviction. The point here bears reiterating. The repackaging of revivalism as something other than religion and the recasting of evangelical rebirth as a rational choice make conversion more palatable for men.

Another motivation for PK's disavowal of organized religion is less related to gender and more a product of the desire to expand the circle of believers at large. As an evangelical movement, the primary goal of the Promise Keepers is not to preach to the choir (that is, those who are already saved). Rather, the Great Commission given to believers and articulated explicitly in the last of PK's Seven Promises commands those who have been saved (born again) to share the "good news" of the Christian gospel with those outside the fold. In this sense, it is not surprising that many of the men to whom I spoke—both at conferences and in interviews—became affiliated with PK through primary social networks. Quite commonly, men had the good news shared with them through relationships with a male family member, fellow congregant, close friend, or colleague. Often these relationships are strengthened as men travel in cadres (brothers, coworkers, fathers and sons) to PK conferences.

Many men initially came to a Promise Keeper conference as "seekers"—a term some evangelicals use for unsaved persons who exhibit a general spiritual demeanor or show a specific interest in the faith. The typical seeker has a checkered past that has left him unhappy but that also strikes him as squarely at odds with religious conviction and church membership. Yet, as these former seekers describe it, something amazing happened when they attended their first Promise Keeper conference. These men were able to reconcile themselves with their pasts, gain a sense of forgiveness for bygone transgressions, and make a commitment to live more righteously—often after responding to the call to faith.

To make sense of this process, it is instructive to compare PK conferences to the "seeker churches" that have emerged on the American religious scene during the last couple of decades. In his outstanding analysis of the seeker church movement, as exemplified by Willow Creek, Kimon Sargeant (2000) reveals how this new breed of churches brings nonbelievers into the conservative Protestant fold by creatively repackaging the traditional tenets of evangelicalism. Seeker churches emphasize spiritual rebirth, scriptural authority, and community cohesion but do so through unconventional means—live theater, film screenings, and recreational activities. In these ways, seeker churches offer the unsaved a non-threatening form of spirituality rooted in orthodox evangelical theology but delivered in a form that lacks the preachy didacticism typically associated with traditional organized religion. Like seeker churches, much of PK's early success lay in its ability to take orthodox evangelicalism, move it out of the church and into the stadium, and then introduce it to men as something other than institutionalized religion.

Yet, even in this cultural domain, paradoxes abound. Although PK periodically disavows organized religion at its conferences, leaders in the movement clearly recognize their dependency on religious institutions to retain new converts. In fact, believer retention is a goal PK pursues in concert with the religious establishment through its distribution of men's ministry materials to congregations nationwide and its placement of PK "ambassadors" and "key men" in local churches. Beyond these structural connections between PK and organized religion, the timing of conference events reveals an alliance between the two. Conferences begin on Friday evening and conclude early on Saturday evening (typically at six o'clock). Conference events end when they do so that men can return home Saturday night for Sunday morning services after their weekend PK "retreat." In this way, PK attempts to pass the baton of new converts off to churches as early as one day after a conference.

Conference programs are also punctuated by messages that evince support for organized religion, and these pro-religious blurbs come more frequently as the program progresses. Wasting no time in building bridges to organized religion after the call to faith, PK leaders encourage men who have accepted Christ during the call to "take the next step" and "seal your commitment" to Christ by being baptized. Obviously, PK leaders recognize the possibility for weekend conversions at a PK conference to be long forgotten by the time Monday morning rolls around. So, in addition to recommending formal baptism, speakers admonish men several times during the conference program to find a "home congregation" in their local community. Though the words used to encourage formal church membership vary from one speaker to the next, the message is invariably the same: church membership will enable men to stoke the nascent flame of spiritual transformation presumably lit during the conference. The fifth of the Seven Promises says as much: "Support the mission of the church by honoring and praying for his pastor, and by actively giving his time and resources." Advice provided in the Choose This Day program reiterates this message:

> WHAT NEXT? After we have [accepted Christ], the Holy Spirit lives within us as sons of God. While we still struggle with sin and failure, the Holy Spirit's power helps us overcome areas of bondage to sin and live godly lives (John 14:16–18, 26; 16:7–14; Romans 6:22). Be sure to get involved in a Spirit-led, Bible-believing church fellowship for accountability and encouragement in your new walk with Christ.

The Promise Keepers' commitment to organized religion is also evidenced in the treatment given to pastors during conferences. PK conferences typically feature a complimentary lunch for pastors in front of the stage area. When combined with the practice of calling pastors up to the stage so that men can cheer in appreciation of clergy, the stage area becomes more and more like an altar as conferences progress. Though not a formal altar, the stage nevertheless comes to approximate an *axis mundi* (spiritual center point) of the stadium in which a conference is held.

Even where the solicitation of donations is concerned, PK is careful to adopt a chivalrous stance toward "Christ's bride"—the church. In both conference talks and distributed materials, men are told to donate funds to the Promise Keepers only *after* they have made financial contributions to their local churches. For their part, Promise Keepers seem to have heeded this advice. A survey of conference-goers conducted in 1995 (near the movement's peak) revealed that nine of ten attendees surveyed made financial donations to their local church (Morin 1997). In this way, as in others, PK conferences blend a revivalism that is quite critical of established Christianity with myriad practices that affirm the legitimacy of organized religion.

Conclusion

This chapter has examined the dynamics of Promise Keeper stadium conferences. These mass gatherings, commonly held in football stadiums during the movement's heyday, provide men with a forum for renegotiating boundaries in the domains of sport, gender and family, and religion. In their most vivacious moments, these events are as rowdy as the football or basketball games that take place in the stadiums and arenas in which conferences are held. Yet PK conferences pair this footloose conviviality with an ethic of respectability that cultivates trust, good will, and gentility among the men who attend them. Conferences also provide men with resources for renegotiating their gender identities and revaluing their family relationships. Conference activities subvert hegemonic masculinity by fostering intense emotional expression and teaching men about humbly serving their wives and children. Yet, by normalizing masculine strength and male leadership in the home, conference activities selectively affirm traditional masculine ideals. Finally, in their most revivalistic moments, PK conferences can be readily distinguished from organized religion. Getting saved at a conference is not about "playing church." At the same time, however, PK endorses organized religion and views local congregations as allies in the retention of new converts. In short, Promise Keeper conferences are both engaged with and distinct from the mainstream cultural domains of sport, gender, and religion.

5

The ABCs of Promise-Keeping

Accountability, Brotherhood, and Confessional Culture

Having explored the dynamics of Promise Keeper conferences, I now turn my attention to men's struggles with keeping promises and emulating godliness once they have joined the movement. The everyday practice of promise-keeping is strongly influenced by the distinctive gender discourses advanced by leading Promise Keepers, as well as by men's points of entry into the movement. As noted in chapters 3 and 4, elite PK advice and stadium conferences give rise to a whole host of cultural contradictions. It is these paradoxes that Promise Keeper men are left to sort through as they gather weekly in small PK groups and forge meaningful man-to-man relationships with their brothers.

In wrestling with these paradoxes, Promise Keeper men employ boundary work strategies that simultaneously facilitate inclusion (solidarity with movement insiders) and exclusion (social distance from nonbelievers) (cf. Lamont and Fournier 1992). Consistent with the metaphor of "iron masculinity," PK accountability groups are designed to "sharpen" the character of PK men who frequent them. The groups accomplish this by placing members in sustained relationships with other godly men. A 1997 survey of select PK conference-goers revealed that half of respondents met regularly with a small group of men (Morin 1997). Thus, the accountability group was a widely utilized resource in PK's cultural tool kit at the movement's peak and continues to be stressed by its leaders today. In this chapter, I peer inside these groups and examine how accountability, brotherhood, and confessional culture are produced within them.

Accountability: Striving for
Faithfulness to the Seven Promises

One of the most distinctive features of the Promise Keepers is men's invocation of the term "accountability." PK men to whom I spoke regularly cited accountability as a governing principle of Promise Keeper affiliation and viewed it as the bedrock of their relationships with one another. PK leaders strongly emphasize the principle of accountability at stadium conferences, wake-up calls, and local men's gatherings. This focus on accountability defines PK against highly individualistic strands of evangelical Protestantism where every believer in his own priest and salvation is attained through a private acceptance of Jesus Christ. To be sure, PK places a strong emphasis on individual conversion and the believer's cultivation of a personal relationship with Jesus Christ—the ultimate godly man. Yet, in stark contrast to predominantly individualistic forms of evangelicalism, the principle of accountability focuses primary attention on the social relationships PK men have with one another. In this way, individual PK men understand themselves and evaluate their conduct in light of their place within the collective body of Christ. And each man's relationship to this body of believers—in the form of PK affiliation and local church membership—is defined by the principle of accountability.

What, precisely, does accountability mean? In a general sense, accountability entails men's mutual and reciprocal responsibility to sharpen or hone one another—again, like iron—in light of the standard of godly manhood. Accountability focuses men's attention away from themselves and underscores the importance of close, personal relationships. Several men I interviewed described the principle of accountability—and the small groups spawned by this ideal—as the most appealing aspect of the Promise Keepers. As Steve, a local PK leader explains, accountability corrects for men's innate tendencies toward isolation, fear, and anger. Steve says that these tendencies have been passed down from Adam to all men:

> With men, you take the way God made us. Men normally want to isolate themselves with other men. They want to get close [to other men only] to have a bunch of acquaintances. Yet God desires for men to have relationships with other men where

they have two or three men who are real close. Who can hold them accountable because they desire to be accountable. Because they want to be godly men and they know they need help. And some men help them to do that.

[Bartkowski:] Where does the tendency towards isolation come from, do you think?

From the garden. . . . That's the way it started out. See, Adam and Eve [pause]. When Adam ate the apple . . . Adam showed his cowardice. The first time, he said: "Eve, let's go hide over here in the bushes," because he knew what had happened. He knew God was fixing to come down on him. And so instead of going [to God to] say: "She ate the apple. I'm sorry I blew it." He didn't [do that]. He went and hid. . . . He was watching her as she ate the apple. And he did not stop her. And he's her protector. God made him as her protector and yet he just sat there, stood there. . . . God came in the cool of the evening. And Adam remarks [to God]: "The woman made me do it." He hid behind the woman's skirt. So every act that he did was an act of cowardice. And so those acts would be passed down. His seed was passed to me and to you. I have Adam's seed in me as the man. His seed has been passed down to us. So, my tendency is fear and anger. Those are the tendencies that I have in my life. And most men have those same fears.

Thus, Steve argues that placing men in close, meaningful relationships with one another helps men to overcome their innate tendency toward isolationism. Male isolationism does not come from God, but stems from what evangelicals typically refer to as "the fall"—the original sin of Adam and Eve. Adam failed to take responsibility in his first relationship (with Eve), and men have been following his bad example with women and other men ever since. Relationships that stress accountability restore the natural order by emphasizing men's responsibilities and obligations toward others.

Other men adopted a less theological tone and offered a personal testimony about the power of accountability. Jeff, who struggles with lust, describes accountability as the "number one thing. . . . The only thing that would work for me is that I have an accountability partner that got in my face. You can't just pick anybody, it has to be somebody you trust and respect." For other men, accountability manifests itself in other forms that might seem mundane to those outside the evangelical fold but are highly significant to Promise Keepers. William says that his accountability group has made a commitment to be more diligent about the "daily discipline" of prayer. He characterizes accountability as "a big plus." In his group, the principle has recently prompted men to ask their fellows:

> "Are you praying with your wife?" I think [our accountability group meeting last] Wednesday had a big impact on that. What happened last Wednesday was we started [to recognize that] prayer needs to be more [pause]. Let's put more emphasis on praying—with our wives and [with] us as a team and also with other men. So yeah, the accountability is from each other. The way to slip out of that is [to say], "Sure I don't need this stuff anymore. I'll go home and do my own thing." It's easy to get back in the old routine.

Thus, at the grassroots of PK, accountability and integrity are not simply abstract notions. Rather, these principles are the central feature of PK men's relationships with one another. The Promise Keepers place a strong emphasis on the formation of grassroots accountability groups among local members. Men are introduced to this feature of PK at conferences after the call to faith and during small-group activities and break-out sessions.

In addition to accountability groups, PK strongly supports men's involvement in dyadic accountability partnerships. Strikingly similar to the twelve-step programs and consciousness-raising groups that have proliferated in the last several decades, PK accountability groups are intended to complement, channel, and sustain the collective effervescence experienced by many men who attend the Promise Keeper stadium conferences. Accountability groups aim to assist PK members in "putting into practice" the Seven Promises to which they are exposed during PK stadium conferences. Because of their small size, accountability groups composed of five to ten men and two-man accountability partnerships provide for friendly oversight of PK members' ongoing "walk with the Lord."

As a small cadre of men who are intimately acquainted with one another, accountability groups are viewed as a perfect complement to the massive stadium conferences through which many men first become exposed to PK. Accountability group attendees recognize that the spiritual high produced by the stadium rallies would ultimately fade without the close peer monitoring and the intense moral scrutiny provided in these small-group forums. Jeff, quoted above, describes the importance of accountability groups as follows:

> [Accountability groups are] a must. They preach that [message of accountability group involvement] at Promise Keepers, and I was glad they did. Without that kind of small group activity, that sharing to get involved in, [stadium conference attendance] won't make a difference. It won't. It will just be a mountain-top experience and you'll fall back into whatever pattern you've been in for your whole life—because that's what you know. . . . PK knows that things like stadium events, that's what they are—they are stadium events. They are wonderful. They are eye-opening. But without something ongoing, the change isn't going to happen. [Accountability groups are] just one of the many tools out there [used by PK]. I think it's a very powerful tool.

Thus, accountability groups are believed to be critical to "sharpening" the man who aspires to godliness. PK men regularly portray accountability groups as the site in which the "hard work" of promise-keeping is actively facilitated and collectively pursued.

Because Promise Keepers view Jesus Christ as the ultimate godly man, PK men hold up the life of Christ[1] as the final standard against which their thoughts, motivations, and actions should be judged. It is in this sense that Promise Keepers aspire to be "men of integrity." Accountability is viewed as the primary means by which PK men can pursue a Christ-like "life of integrity." Accountability therefore fosters an openness to men, who allow their conduct to be scrutinized by others in light of the Seven Promises. And because the assumption going in is that "all have sinned and fall short of the glory of the God" from Adam to the present day, there is no shame in a man confessing his struggles with problems in his life. Quite to the contrary, making oneself vulnerable is viewed as an act of courage.

The principles of accountability and integrity build an ethic of judgment—authority, truth-seeking, and justice—into PK men's small-group interactions (cf. Bartkowski 2001a; Becker 1997). With its emphasis on moral certitude and social hierarchy, this ethic of judgment invokes core elements of the Rational Patriarch archetype. Manly authority and leadership also draw on the King, Warrior, and Mentor pillars of masculinity from the Tender Warrior archetype. With these ideological backdrops, accountability functions through open exchanges that enable men to engage in a sort of mutual scrutiny that makes each man his "brother's keeper." Yet, far from being invasive or heavy-handed, such scrutiny in accountability groups and partnerships is offered out of love and concern—with nothing less than one's eternal salvation at stake. In a way that would not make sense to people situ-ated outside the movement, accountability is appreciated by PK men for its ability to reach into their souls and eradicate the notion of a private realm and inner sanctum. Knowing that they will be held to a standard of integrity (the Seven Promises) at weekly accountability meetings, every man becomes not only his brother's keeper but his own keeper as well. In this way, accountability within the Promise Keep-ers simultaneously disciplines and liberates men. Prodded into lead-ing a disciplined life of integrity, men are liberated from their greatest enemies—sin, damnation, and isolation from the ultimate brothers, Jesus Christ and God the Father.

When I asked PK men why they attend accountability groups, many of them responded by invoking terms consistent with an ethic of judgment and the Rational Patriarch or Tender Warrior archetypes. In various ways, Promise Keepers claim that regular attendance at account-ability groups holds each man's "feet to the fire"—with that fire being the pursuit of godly living according to biblical standards of right and wrong. As such, accountability groups provide a forum for gently re-proving men who are wrestling with severely strained relationships at home, temptations of sexual immorality, or difficult dilemmas at work. All of these topics are openly discussed in accountability groups, with PK brothers offering advice and, where needed, admonitions typically rooted in biblical passages. And the life of integrity wrought through these brotherly exchanges would seem to have its own rewards, as PK men say that they have developed more fulfilling relationships with their wives, children, friends, and business associates through diligent attendance at accountability groups.

Because the very notion of accountability resonates with an ethic of judgment and ideals of traditional masculinity, a good deal of the work accomplished in accountability groups entails the drawing of exclusive boundaries. Most notable among these is the absence of women from accountability gatherings. Critics of the Promise Keep-ers have suggested that the very notion of a men's movement—an or-ganization that excludes women by design—can preclude authentic egalitarianism by derogating women as an "other" (an out-group) against which men define themselves (Messner 1997: xiv). I went into the field expecting this practice to be regular fare in accountability groups, but it was not. And when the rhetoric of gender difference did emerge, it was not in the service of denigrating women. In accountability fellowships, the language of gender difference, when it emerged, lauded traits commonly attributed to the "fairer sex"—sensitivity, communicativeness, and emotional expression. What's more, the practice of women's exclusion created a homosocial (that is, same-gender) environment in accountability groups characterized by "loose essentialism." Taking the baton from interactions at PK conferences, men in accountability groups reported that they could get together in an all-male fellowship and "let down their guard." Paradoxically, they could become "more like women" than they thought would be possible if women were present.

Thus, PK men emphasize the positive consequences brought about through the exclusion of women from PK small groups. Larry, who regularly attends PK accountability groups, argues that it is women's absence from such gatherings that enables men to set aside their inhibitions. And it is only in this all-male context that men can be held accountable for the most private and personal dimensions of their lives. Larry says that men and women are "wired up" differently by God, and explains: "I can't tell you how many Sunday school classes and situations I've been in where the women are more verbose. . . . So a lot of the times the men will just—especially the more quieter and reserved ones—won't say a word. But when you get women out, and [men] feel like it's a non-threatening atmosphere, they feel safe. It's in a small group that they'll open up. They will open up and share what's going on inside."

"So," I ask, "some of the men might feel threatened by sharing in a mixed group, you're saying then?"

"I don't know that it's conscious, but I think it's a subconscious thing," he replies. "You know, it is just a fact. If you've got fifty men in a meeting room together and they're having a really honest sharing session, and a woman walks in—it changes the whole dynamic."

Beyond women's exclusion from these all-male encounters, PK accountability groups are a forum for men to reinforce the importance of male family leadership. My field notes from PK small-group gatherings are littered with references to men as "leaders," "heads," and even "patriarchs" of their families. In casting men as domestic patriarchs, PK members eschew a marital egalitarianism and thereby reject the secularism and feminism such commitments would seem to imply. In this way, they underscore their cultural distinctiveness from mainstream American values that have democratized family life in the last few decades. Nevertheless, these men are not oblivious to feminist criticisms of patriarchy, and their strategies of cultural distinction are overlaid by evidence of social engagement. Social engagement facilitates the building of bridges to the American cultural mainstream. Almost to a man, accountability group attendees asked to elaborate on male leadership in the home invoked the neopatriarchal language of a husband's servant-leadership. In some cases, this Tender Warrior imagery was interlaced with Expressive Egalitarian references to mutual submission. The use of such contradictory language by PK men underscores the uneasy tension between patriarchal convictions and egalitarian sensibilities manifested within the Promise Keepers and, more broadly, within contemporary evangelicalism.

Finally, there are leadership structures—both formal and informal hierarchies—that often emerge within accountability groups. Leadership within accountability groups can be based on formal organizational ties with the Promise Keepers (Key Man, Ambassador), as well as on the length of a man's tenure as a born-again Christian or Promise Keeper. The actual implementation of leadership within these groups may entail calling the accountability meeting, initiating the discussion (sometimes by way of introducing a "theme" for that meeting), or charting the temporal trajectory of the meeting (such as the transition from fellowshipping to thematic discussions to prayer time).

Yet, consonant with the notion of servant-leadership, these asymmetries do not lend themselves to heavy-handed exercises of power within accountability groups. In fact, some local Promise Keepers view them as benevolent and empowering. Several men compared accountability groups to the man-to-man relationships enjoyed by Paul, Peter, Timothy, and Barnabas in the Bible's New Testament. Paul, a gifted writer, was a prolific contributor to the New Testament. Peter is said to have been appointed by Jesus Christ himself as leader of the church and mentor of the apostles. Timothy was Paul's protégé, his apprentice in mission work. And Barnabas is characterized in the Bible as one of Paul's best friends. As the analogy goes, these relationships were marked by both vertical ties of inequality (mentor/protégé) and horizontal ties of fellowship (friends, peers). As Al, a PK leader on the local scene, sometimes tells those who attend his weekly men's gatherings:

Men, we should aspire to be like the apostle Paul. We ourselves need a mentor. We need someone to mentor. And we
need a close friend—a buddy. So, find a man to mentor you—
someone who will hold you accountable. Follow his counsel.
He will be for you what Peter was to Paul. Then, find another
man to mentor—a man for whom you will need to set a godly
example. He will be your Timothy. Finally, make sure you have
friends—buddies you can have fun with who will keep you
from feeling isolated. They will be your Barnabas.

In this sense, acting as a mentor is not an invitation to dictate how
another man should behave. Rather, such "leadership" entails "serving" as an example and source of support to someone who is younger
either in chronological age or in terms of his "faith walk." As a men's
minister and local pastor, Al personally embraces and advocates a
model of servant-leadership in which mutual submission figures
prominently.

Solidarity: The Bonds of Brotherhood

The concept of brotherhood[2] is another defining
feature of the Promise Keepers. Through the deployment of such fraternal language, PK men engage in another form of boundary work oriented toward solidarity. PK boundary work predicated on solidarity
stresses men's connectedness. Moreover, men's solidarity hinges on
an ethic of compassion that privileges a heartfelt sensitivity toward
men's shared struggles. So, whereas accountability is predicated on
an ethic of judgment, the notion of brotherhood unites and levels men
under the banners of equality and companionship. Here again, brotherhood is not simply an abstract principle in PK gatherings. Rather, it
is an ideal that produces powerful real-world effects in PK men's social interaction.

Larry, who generalized about "reserved" men and "verbose" women
being "wired up differently" (quoted above), values the compassionate and companionate aspects of accountability group interaction. Larry
believes that man-to-man companionship is the perfect corrective
against the excesses of masculine stoicism and self-interest:

The most appealing [aspect of PK is its] emphasis on linking
men up. The statistic was shared very early on with me that
ninety-five percent of most men don't have a friend. So, the
idea of linking men up in small groups—the accountability

groups—just to hang out together and be a friend. I felt like that was really significant. . . . And to help men be in relationship with one another with their wives and with other people in the community. . . . I come from a very structured, if you will, a kind of regimental background.

Larry pauses momentarily, then continues:

My approach to meeting with people [is that] I often times would tend to, not necessarily impose my structure on them. I probably need a more gentle word than "impose." But I would sort of have a background idea in mind. I'd have my agenda and the relationship would kind of follow from that. So I think Promise Keepers helped me refocus my goal in meeting with men. To make the friendship and the relationship number one.

How do accountability groups "link up" PK members into a companionate brotherhood given the utilitarian and pragmatic sensibilities of many of these men? Among the more striking aspects of these gatherings is the way they use social space to generate feelings of equality, connectedness, and companionship. Accountability groups typically consist of some sort of circular space—often chairs arranged tightly together in a closed circle—regardless of the number of men attending the group. When men arrive during the course of these meetings, the circle of attendees is typically expanded to include the new arrivals. Thus, an accountability group culture is created that counters men's tendency toward isolation and withdrawal. The distinctive culture produced through accountability groups instead integrates men within a circular brotherhood. The spatial geography of these gatherings is designed to assist men in achieving two key goals embraced by Promise Keeper accountability groups and the organization at large—the recognition of equality among all men, and the fostering of intense intimacy with one's PK compatriots.

PK accountability group circles symbolize men's longing for solidarity and need for reconciliation. Consistent with the PK discourses of Racial Reconciliation, the Expressive Egalitarian, and the Friend Pillar of the Tender Warrior archetype, accountability group circles aim to "break down walls" that often divide men one from another. Several accountability groups within the central Texas area consist of members who differ in age (teens to retirees), race (Anglo, African-American, Hispanic), and social class (college professors seated next to auto mechanics who were themselves adjacent to unemployed men). In addition to eradicating these forms of social stratification, local accountability groups aim to build bridges across Christian (though mostly Protestant) denominations—Methodist, Baptist, Assembly of God.

The circular geography of the accountability group places men with these diverse backgrounds and life experiences face-to-face. Each man in the circle is flanked on either side by his fellows, and this close-quarters arrangement stimulates conversational exchanges that often flow freely and openly from one participant to another. The inscription of space in PK accountability groups, then, aims to level the pernicious social hierarchies that pit men against one another in various social arenas (secular and religious) "outside" the circle. This form of boundary work, then, aims to be wholly integrative.

Accountability group solidarity—and the integrative equality it implies—resonates with longstanding evangelical Protestant themes of equality among all Christians ("the priesthood of all believers"; "all have sinned and fallen short of the glory of God"—Bartkowski 2001a; Juster 1994). In most recent memory, such themes have been raised by biblical feminists and equality-minded evangelicals who criticize the authoritarian sensibilities of other leading conservative Protestants (Bartkowski 2001a). Although many Promise Keepers would probably not see themselves as heirs to the egalitarian legacy of evangelical feminism, the very structure of PK accountability groups and much PK rhetoric has clearly been informed by biblical feminist critiques waged against seemingly un-Christian forms of domination and exclusion.

Of course, the very term "brotherhood" desexualizes the intimate bonds forged within the PK fraternity. In an effort to disentangle intimacy from sexuality, many PK members characterize their strong emotional attachments to one another under the rubric of familial bonds. It is no accident that PK men—leaders and members alike—often refer to one another as "brothers." In a telling (though by no means universal) commentary, one member of PK remarked that perhaps the most redeeming aspect of the Promise Keepers is that the members "love each other—but in the right way, like brothers." By using familial references to refer to their PK "brothers," many Promise Keepers imply that "brotherly love"—like actual sibling relationships—can be intensely emotional without being "tainted" by sexual desire.

Nevertheless, mere rhetorical references to brotherly love do not thoroughly manage the bonds of intimacy for all Promise Keepers alike.

PK members are not literally family, and the vast majority of them do not share actual biological ties. Consequently, men's bodies sometimes become implicated in the desexualization of this brotherly love. Such was the case with Abel. Abel, who was reared largely by his Catholic mother, openly acknowledges his own effeminate demeanor and its impact on his relationships with some of his PK brothers. Abel attributes his "high, squeaky voice," his obvious lisp, and his distinctively "feminine way of walking" to his mother's overriding influence on him as a youngster. Alongside these effeminate qualities, Abel has a penchant for rejecting his PK brothers' handshakes in favor of hugs. Abel's proclivity for tactile affection sometimes produces discomfort for the PK members who happen to be on the receiving end of his warm displays of brotherly love. In such cases, the persistent Abel says that he can usually win over his uncomfortable compatriots, essentially convincing them that there is nothing unmanly in openly displaying his affection for his brothers.

Interestingly, as Abel uses the word "brother" during our conversation, he often flexes one of his arms while clenching his fist. In striking this restrained pseudo-bodybuilding pose during our conversation, Abel uses his otherwise feminine body to contrast for himself—and, most likely, for his PK compatriots—the strength and power of brotherly love with more suspect forms of male-to-male contact. Abel's body serves as a site for the literal reproduction of muscular Christianity because his expressive social practices and feminine demeanor risk subverting this traditional manhood altogether.

Confessional Culture in PK Accountability Groups

Enclosed PK accountability circles, then, both unite and divide. As a unifying force, accountability groups facilitate powerful bonds of trust and vulnerability among PK insiders who share with one another their innermost fears and foibles. For PK men on the inside of this circle, accountability group attendance has immediate practical ramifications—namely, the facilitation of emotional sensitivity and extreme vulnerability. Yet, such vulnerability is made safe by sharply dividing the companionship expressed within the circle from the more narrow "worldly" framework that reduces masculine intimacy to either eroticism (expressed within heterosexual relationships) or sports (sanctioned within all-male gatherings). Consequently, the circular geography of accountability groups is designed to distinguish the secure confines designated for intimate brotherly exchanges from erotic or violent displays of masculine emotion.

Like the Expressive Egalitarian archetype manifested in the PK discourse of liberated masculinity, many men remark that they can "be themselves," "become transparent," and "let down their guard" within accountability groups. When I first sat in on accountability groups and other small-group PK gatherings, I was unprepared for the blatantly confessional character of these encounters. In such forums, men talk openly about a range of otherwise highly private topics they would be hard pressed to lay bare in the "outside world"—various problems with the law; assorted sexual temptations; thorny interpersonal dilemmas with their wives, children, colleagues, and friends. One interview respondent even recounted how, at an accountability group meeting he had recently attended, otherwise "strong men" ended up weeping profusely and rolling on the floor in anguish after learning that the vast majority of them had been sexually abused as children. In this circumstance and others like it, a man's sharing of his innermost struggles with a select group of equally vulnerable compatriots is accompanied by a powerful emotional discharge (cathexis, in the Freudian sense) that has been remarkably absent from men's peer relationships.

It is in this sense that accountability groups create a distinctive confessional culture for PK members. To be sure, the PK confessional culture is significantly less formal and hierarchical than the traditional Catholic sacrament of the same name. Nevertheless, there are striking parallels between PK confessionalism and the Catholic rite of Confession—renamed Reconciliation within contemporary Catholicism. Like the Catholic sacrament of Confession/Reconciliation, PK's confessional culture is cathartic in character and is loosely organized around a multistep process of repentance:

- admission—the penitent's public acknowledgment of his transgression;
- contrition—the sorrowful penitent's stated intention to repent from his sin; and
- absolution—forgiveness despite wrongdoing and, ultimately, freedom from one's sinful past.

A twenty-year-old first-time participant in one accountability group was moved nearly to tears by conveying a series of misadventures in his recent past that had included, among other confessed transgressions, a conviction on felony charges and jail time. He explained how, after having been abandoned by a girlfriend who had borne him a child, he faced the challenge of raising his young daughter on his own. As this young Latino man completed his admission of past improprieties and vowed to continue his turnaround, his initially somber tone visibly gave way to giddy relief. On the heels of his cathartic discharge, this newcomer reflexively called attention to the overwhelming sense of relief produced by exposing his checkered past to other men who would still, he hoped, accept him as a "brother in Christ." Recognizing their young brother's vulnerability, several of the older men took the opportunity to reaffirm this bold newcomer and reciprocated his transparency by proceeding to share their own life's struggles with other men in the circle. Through such exchanges, accountability groups directly subvert traditional forms of masculinity that decry sissified, soft men and lionize manly toughness.

Confessional culture and the accountability-brotherhood dialectic that makes it possible often entail persistent struggle and a more circuitous path to ultimate absolution. Jeff, who described accountability groups as the perfect complement to the "mountain-top experience" of PK stadium conferences, testifies to this fact. Through his involvement in PK and its accountability fellowships, Jeff ultimately overcame his "incredibly shaming" problem with masturbation—a sexual practice that he now recognizes was an "intimacy killer" in his marital relationship.[3] Jeff's narrative reconstruction of his struggle with masturbation highlights each of the core elements of PK confessional culture—admission, contrition, and absolution.[4] At the same time, his account reveals that godly men's ultimate triumph over sin often requires the creative application of PK's cultural repertoire.

It was at Jeff's first PK conference that he decided to share this thirty-year struggle with his brothers during a small-group prayer session. In offering this admission, Jeff felt a tremendous sense of relief. The PK conference had helped Jeff to cultivate a genuine spirit of contrition about his thirty years of masturbation. While he had long felt guilty about his autoerotic practice, this spirit of contrition moved him to feel genuine sorrow for his transgression. He had resolved to commit this sin no more.

Despite Jeff's facile entré into PK confessional culture at this stadium conference, absolution for this sin proved to be more elusive. When Jeff tearfully admitted to his longstanding struggle with masturbation, the men in his stadium conference prayer group were shocked by his confession. Jeff describes the other men's collective reaction as "jaw-open." In spite of their initial reaction, Jeff had hoped that his brothers would help him to avoid this sin on the heels of his conference-inspired contrition. He requested that his prayer group partners check up on him to encourage him in his fight with autoeroticism. He desperately wanted them to hold him accountable to the PK standard of sexual purity. Within PK, sexual purity is considered a core component of living a life of "personal integrity." This expectation seemed most reasonable. Stadium conference prayer groups are instructed to exchange contact information and to hold one another accountable to PK standards of godly manhood. Yet, despite the PK edict of accountability, none of his brothers in that prayer group ever contacted Jeff. Jeff admits to feeling deeply disappointed by this development. But as Jeff has since come to understand it, the men in his prayer group "had the same difficulty [with masturbation]. It just simply hit too close to home." His problem, he now surmises, was their problem as well—and they did not wish to be held accountable for changing their behavior.

Undeterred by this disappointing development, Jeff forged ahead with his involvement in PK. Some time later, he was able to quit masturbating with the help of an accountability partner he met at a men's retreat. As Jeff recounts: "I had tried on my own [to quit masturbating] and thought, 'I can beat this. I can beat this.'" But, on his own, Jeff could not achieve victory in this struggle. The turning point for Jeff occurred "when [he] finally got to the point where [he] gave it over to the Lord, and found again it was the accountability part." Jeff now firmly believes in the transformative power of brotherly accountability: "Believe me, this is something that you don't want anybody asking you about. You can imagine. You don't want somebody calling you up [to ask you if you have been masturbating that week]. And when they do, you certainly don't want to have to say: 'Man, I just, you know, I've fallen again. I just can't do anything about it.'" Thus, the norm and practice of accountability provided Jeff with an avenue for resolving his longstanding private trouble. Yet, this avenue toward resolution was long, winding, and fraught with obstacles requiring Jeff's careful and determined navigation.

On advice he had received at his first PK conference, Jeff had initially gone home to confess his habit of masturbation to his wife. "They had told us, not specifically about [masturbation], but if you have got these [sexual] things going on—if you've been unfaithful or any of this stuff—the number one thing you have got to do is go home and tell your wife. Go home and tell her now—which I thought was bold. And I thought it was incredible." I asked Jeff to recount his wife's reaction.

Oh boy. She didn't [pause]. It was almost like [the men's] reaction [at the initial PK prayer session]. She had no idea. She was stunned. Again, that was one of those things that made me aware of how important Promise Keepers is. Because, she really isn't built for that. . . .

[Bartkowski:] So a group of guys could hold you accountable in a way your wife could not?

She could, but I think there are certain issues [pause]. . . . My friend terms it [this way]: "They are not built for that type of warfare." [My wife] didn't understand. She loved the intimacy aspect of it, the fact that I was opening up to her. But it's not something I could repeatedly ask her about or have her ask me about.

[Bartkowski:] Because she doesn't struggle with that issue, you're saying?

Exactly. She doesn't understand.

From start to finish, Jeff's narrative of tribulation and triumph over masturbation weaves together themes that highlight the interconnections between the ABC's of promise-keeping—accountability, brotherhood, and confessional culture. Within the context of Jeff's narrative, brothers—that is, men like Jeff, his accountability partner, and those in his conference prayer group—must struggle more vigorously with the burden of sexual sin. Men must wage "war" against sexual temptation. The uniquely masculine character of autoerotic impulses is further underscored by the fact that women—specifically, Jeff's wife—do not wrestle with masturbation as their male counterparts do. Women are simply "not built for that type of spiritual warfare." And yet, after brothers openly confess their shared struggle with sexual sin, the principle of accountability must be applied if men are to wage a successful spiritual war against sexual immorality. While other men may struggle with different areas of concern (a controlling temperament, broken family relationships, unemployment), the underlying motif of PK men's narratives is remarkably similar. The problems that stem from "men's issues" would seem to require a distinctively masculine solution—the Promise Keepers. "As iron sharpens iron, one man sharpens another."

Conclusion

In this chapter, I have explored the boundary work that is undertaken in Promise Keeper accountability groups. Accountability groups meld together exclusionary social practices (male-only meetings) and inclusive forms of interaction (interracial and interdenominational fellowships). By deftly bringing together social practices of inclusion and exclusion, accountability groups become a forum for clarifying men's identities and "sharpening" the character of PK members who aspire to become godly men.

Each of these boundary work strategies resonates with several of the godly man archetypes embedded within elite Promise Keeper discourse. With its emphasis on judgment, unyielding moral standards, and social hierarchy, accountabilility invokes themes from the Rational Patriarch archetype of godly manhood, along with its Tender Warrior counterpart. This boundary work strategy defines men's relationships with one another in terms of a benevolent hierarchy—mentor/protege, newcomer/veteran, elder/younger brothers. Within PK, authority is equated more with responsibility than with power. Mentors are charged with setting a godly example for their protegés.

By contrast, PK boundary work centered on the concept of brotherhood creates social solidarity and "breaks down walls" that typically divide men. Solidarity among Promise Keepers is cultivated through close-knit fraternal bonds that themselves give rise to companionate masculinity. The practice of fraternal companionship enables men to cultivate relationships that can be characterized as "best friends" and "close buddies." Solidarity stresses unity and togetherness among men, thereby drawing together themes from the Expressive Egalitarian and Tender Warrior archetypes (the Friend Pillar of masculinity in the case of the latter). Moreover, the social boundaries that are trangressed in multiracial and interdenominational accountability groups resonate with the racial reconciliation motif of PK's Multicultural Man discourse.

Finally, PK boundary work based on cathexis lends an emotional charge to men's relationships within PK. Promise Keeper accountability group meetings create a therapeutic ethos in which men feel free to confess to one another their innermost feelings, fears, and failings. Through a free-flowing interactive sequence of admission, contrition, and absolution, individual men share their innermost struggles and

sins with other men in their accountability group. Men in the accountability group, in turn, are charged with validating the penitent's pain,
offering man-to-man forgiveness, and holding the now-forgiven sinner accountable for pursuing moral uprightness thereafter. The confessional culture of PK gives men a social forum for wrestling with
and, at times, overcoming their personal demons. Cathartic boundary
work draws force directly from the Expressive Egalitarian archetype
in which godliness is defined as liberation from the stoicism of traditional masculinity.

Akin to Promise Keeper stadium conferences, accountability groups
preserve a sense of social order—God's order—and, in so doing, liberate men to explore the unfamiliar terrain of intimacy and solidarity. Accountability group interaction is therefore characterized by a
set of antinomies. Within these fellowships, hierarchy becomes
intermeshed with equality, rational discipline is intertwined with emotional expression, and cultural distinctiveness converges with social
engagement. These productive contradictions create an atmosphere in
which committed Promise Keepers can collectively pursue the shared
objective of becoming godly men.

6 | Multicultural Evangelicalism

Racial Reconciliation and Cultural Diversity

The sixth of PK's Seven Promises claims that biblical unity is only possible through the eradication of social barriers that separate men from their fellows. The Promise Keepers identify racism and denominationalism as two of the most pernicious barriers that divide Christian men. How have the Promise Keepers sought to "break down the walls" separating men of faith? Have they succeeded or failed in this endeavor? To what extent have the Promise Keepers made the Multicultural Man archetype discussed in chapter 3 a reality? This chapter explores these issues.

The first portion of this chapter examines how cultural diversity is evidenced at PK conferences. In many respects, PK conferences are multicultural affairs. Conference rhetoric, logos, and social practices are specifically designed to break down barriers that divide Christian men from different racial and denominational backgrounds. At conferences, PK leaders pursue this goal by emphasizing attendees' shared gender and religious status—their brotherhood in Christ. Given the racial segregation that characterizes American religious denominations, the anti-establishment tenor of PK revivalism also serves the ends of racial inclusiveness and interdenominational fellowship.

Cultural diversity meets consumerism backstage at PK conferences. The backstage "resource area" at PK stadium events presents conference-goers with a veritable bazaar of multicultural goods available for purchase. Many of these goods are designed to promote racial reconciliation and to underscore the movement's commitment to cultural diversity. A diverse lot of evangelical ministries also purvey information and solicit members backstage at PK conferences. These ministries cater to men of various stripes, enhancing the multicultural ethos created at Promise Keeper stadium events.

Despite the emphasis on cultural diversity at PK conferences, some practices undertaken there run the risk of reinforcing racial difference. This is especially the case at climactic moments of racial reconciliation, when a man representing his particular "racial community" confers forgiveness on a brother seeking to overcome his personal prejudice against those of another color. Thus, the Promise Keepers' relationship to race is much like that concerning sport, gender, and religion— it is one of paradox.

The second portion of this chapter explores the effects of PK's multicultural brand of evangelicalism on men's lives. Defining racism as a personal sin enables men to confront their hidden racial animus and to develop interracial friendships that were previously absent in their lives. Interview accounts reveal a great deal of positive change in men's lives that has been brought about by grassroots efforts to combat racism. Yet, despite these admirable developments, the Promise Keepers' commitment to eradicating prejudice "one man at a time" generally forestalls discussions about the structural character of racial stratification in American society.

Eradicating Race, Destabilizing Denominationalism: Breaking Down Walls at PK Conferences

The Promise Keepers' commitment to racial diversity is quite evident at their stadium conferences. At any conference, speakers are selected for more than merely their ability to touch the hearts of men. They are also chosen with an eye toward fostering a racially diverse religious movement and appealing to men across the racial spectrum. Thus, many conference programs feature speakers who are religious leaders in white, black, Latino, and Asian American communities. PK's commitment to racial diversity is genuine enough, but it is also a product of the particular moment at which it emerged on the fast-changing landscape of American masculinity politics. For the time being, PK seems to be the last in a long line of popular men's movements organized first around gender (men's liberation, mytho-poeticism), then around gender and race (Afrocentric men, the

Million Man March), and now around gender, race, and evangelical religion (the Promise Keepers). It is noteworthy that PK's Stand in the Gap conference was held on the National Mall in Washington, D.C., in October 1997, two years almost to the day after the October 1995 Million Man March. Both the size and the timing of the PK march on the National Mall portrayed it as the heir apparent in the vast array of men's movements that had come to dot the American cultural land-scape in recent decades.

Aside from featuring a racially diverse slate of speakers, PK con-ferences demonstrate the organization's concern with race in a num-ber of different ways—all of them intended to challenge racism and unify the body of believers. In some instances, racism is challenged directly as a patently un-Christian orientation and men are told to re-pent of this sin. At other moments in conference programs, racial preju-dice is addressed more subtly—though still critically—through symbolic and practical representations of godly manhood that subvert the color line.[1]

During each conference, PK leaders spend considerable time re-viewing the Seven Promises, and particular talks are organized around the themes raised in the Seven Promises. At Choose This Day-San An-tonio, Noel Castellanos (President of the Latino Leadership Network in Chicago, Illinois) spoke on the issue of racial reconciliation. The standard approach to this issue among PK leaders is to decry the "sin-fulness" of racism, particularly that within the Christian community. They also commonly call attention to the pernicious consequences of racism for Christians and their unsaved neighbors. Within Christendom, racism is sometimes likened to a "fracture" on the "body of Christ." Here, the metaphor is one of injury—and self-inflicted injury at that. Christians who hold racial prejudice against brothers are literally sin-ning against the body of Christ. Because body parts only work in uni-son, animus harbored against another body part (that is, Christian men of another race) is condemned on both practical grounds (as self-defeating) and spiritual grounds (as contrary to God's will for "his children").

At the same time, racism is believed to have negative consequences for the relationship between Christians and the "ungodly world" in which they live. Recall that the goal of evangelical Protestantism is to evangelize the unsaved. The Great Commission identified in the last of PK's Seven Promises entails sharing the "good news" of the gospel with those who have not heard it. Racism undermines this mandate.

Racial divisions among the body of believers, and racism that is manifested toward the unsaved, make Christian men less effective missionaries to nonbelievers in the "outside world."

PK has produced an array of videos designed to challenge racism, and selections from these are shown on jumbotron screens at conferences. At Choose This Day, one video began by featuring video segments of a white man and a black man speaking separately and in alternating sequence—first the black man, then the white man, then the black man again, then the white man again. Each man's face was positioned apart from the other, with the black man to the right side of the screen and the white man to the left. As each of these men admits to his hidden prejudices and begins speaking about how he has overcome racial animus, the images featured in sequence begin to converge near the center of the screen—until they are at last talking to one another (rather than past one another) in a face-to-face dialogue.

While racial reconciliation and the eradication of social divisions is featured prominently in all conferences, the theme of the 1996 conference series—"Break Down the Walls"—put this issue on top of the organization's agenda. The logo for the series was telling. The words "BREAK DOWN THE WALLS" appear in tan letters with the last word—WALLS—printed in a thick font that resembles crumbling stone. Above the word "walls" are three artistically rendered men wearing the same blue shirt but of very different skin hues—ostensibly, men of different races. Behind them is a brick wall that is beginning to crumble. Among these three protagonists, what appears to be a black man sounding a trumpet is positioned to the left. A white man, also sounding a trumpet, is featured to the right. A brown man, praying earnestly with hands clasped, is situated in the center. Despite the predominant color of these characters (black, white, brown), the texture of each man's face is complicated by a number of different shadings—white on black, black on white, and both white and black on brown. The scriptural passage on which that conference series and its emphasis on racial reconciliation was predicated is found in Ephesians 2:14—"For He Himself is our peace, who has made the two one and has destroyed the barrier, the dividing wall of hostility."

As might be expected from the language in the sixth of the Seven Promises, racial representations within PK are never just about race. They also address denominational divisions and other forms of social cleavage. Where breaking down denominational barriers is concerned, PK seems to have been successful—at least in attracting evangelical men. The anti-establishment, revivalistic character of the Promise Keepers not only makes religion palatable to men and "seekers" (the unsaved—see chapter 4 of this volume); it also has the benefit of allowing Promise Keepers to critique and distance itself from the denominational divisions that create factionalism among evangelical Christians. Given the noteworthy theological differences between Southern Baptists, American Baptists, the Church of God, the Assembly of God, and other conservative Protestant denominations, the Promise Keepers' opposition to organized religion gives it broad appeal. What's more, denominationalism in American religion intersects with race. In a world where predominantly white evangelical organizations like the Southern Baptist Convention are readily distinguishable from black evangelical organizations like the National Baptist Convention and where pentecostals splinter into white and black factions, the Promise Keepers are able to challenge racial separatism among born-again Christians by attacking the divisiveness of denominationalism.

Promise Keepers' pursuit of racial reconciliation is not only inflected by its critique of denominationalism but also intersects with its construction of gender. Visual depictions of the male body—at once deeply gendered and boldly multiracial—figure prominently in virtually all PK media. The series logo featured in mammoth form as the stage backdrop for the 1999 Choose This Day conference series was particularly telling in this way. Exaggerating the traditional masculine features of the male body, the man in the logo is no wimp. He boasts extremely broad shoulders and long, powerful legs and arms. He has a square chin and strong jawbone. Given PK's emphasis on multiracial evangelicalism, it is hardly surprising that the man in the poster's foreground is dark-skinned (a shade of brown). Interestingly, he is flanked by an army of even darker (black) men standing in his shadow. Nevertheless, the fact that these men are positioned in the shadows leaves their blackness ambiguous—it can potentially be seen as either a product of their skin color or the effect of the shadow that is cast over them.

Even more intriguing, the blackness of the protagonist is balanced by a different color scheme on an inset picture. In the lower right corner of this logo is an inset drawing of the body of a large white man, shown from below to emphasize his imposing stature, guarding the doorway to his home like a gladiator. His home is shown as a black shadow behind this towering figure of masculinity. The caption reads:

CHOOSE

AS FOR ME AND MY HOUSE

THIS

WE WILL SERVE THE LORD

DAY

Joshua 24:15

The compact disk version of the logo is especially intriguing. The disk jacket, a replica of the Choose This Day logo, features the black-white color scheme described above. However, the compact disk itself offers yet another color scheme over this same portrait. On the disk itself, the protagonist's body is no longer black, but rather a yellowish brown. Within this montage of images, then, men's bodies are vividly racialized (black versus white), racially ambiguous (background men), and marked by a race that is fluid and flexible (changing from brown to black, and then from white to yellow).

Consuming Cultural Diversity:
Backstage at Choose This Day

The backstage area of any PK conference reveals a veritable cultural bazaar in what is commonly referred to as the "resource area." Between conference speakers, a man steps on stage and advertises several of the items for sale backstage at the resource area. At Choose This Day-San Antonio, this job fell to a man affectionately known as "Roscoe the Resource Dude." The live "commercials" brought to us between speakers by Roscoe underscore the vast array of consumer goods available for purchase backstage. Diversity is not just a matter of racial, denominational, or cultural background at PK conferences. Diversity also entails being able to purchase objects of one's choosing from the array of what conference catalogs describe as "Tools to keep your PROMISES everyday."

It quickly becomes apparent to one arriving backstage that the re-source area is a marketplace of multiculturalism. At Choose This Day, what seemed to be several hundred different book titles were for sale in the resource area. Many of these volumes address issues of racial reconciliation, including Tony Evans's *Let's Get to Know Each Other: What White and Black Christians Need to Know about Each Other*, as well as Raleigh Washington and Glenn Kehrein's *Breaking Down Walls: A Model for Reconciliation in an Age of Racial Strife*. This latter volume comes complete with an accompanying workbook and video. These and related volumes are all advertised in glossy color on a page of the Choose This Day program under the title, "Reconciliation Books." Compact disks ("Take 3 CDs home today! Get 11 more FREE!") are also well stocked. These disks, also conveniently available in audiocassette, are advertised in the Choose This Day catalog as well.

The plethora of advertisements and consumer options at PK conferences underscores the multiple meanings of the word "choice" (Bartkowski and Regis 2003). In a spiritual sense, choice is central to the evangelical faith. As discussed in chapter 4, evangelicals contend that faith is a matter of choice. Believers must choose to "accept Christ." Yet, beyond this obvious spiritual meaning, it strikes me that the word "choice" might also have another meaning at Choose This Day. Given the breathtaking array of consumer goods available in the backstage resource area, choice here has an economic meaning—one that is un-spoken but nevertheless apparent. In this latter sense, choice entails supporting the Promise Keepers' ministry and formalizing one's ties to the movement through the exercise of consumer preference. At any given conference, Promise Keepers can choose from the wide array of support materials, memorabilia, and accouterments that are available for purchase backstage.

What's more, consumer choice meets cultural diversity in the back-stage resource area and in the conference program catalog. Given the Latino presence in San Antonio, one page of the Choose This Day-San Antonio catalog advertises various resources in Spanish ("Recursos En Espanol"). Included among these are the best-selling volumes *Siete Promesas de un Cumplidor de su Palabras* (*Seven Promises of a Promise Keeper*) and *El Poder de una Promesa Cumplida* (*The Power of a Promise Kept*), and the popular PK music CD *Canticos de Adoración y Alabanza para Cumplidores de Promesas* (*Praise and Worship Songs for Promise Keepers*). The bottom of the Spanish resources page, which features no English whatsoever, tells men: "Visita La Libreia de

Cumplidores de Promesas y Lleva Magnifico Productos Hoy a su Casa" ("Visit the Promise Keepers' Resource Center and Bring Home These Great Products Today").[2] Of course, each of these advertised items is available backstage at Choose This Day-San Antonio. The multicultural fashion giant Benetton, famous for its "United Colors of Benetton" advertising campaign, would seem to have nothing on the Promise Keepers. PK reveals its own colors as the Benetton of the evangelical world.

Multicultural evangelicalism and consumer preference are not only purveyed in the conference catalog through Spanish advertisements; they are quite evident in other ways as well. At Choose This Day-San Antonio, PK simulcasts a Spanish-language translation of each conference talk on a local AM radio station. Apparently aware of this option, a few men bring portable radios with headphones to the conference. In this way, they get to partake of conference festivities and instruction while hearing speakers address them in the language of their choice.

Moreover, virtually every advertisement page in the conference catalog features PK accouterments being sported by a racially diverse group of models—Latino, African American, Asian, and white. As might be expected, each item in PK's clothing line features the letters "PK" embroidered in one of many fashionable colors. Beyond this point of commonality, the available options are mind-boggling. T-shirts, dress shirts, and even "Gen-X stompwear"—all in 100% cotton. Straw hats, baseball caps, bucket hats, and even wool "bomber" jackets to "fight off the chill" are all advertised in the catalog and readily available backstage. PK sells jewelry of all sorts, including specialty wrist watches, collegiate rings, and sterling silver band rings. Coffee mugs to suit busy lifestyles are also for sale, including a manly, oversized 20-oz. mug billed as "Perfect for coffee at home or at work."

Adjacent to the resource area are a panoply of information booths staffed by a host of Christian groups, all of them purveying their particular set of wares. The booth of *The Christian Businessman* magazine bills itself as "The Premiere Magazine for Complete Success." This month's issue of the glossy Christian counterpart to *Business Week* features an appropriately "PK" cover story, as Darrin Smith (a black professional football player) offers investment advice. The title of the article deftly melds the language of sport and finance. For Smith, "Investing is not an option play." Shepherd Values Funds, an evangelical Christian investment group, highlights the moral nature of investment. This evangelical investment group shows itself to be engaged with the rise of "socially responsible" investing that is so much in vogue through-out the cultural mainstream, albeit with a conservative religious twist. Playing on a double entendre of the word "values" (moral conviction, financial worth), the booth informs passersby that "stewardship" en-tails ensuring that "your investments share *your* values." Nearby, the Christian Outdoorsman organization staffs a booth. An evangelical or-ganization for hunters, hikers, and others who love God's earth, the Christian Outdoorsman is soliciting new members with "a special 20% Promise Keepers discount." To make the offer even more enticing, they will provide a free T-shirt, available in sizes ranging from small to XXX-large, with each paid membership.

Jews for Jesus also have a booth in the backstage area. The booth placard reads

JEWS F✡R JESUS

thereby conveying their dual identity—unabashedly Jewish and unapologetically Christian. Members of Jews for Jesus are distribut-ing flyers with membership cards that ask the applicant if he or she is "Jewish" or "Gentile." The headline on the distributed flyers reads: "Jewish people are coming to Y'shua*," with the asterisk informing the reader at the bottom of the flyer that "Y'shua" is "the Jewish way to say Jesus." It continues: "Throughout the ages, there have always been some Jews who have believed in Jesus. Yet now, more than at any time since the Jewish apostles of Jesus ministered 2,000 years ago, Jewish people are finding grace and salvation in our Lord Jesus Christ." In a clear show of fellowship with evangelical organizations like the Promise Keepers, the Jews for Jesus flyer declares its members' belief that the "Scriptures of the Old and New Testaments are divinely in-spired, verbally and completely inerrant in the original writings and of supreme and final authority in all matters of faith and life." It also declares their belief in salvation only through Jesus Christ, "the Mes-siah [who] died for our sins, according to the Scriptures, as a repre-sentative and substitutionary sacrifice [and] that all who believe in Him are justified not by any works of righteousness they have done but by His perfect righteousness." Here in the backstage area, as on the front stage, cultural difference surfaces but is trumped by shared religious convictions.

Various "partner ministries" that have "teamed up" with PK occupy backstage booths as well. During the 1999 conference series, PK joined forces with Lighthouse Ministries, whose catchy slogan is "Prayer-Care-Share." Lighthouse and this memorable aphorism were mentioned from the podium on several occasions by conference speakers. The product of this cooperative effort—the Promise Keepers Lighthouse Kit—is also for sale backstage. The kit contains an evangelistic video entitled *Jesus*, and an envelope of lighthouse stickers that can be readily attached to the Promise Keeper's front door. These stickers designate the Promise Keeper's domicile as a "lighthouse." The kit also features the "Lighthouse Guidebook" ("Everything you need to know to 'power-up' your lighthouse"). This guidebook outlines strategies for bringing more men and families in each Promise Keeper's neighborhood to the Christian faith. Finally, the kit provides *A Revival Primer*, a booklet written by PK's own "Vice President for Revival and Awakening," Dale Schlafer. This primer tells Promise Keeper men how they "can become of a part of what God is doing to renew his people throughout the world."

In all these ways, backstage "resource areas" enhance the multicultural ethos of Promise Keeper conferences. The cultural bazaar available to Promise Keepers in these backstage areas shows a commitment to cultural pluralism by providing diverse resources, variegated organizations, and consumer choices aplenty.

Performing Race: Reconciliation Amidst Reification

The Promise Keepers also challenge racial divisions in American society through creative social practices undertaken at stadium conferences. Many of these practices aim to problematize the very concept of race. Some are directed at erasing the color line, that is, the boundaries that leave whole communities and people's everyday lives racially segregated. Hence, much of what goes on at PK conferences entails subversive performances that destabilize the notion of race in the pursuit of racial reconciliation. PK speakers offer critical expositions of racism and sometimes engage in performances that parody race. Yet, like sport, gender, and religion, PK's engagement with race is characterized by paradox. Even as some conference practices undermine the veracity of race as a natural category, others reinforce the significance of color. Hence the color line is at once erased and accentuated at PK conferences.

Race at PK conferences sometimes seems as fluid as it is on conference logos, where mixed colors leave the racial status of artistically
rendered characters ambiguous. One of the more memorable performances of racial transgression was accomplished in a spontaneous
fashion by Isaac, the Latino emcee of Choose This Day-San Antonio.
Between conference speakers, Isaac donned a pair of dark sunglasses
and performed a stunningly exact cover of James Brown's "I Feel Good"
with the stage band. Isaac's imitation of Brown was flawless, even down
to the famous black singer's signature yelps of "Ow!" interjected with
perfect timing. Isaac self-consciously called attention to the subversive character of this performance by remarking that some of his friends
know him best as the only Latino who can perform an exact cover of
James Brown.

As it turns out, other forms of music at PK conferences lend themselves to the subversion of racial categories. When the Katinas took
the stage at Choose This Day-San Antonio, they were introduced as
being "of Samoan race." Yet, despite this reference to a seemingly fixed
racial heritage, the band's music is not identifiable as belonging to any
particular racial category. The Katinas' music is multicultural and de-
fiant of genre. The group deftly mixes the rhythms of calypso, rock,
rhythm and blues, and hip-hop. Moreover, as a Christian "crossover"
band, the Katinas have wide appeal among both evangelical and mainstream audiences. Quite notably, the Katinas sing in both English and
Spanish, clearly a factor that contributes to the adoration of the band
by loyal fans in Southwest Texas—many of whom are Latino. Thus,
while the race of the Katinas would seem to be unambiguously Samoan,
their musical performances cut across "ethnic" genres such as "Tejano,"
"hip-hop," and "R&B" while transgressing cultural boundaries that
distinguish "Christian music" from its "mainstream" counterpart.

At Promise Keeper conferences, subversive performances of race
often simultaneously play with other social categories—gender, regional
culture, and even sexuality (though in this last case only obliquely).
At Choose This Day-San Antonio, some PK leaders periodically laced
traditional evangelical notions of godly masculinity with a "Tejano"
(or "Tex-Mex") flavor. Tejano culture is central to San Antonio's collective identity, and makes this Texas *ciudad* (city) an attractive site
for national conventions and tourists alike. Tejano cuisine, often simply called "Tex-Mex" at the myriad local restaurants in which it is
served, is a distinct amalgam of American and traditional Mexican fare
as developed by Latinos in Texas. Texas residents, whether or not they

are Latino, quickly become aware of the cultural and culinary differences between "Tex-Mex" and its counterparts in other largely Latino areas of the country such as California, New Mexico, and New York.

Now and again, Isaac used his role as emcee to "Tejano-ize" the conference program, one time playing Tex-Mex off against its Latino rival in the United States, California. Isaac compared a gargantuan Texas jalapeno to a tiny California jalapeno to highlight the fact that "everything is bigger" in the Lone Star State—including men's love for Jesus. Not surprisingly, this comparison attracted the attention of virtually every one of the fifty thousand men in attendance at San Antonio's Alamodome. As Isaac held up the minuscule California jalapeno, men booed loudly. And when Isaac raised the gigantic Texas jalapeno above his head, the men erupted in a boisterous cheer. Finally, with the chants of conference attendees urging him to consume the Texas chile, Isaac proceeded to bite into the oversized jalapeno. As his eyes began to tear, his cheeks reddened, and his face began to sweat, Isaac then proceeded to play out a parody[3] of the stoic "macho" man by choking out over the microphone, in obvious physical distress, "No man, it's not hot at all." This sardonic remark was greeted with profuse laughter and cheering by PK conference attendees. Thus, at their most subversive moments, PK conferences redraw the intersecting boundaries of race, gender, sexuality, and regional culture through complicated—and sometimes satirical—performances.

Whether it takes the form of cleverly produced films, richly textured logos, multiracial music, or comedic parody, the performance of race at PK aims to promote racial reconciliation. Hence, PK conferences strive to create an atmosphere in which men can set aside their inhibitions and cross racial boundaries. And crossing the color line at PK conferences is not a mere abstraction. It is pursued through tactile, face-to-face interaction among men of different races. PK turns racial reconciliation into an embodied encounter in a number of ways. As "break-out" groups and small-group prayer circles are formed, conference attendees are urged to join up with men they do not know and are especially encouraged to form groups that are racially diverse. This can be difficult, because racial minorities are literally and markedly a numerical minority at what have been predominantly white PK conferences.

Although racial reconciliation is addressed by many speakers at any PK conference, there is a point at each conference when this topic takes center stage. Typically, there is one talk set aside solely for the subject of racial reconciliation. Commonly, it is during or soon after this talk that men are encouraged to find a man of a "different race"—someone who is "not your color"—and personally confess their own prejudices while requesting this brother's forgiveness. It is not uncommon for men of different colors to embrace one another at this time. A quick perusal of most PK conference programs, which are distributed as men first enter the stadium or arena, would prepare men for this experience—if not for hugs, then at least for interracial hand-holding and close-knit, arm-in-arm prayer circles. Hence, many of the pictures featured at the PK website and in conference programs show men of various races (African American, Asian, Latino, Caucasian) sitting next to one another, holding hands in prayer, or tearfully embracing. The Choose This Day conference program featured an array of color photos depicting close interracial contact among men from various backgrounds.

Close physical contact among brothers of different colors and interracial embraces are intended to be doubly subversive. First, they aim to undermine conventional gender norms that look askance on public displays of affection among men. Like many of the practices discussed in chapter 4, a warm embrace among two men challenges the stoicism, detachment, and independence valorized through hegemonic masculinity. Second, close interracial contact is intended to break down the walls created by the segregation of everyday life in U.S. society. As explained by several regular conference-goers, the goal here is change men from the "inside out," doing so "one man at a time." In this way, Promise Keeper conferences provide an avenue through which men can undertake a literal, embodied transgression of the color line.

Yet, despite their subversive character, these transgressive acts are contradicted by the ways in which they risk reifying the color line. If one is to cross a color line, that line must be readily recognizable and then trangressed. The very notion of finding a man who is "not your color" and then seeking forgiveness from that man reinforces race in three ways. First, it suggests that race is indeed reducible to the color of one's skin, for it is only from someone of a decidedly different hue than oneself that forgiveness can be obtained. Thus, blackness, whiteness, and other "obviously" embodied racial characteristics become salient in this context. To be sure, they are salient not in the sense of promoting prejudice. But nevertheless, during the liminal moment when black, brown, and white bodies are careening around in search of absolution, skin color becomes the primary currency through which prejudice may be expunged and excused.

Second, this practice reinforces race because once the skin color of a brother is used to determine his racial status, he represents his "community of color" to the supplicant who is seeking forgiveness for his prejudice against that community. Hence, skin color emerges here both as signifier (notions of a physical essence) and signified (racial groups as a broader concept represented by this essence). During these acts of racial reconciliation, skin color is a signifier in that it "plainly" indicates the race of each man—black, white, brown, yellow, what have you. Given their divergent races, these two men can exchange an embrace, cathartic confessions, and words of forgiveness with one another. Yet, at this very same moment, skin color is also signified because it represents a broader phenomenon—namely, distinct communities of color in America. Thus, during these acts of mutual forgiveness, the color of each Promise Keeper's skin becomes a symbolic representation of his membership in a broader racial group, such as "black America," "the Latino community," or "white people."

The problem here is one of racial homogeneity and representation. Is one black man capable of forgiving his white brother's sinful prejudice against "the black community"? Is a lone white man capable of doing the same for a black or Latino brother? To be sure, this climactic point in any conference program is poignant and, given the segregated everyday worlds in which many Americans travel, appears to be quite radical. Yet, behind this moving act of contrition lurks a tacit assumption that there exists within America homogeneous communities of color. Here, the ideology first articulated in Bill McCartney's essay on racial reconciliation (see chapter 3) in *Seven Promises of a Promise Keeper* becomes social practice. Recall that, when attending a funeral of a former University of Colorado football player, McCartney (1994: 158) "had come in touch, for the first time, with the pain, struggle, despair, and anguish of the black people." Based on the notion of racial homogeneity, a single representative of a racial community can begin the process of absolution from the sin of racism.

By all estimates, whites outnumbered blacks and men of color at PK conferences. For example, one systematic survey of PK conference-goers revealed that 93 percent of attendees were white (versus 74 percent for the general population), with only 2 percent black attendees (versus 12 percent for the general population) (Morin 1997). However, other data suggest that representation of African Americans at PK conferences and within the broader movement was closer to 14–16 percent, exceeding that of the general population (see Everton 1999). Yet, even if nonwhite representation at a particular conference proves to be robust, whites are still a numerical majority at such an event (as they are in the general population). Regardless of the numbers and what one makes of them, these disparate proportions have noteworthy implications for acts of confession and absolution that are to be traded across the color line. A currency of color and racialized economy of contrition readily emerge at PK conferences. Among the barterers in this economy of contrition, there is an overabundance of white men and a comparable lack of men of color. Given the rules of reconciliation that demand securing forgiveness from a man across the color line, darkness becomes valued because it is a scarce commodity. Hence, it is not uncommon for one black man to confer collective absolution on a host of white men seeking his forgiveness. Given the relative dearth of men of color at conferences, white brethren are sometimes lined up (literally rather than just metaphorically) to be forgiven. Thus, the abundance of whites at conferences makes darkness a prized—and, potentially, a fetishized—commodity in the exchange of racial reconciliation.

Finally, the accomplishment of interracial forgiveness at PK conferences reifies racial difference by obscuring the structural character of racial stratification in America. As calls go out to men of different races to "forgive one another" during climactic moments of racial reconciliation, one imagines a segregated America in which racial groups are separate but equal. Yet, if sociological evidence is to be believed, this view of America is imaginary indeed. When compared with their black and Latino counterparts, white men continue to enjoy structural advantages that include greater odds of receiving a college degree and gaining entry into a professional career coupled with lower relative likelihoods of ending up in prison or on death row. The mandate for men to forgive *one another* situates men on a level playing field. While it may be true enough that all are stained with the sin of racial prejudice, the structure of race in America systematically confers privileges on white men that are not equitably distributed among their brothers of color. This is not to say that all white men in America are well-off while their brothers of color are not. But a critical interrogation of race in America must acknowledge that while personal prejudice is one side of racism, structural inequality is another. This latter form of racism, which may be institutionalized in ways that are largely invisible to the individual actors involved, is clearly more intractable and arguably more significant.

Up Close and Personal: Racial Reconciliation in the Trenches

Admittedly, this critical interpretation of the climactic moment of racial reconciliation at PK conferences does not tell the whole story. The practice of racial reconciliation at conferences is intended to be a starting point rather than a final act of contrition. The tearful embraces shared by men of different races on the football fields and in the stadium seats at conferences are supposed to give way to farther-reaching changes in men's churches, accountability groups, and everyday lives. Thus, to appraise the broader influence of racial reconciliation on Promise Keeper men, it is to these men's everyday lives that we must turn.

To what degree has Promise Keepers facilitated racial reconciliation among men who have joined the movement? The twenty men I interviewed feel that the Promise Keepers' emphasis on racial reconciliation has brought about palpable changes in their lives. In the trenches of everyday promise-keeping, racial reconciliation is aided not only by recalling memorable conference experiences or reading the commentaries of leading PK authors on the subject. It also is bolstered through local networks that include accountability groups and even through email notes sent out via local distribution lists.

Steve, a prominent leader of the Promise Keepers in central Texas, commonly raises the issue of "breaking down the walls" with men in accountability groups, training seminars for local members, and his extensive email list. Through these various forums, Steve urges local Promise Keepers to bridge the chasms that so often divide believers along the lines of race, denomination, social class, and even spiritual development. One of Steve's daily email messages underscores this very point[4]:

By All Possible Means
1 Corinthians 9:22
"To the weak I became weak, to win the weak. I have become all things to all men so that by all possible means I might save some."
Find the common ground and meet people where they are. Paul was a pillar of strength. However, from a position of strength, he wouldn't have been very effective with the weak. . . . Do we have a select crowd with which we comfortably associate? Do we have trouble talking about God with people

of different income levels, different education levels, different talent levels, different spiritual levels? We each have a
message to share and we're encouraged to share that message
with ALL, so that some might be saved. Please continue to
share these messages with others—so that by all possible
means some may be encouraged and be drawn closer to God.
Have a Great Day!
God Bless,
Steve

Yet another message delivered from Steve to many of his PK brothers
is predicated on a metaphor of teamwork that melds PK's emphasis
on breaking down social barriers with the movement's cultural appropriation from the world of sport:

Paul gives a great encouragement in his letter to the believers in the city of Philippi. [In] Philippians 1:3–6, [Paul says]:
"I thank my God every time I remember you. In all my prayers
for all of you, I always pray with joy because of your partner-
ship in the gospel from the first day until now, being confident of this, that he who began a good work in you will carry
it on to completion until the day of Christ Jesus."
　The day that God first touched our lives, we became partners in the gospel. And on that day, God began His work in
us. God has a wonderful plan for each of His children—no
matter what stage we are in. Be confident that our Father will
finish the work he [has] begun. I praise God [that] we are partners in the gospel. We may be serving in different capacities,
different ministries, or different churches, but we're all on the
same team.

Beyond this grassroots prompting, what sorts of practical changes
have taken place in men's lives because of the Promise Keepers' emphasis on racial reconciliation? Interview data culled from central Texas
Promise Keepers suggest that such changes occur on several levels.
To begin, many of the men I interviewed suggested that the Promise
Keepers' perspective on racial reconciliation has highlighted the pernicious workings of prejudice—often unconscious—in their own hearts.
This was especially the case for several of the white men I interviewed,
many of whom acknowledged that admission of their prejudices was

fostered by accountability group involvement. The Promise Keepers' efforts to reconcile men of different racial and social backgrounds prompted several interviewees to engage in introspection about their own feelings toward their brothers who were culturally quite different from them. Often, this introspection led to self-admissions and then public confessions about stereotypes they harbored toward others. Thus, the confessional culture generated in Promise Keeper accountability groups (see chapter 5) fostered admissions of previously covert prejudices.

One of the men I interviewed recounted how a white PK speaker confessed his own covert racial animus to a large crowd at a local conference. This speaker admitted to a habit of which he had been unaware prior to coming into PK—namely, washing his hands soon after he shook the hand of a black man. (He did not rush to wash his hands after handshakes with white men.) During this painful admission, the speaker confessed that he had been acting on unconscious thoughts of getting his right hand "dirty" by shaking hands with black men. This speaker's admission had prompted each man at the PK conference, including the interviewee sharing the story with me, to reflect on his own reactions to meeting men of a different race as well. The man who recounted this story told me that he too was guilty of harboring prejudice toward men of color—though he had not been aware of it prior to joining the Promise Keepers. After a concerted effort to expand his friendship circles to include men of different racial backgrounds, he now finds himself "more sensitive to brothers" whose race differs from his own.

Several white interviewees reported a newfound understanding of the experiences commonly endured by their brothers of color. Often, empathetic feelings surfaced in subtle and unexpected but nonetheless significant ways. In cultivating close friendships with evangelical men of color, one man began frequenting restaurants with his new friends. He quickly began to realize something that had never occurred to him when traveling within his circle of white friends. When he went out to eat with black and Latino men, he noticed that waiters were often considerably more conscientious in taking care of white customers—filling cups, checking on food, busing dishes—than they were with black or Latino patrons. Experiences like these made this man aware of the privileges that he as a white man enjoyed, but of which he had been previously unaware. This particular man testified that PK has helped him to overcome these and other "blind spots." Given this subtle yet persistent form of discrimination against his new friends, this man goes "out of [his] way" to show his "brothers of color" that "they're special" to him.

For men with progressive political sensibilities, the Promise Keepers' forward-thinking stance on racial reconciliation serves as a welcome counterbalance to some of the movement's more traditional rhetoric on gender. In such accounts, race and gender intersect in an intriguing way. Though such men were admittedly a small fraction of those interviewed, PK redeems itself from gender traditionalism by adopting a progressive approach to racial integration. Nowhere was this pattern more clearly evidenced than in the account of Andy, a Promise Keeper who described himself as "open-minded" about both gender and race. When I asked Andy about the most appealing and least appealing aspects of the Promise Keepers, he lauded the forward-thinking emphasis on racial reconciliation and PK's attempt to eradicate other social barriers that divide men. In fact, given his Jewish heritage (which he mentioned to me early in my interview with him), Andy thought that the Promise Keepers' efforts at reconciliation needed to be pushed beyond Christian boundaries to include outreach to men of non-Christian faiths. As Andy put it:

> The most appealing aspect to me was attempting to unify— to bring together—men of all denominations, races, and belief systems into a single [group]—into a common thread. . . . [But] that doesn't go far enough, actually, in my mind. In my mind, it should be more than just a Christian-type of an effort. You have to remember, my background, since my father was Jewish. So, I've got that side. But I look beyond everything and say, "This is a chance to start bringing people together." It's a great start. That's probably one of the most appealing things to me.

In the same breath, Andy was quick to criticize the movement's traditionalist approach to gender:

> Least appealing, might be some of the more controversial statements that some [men in the] Promise Keepers make. And you know, to me those are dividing points. Those are points when things get a little bit stressed. When people take too strong a stance on some of the areas—some of the issues which I don't think are fundamental to the cause or to the beliefs. But [these men] try to [portray themselves as] representative [of all Promise Keepers].

[Bartkowski:] Any particular issues come to mind?

Oh, there are issues about, you know, there are some men that like to purport that women should be subject to or underneath men. And [they say that] this is very important—that it's stated in the Bible and therefore that's the way it is. I don't feel that way. I'm more, a little more open-minded in that respect.

Despite the thorny issue of gender traditionalism, Andy's last words return to the corrective that he believes the Promise Keepers provide concerning racial and religious separatism. In Andy's eyes, a mere "tolerance" of men from different racial and religious backgrounds is insufficient. Andy believes that PK and Christianity in general require men to do no less than embrace cultural difference and build meaningful relationships with men who differ from them:

> One of the messages that I got out of [the Promise Keepers] was that it's not enough to simply be accepting of other men—men of other colors, denominations, and so forth. We need to reach out to one another and we need to go beyond simply saying, "Oh well, I'm not biased, and therefore I've solved the world's problems." I think that's one of the messages and probably one of the most important ones I got out of it.

Several white Promise Keepers to whom I spoke reported similar transformations but shared their longstanding struggle with prejudice against men of color. Harry, a white Promise Keeper in his late fifties, was raised during the segregation era in the South. He admitted to harboring racist attitudes given the fact that he had come of age in the Jim Crow South. Although his view of blacks changed somewhat when he fought alongside them in the military, prejudice had led him to draw the line at men he called his friends—men who were, by and large, white. His involvement in the Promise Keepers provided the incentive he needed to begin to cultivate genuine friendships with black men in spite of his segregationist heritage. Harry explained:

> For me, being born and raised in Mississippi, [race] has been a real challenge. When I was growing up in Mississippi, they still had the white and colored signs over water fountains in Biloxi. So, I was raised with a lot of personal bias. Then, when I was in the military, I realized that black guys are okay—especially when we're getting shot at and they're right there with

me. Then I get out [of the military]. And then one of these
[Promise Keepers] guys said, "You have all these white friends,
you have very few black friends."

Upon hearing remarks like these (which are commonly articulated by
Promise Keepers), Harry realized that he continued to harbor racist
attitudes, though on a more covert level than those with which he had
been raised. He was no longer overtly prejudiced against blacks, but
he didn't really have any African American men among his close
friends. Yet, in part due to his involvement in PK, he has begun to
make significant changes in his life. With his recent move to the central Texas area, Harry has made a self-conscious effort to attend a church
that is racially integrated. Whites and Latinos are both well represented
in this congregation. And he is quite pleased that his church has, in
his words, begun "reaching out to the black churches in the area."
     What forms does such outreach take? White interviewees lauded
the new outreach efforts undertaken by their congregations. In fact,
all of them participated in such efforts, and several spearheaded them.
Most common among the congregational outreach efforts mentioned
by PK men were jointly held worship services. These worship services
were typically designed so that one church would "close its doors"
on a given Sunday. Congregants at both the "black church" and the
"white church" involved would then meet for a common service at
the church building that had been designated in advance as the site
for joint worship. Soon after, the church sponsoring the first joint service would close its doors and all congregants would meet at the other
church. Sometimes these services even rotated among a network of
churches linked in a relationship of interracial fellowship.
     While interracial worship services could hardly be said to eradi-
cate racial stratification within churches or outside of them, they do
create opportunities for interracial alliances and interdenominational
dialogue. They also foster resistance against the racism that has been
institutionalized in many faith communities—white churches here,
black churches there, and so forth. And, in the words of one Promise
Keeper who participated in them, these rotating services "got people
out into parts of the community where they don't typically travel."
Given patterns of racial segregation in local communities, the churches
linked in such fellowships were often located in different neighborhoods—locales that were respectively racialized as the "white," "black,"
or "Latino" part of town. Often these locales were divided by clear

social or geographical markers, such as an interstate highway running through town, or other indicators that demarcated the impoverished "south side" from the more affluent "west side." In several instances, faith communities formalized these ties across racial and denominational lines by creating a relationship of "sister churches" between them.

Here, then, were the beginnings of structural change in central Texas evangelical communities to which Promise Keeper men had apparently contributed. PK conference-goers hugging one another in pursuit of racial reconciliation had "fanned out" and were now catalysts in a collective mobilization against racism within churches. Embracing bodies had given rise to whole groups of religious believers making periodic pilgrimages across town to worship with faith communities quite different from their own. The effects of such joint worship services and collaborations should not be overstated. Perhaps the most genuinely revolutionary act would entail the wholesale integration of such congregations into multiracial faith communities. However, these outreach efforts represent what might be not just the beginning of "changed hearts" among evangelicals in central Texas, but the prospect for newly cultivated social relationships among whole groups of people who have long lived in separate worlds.[5]

What did the interviews I was able to conduct with Promise Keeper members of color (five thorough in-depth interviews and many more unstructured field interviews) indicate about how these men evaluated the movement? As might be expected, these men were equally laudatory of the Promise Keepers' emphasis on racial reconciliation. Yet, because many of these men had been on the receiving end of prejudice and discrimination, the substance of the narratives in their commentary was often quite different. When asked about the meaning of racial reconciliation, Jesse, a Latino Promise Keeper, began by suggesting that there is a strong kinship between Jesus Christ and oppressed groups. He then proceeded to describe the prejudice he has faced, and the distinctly Christian strategies he as a Promise Keeper uses to combat it:

> Well, you know, Jesus was a Jew. He was not blue-eyed and blonde-haired. I've met some fine Christian people who felt that Jesus was blonde and blue-eyed. I'm kind of like, "No. You think about the concept [of Jesus], and that's really in front. Because [Jesus] was a lower-class citizen from a slave group,

being that Rome was in charge of Israel. And no, He was not part of the dominant group." In our society, we've erected barriers. I can tell you names of churches where you won't see a black or brown face. That's sad. I can tell you names of churches where you won't see a white or light-haired person at all. I think what the Promise Keepers are trying to do is to help us realize that the Bible scripturally states [that the gospel must be proclaimed to] "every tribe and every tongue." I can't say, "It's not for you, because you're not my race." I can't do that. It's ludicrous for me to call myself a Christian. It's unfortunate that I have not only heard that, but [I have] experienced that. I just tell them, "I think you're wrong. In fact, I know you're wrong. I don't think you can find what you're thinking in the Bible." Of course, it got me into some debates about race. But there are no racial barriers in the Bible. There are none. Jesus talked to the Samaritan people. And if you don't understand the cultural context in that, you're not going to understand what that great leap was. The Ethiopian . . . I guess it was Mark in Acts [of the Apostles], who He witnessed to. There is no race line here.

Jesse then proceeded to discuss how his own involvement in PK, and that of his pastor, Gino, has brought about racial reconciliation in his home congregation. Jesse's home church shares a building with several other churches. Traditionally, black Africans have used the building on Saturdays and Latinos have used it on Sundays. For as long as this arrangement has existed, it seemed like a necessity because the Latino church holds their service in Spanish. Yet, after attending Promise Keepers events and hearing the message of racial reconciliation, the apartheid-like quality of this arrangement dawned on Jesse and Gino. They decided, with the help of some leaders in the church, to make a change and not let linguistic differences act as a barrier to deeper fellowship. Jesse explains:

The Promise Keepers have made a big effort to try and break some of that [racial barrier] down. Our pastor, Gino, is involved in that. Because he has confronted the whole congregation about how we suddenly or inadvertently think that way. And we have challenged him as well. What he has done is, he has talked with other pastors and we have had an intermingling of black and Hispanic people in our church. One thing good about our church is that we [pause], I don't know if we rented it out to them, but we let them use [the buildings]. We let other churches, like the African church, use our buildings on like Saturday afternoons and then the Hispanic church uses it on Sunday afternoons. So, what we told Gino—me and the men's leader—[is that] we need to have a service, and we did, where we have everybody there and have a translator at the front.

Here, then, is an example of interracial fellowship stimulated by the Promise Keepers that entailed not reaching out across congregational boundaries (as described above), but rather facilitating interaction among churches situated within one congregation. By this account, such interracial fellowship has not radically altered the nature of the relationship between these groups, at least to this point. The Latinos own the building complex, whereas the blacks apparently rent the facilities. The Latino church meets on Sunday, the traditional Christian day of worship, whereas the black church meets on Saturday. Yet, at the same time, involvement in PK had created a new sensitivity to the segregated nature of this relationship and had engendered a desire to overcome the linguistic barriers that often divide communities of color from one another.

Several of the men of color to whom I spoke explicitly rejected criticism of PK as a men's movement for whites that included some token racial minorities simply to wave the banner of multiculturalism. These men were among the most articulate concerning the care needed to navigate between the Scylla of Christian unity and the Charybdis of cultural diversity. Jamon, one of the black Promise Keepers I interviewed, explains that the Christian "walk" entails simultaneously recognizing all believers' oneness in Christ and each believer's distinct cultural background and unique talents. Jamon alludes to the scriptural metaphor of the "body of Christ" to illustrate this point:

Those of us in the body are called to walk, not against our culture, our cultural background, our cultural beliefs necessarily. Or laying down our diversity, gifts, et cetera. But instead, [we are called] to say, "That's not going to control me. What's going to control me is my love of the Lord." Instead of being ethnocentric, if you will, being Christocentric. . . . Getting to that point brings alive the scripture that says, "One body, yet many members." So, realize that there are many walls that divide even the Christian faith, let alone all societies— sex, male-female, generational walls, cultural walls, even among the same race, racial walls, geographic walls, denominational walls. It's always been a concern of mine that the body would reflect one body, so that we would work toward bringing the walls down, laying aside our personal grudges and beliefs [by] saying "Okay, we're going to reflect it."

Jamon is pleased that the Promise Keepers have not promoted a homogenizing form of cultural accommodation in which nonwhites are essentially asked to be white. In fact, that was one of the features of the movement that most appealed to him.

The Promise Keepers, to me, was an organization that was trying to help tear down some of the walls. Primarily, racial walls. So, it was a natural fit for me. My heart was right there. Here is a man [Bill McCartney] who, I felt, was actually walking it out. He wasn't [just] talking about [reconciliation]. He wasn't dealing with it from a standpoint of, "I'm over here. You guys are over there. Get your lives together." But [he] was dealing with the reality of it. All the ups and downs of trying to live out a life. So, that was an attraction to me.

Jamon proceeds to provide an illustration of the Promise Keepers' commitment to racial reconciliation from a conference he attended. Despite the conference's interruption by severe weather, the men in attendance remained in the stadium and took seriously the mandate of racial reconciliation. As he explains:

I went up there with some of the men from the church that I used to pastor. My fellow co-pastor, plus we traveled with a white brother of mine. My church was mixed, but it's predominantly black. [We went] with a gentlemen from a predominantly white church, who is the minister of music there. He and some of his guys. And we traveled together and we had a great time. . . . In the midst of the meeting, storms opened up. The stadium—it was an open stadium—and they didn't cancel the meeting. They didn't say, "Everyone go home." We [took cover in] a gymnasium and it was neat. Guys just being guys. [We] didn't whine and complain about the rain, being wet, et cetera. [We] wound up throwing the football in the gym, talking and singing, and that kind of stuff. Then the rain ceased. We went out and ate cold barbecue, roasted chicken. They fed everyone. We were charged for a meal, and continued on with the service, the meeting.

After the severe weather had passed at the conference Jamon attended, racial reconciliation took center stage. As at other PK conferences, reconciliation took the form of exchanging embraces, trading tearful admissions, and mutually conferring forgiveness on brothers of different racial backgrounds. As Jamon recounts, white men had crowded around him to ask for his forgiveness of their prejudice:

> One of the things that stuck out to me in that meeting was a time, it might have been Tony Evans speaking, but at some point he said, "All right, I want you to get together with someone you didn't come here with and speak your heart and repent. If you have anything to repent for. Any thoughts or actions you've taken that [are] racist." I was standing there and about four or five guys came up to me like this, [including] one of the spokespersons from either East Texas or Louisiana. And the guy started talking. He could barely get the words out of his mouth. He was pretty choked up. I believe he had some tears. He said, "I just want to apologize for some thoughts I've had that black people were less than human. Just some bad thoughts." And the other guys that were with him were nodding their heads [and saying,] "I just need to apologize and repent for that." I said, "Well brother, that's a two-way street. I've had some thoughts that weren't right myself." I understood. And so, I could tell he was being sincere. . . . That was a touching moment and there were other meetings [across racial lines] around going on. That's what it's about. It's about recognizing that, you know, I'm not perfect. I've done some things wrong. And if you want to push on it, we really want to reflect Christ. We've got to take care of everything in our lives, [and] have everything match up [with Christ's example]. And this is an area in which the church has fallen short.

Found! A Multiracial Promise Keeper: Abel's Narratives of Racial Reconciliation

In some instances, men of color were able to re-count stories in which their fears stemming from a history of antago-nism toward whites gave way to racial reconciliation. One of my interviewees, Abel, told me of a memorable encounter at a Promise Keepers conference. Abel's encounter underscores how masculine gen-tility and racial reconciliation sometimes converge at conferences. As Abel explained, "I was standing in line to get a hot dog." Then he re-alized that behind him was "this big burly guy [with] broad shoul-ders." Abel said that his knee-jerk reaction was to be "really scared of him." In fact, he told the man, "Why don't you go ahead? I'm over here talking to my friend." Abel's fears arose based on the man's physi-cal girth and his whiteness, combined with the fact that they were in a large crowd of men at a stadium. Yet, he soon found out that these fears, which seemed quite justified given his personal history, were unjustified in this particular setting:

> Normally, I'd be scared of him. Scared of him because I'd think that he would want to chew me up, or crunch me down, or step on me or whatever. But he was the nicest person I've ever met. That's one of the things that I'm talking about [regard-ing racial reconciliation]. I view this guy as a mean, ugly, white guy because all my life I've been stepped on. I mean, [I am] this little, puny, Mexican dude. I was scared of this guy. The fear was there. . . . Instead, my fear subsided. In fact, when he spoke to me, it made me feel good.

Abel's case is an interesting one. Although he describes himself here as a "Mexican dude," his race (like that of the artistically ren-dered characters in PK logos) is most difficult to pin down. In the short survey I administer to respondents before conducting in-depth inter-views, Abel described himself as "Caucasian with Hispanic ethnicity." Yet, during the interview, he alternately described his race as "His-panic," and "mostly mestizo Indian . . . mestizo, meaning 'many blacks' . . . [with] some French and Spanish roots, my dad being the Spanish part, because he is white. He's whiter than you are," he says, smiling and pointing at me. Yet, Abel comments on what he calls his own "dark-ness," telling me that "when [my dark brother and I] burn [in the sun], we bronze. We don't tan." His other two brothers are fair-skinned.

Abel's complicated racial status affects the way he views race and PK's efforts at racial reconciliation. As the foregoing account illustrates, Abel is very critical of white privilege. As a "little, puny Mexican dude," he has had his share of tangles with whites. Yet, sometimes he speaks of himself as if he were white. Nevertheless, the message he imparts is consistent. In God's eyes, skin color doesn't matter. As Abel explains:

> The Promise Keepers are interested in having racial reconcili-ation in all these things that we have been hearing about— blacks and whites, Mexicans and whites, Orientals and whites. Always the whites are involved there. You know, we're all made perfect. We're all made perfect. We have this skin color, because that's just the way we were made. . . . The Promise Keepers are trying to teach us God's view of His perfection in us—that He made us all equal. He made us all the same in his own perfection, to be brothers and sisters. But, because of the circumstances in history—in man's history, not God's history—in the fact that we didn't get to learn who we were to each other, we immediately jumped to the judgment and conclusions that we were the best race—speaking of whites. We were the best race, because our skins were white and we read the Bible and we didn't know that they did, too. We didn't believe their Bible, because we didn't think it was the same Bible they were reading that we were reading, which it was. They were reading the same Bible that we were. But yet, the Caucasians or the white race or the white-skinned people took their color and . . . made [that color] the best one. . . . What I'm trying to get at is: We're all made the same. We all read the same Bible. We all serve the same God. We're all created from the same God. So why are we fighting? . . . Why can't we live together as brothers and sisters in Christ? . . . So what the Promise Keepers are trying to say is let's come together and let's talk about what is really bothering us. Let's learn through Scripture who we really are in Christ, who we really are in God. Not who we are in black and white, in being Baptist, Method-ist, and all those other [denominations]. What is the real thing here? The real thing is that we're all born of God.

While it may be true enough that skin color does not matter in the eyes of God, Abel seems doubly aware of its importance in social

life. On the one hand, Abel recognizes that the valorization of whiteness is a primary source of racial oppression—whether manifested as
antagonism toward blacks, Mexicans, or "Orientals." On the other hand,
Abel's mestizo heritage complicates traditional racial categories. And
here, it is not just categories of color such as Mexican or black that
become blurred, but the reference category of "white." Like the artistically rendered Promise Keepers that appear in the movement's logos
and the PK leaders who satirically efface racial categories during conferences, colors bleed into one another throughout Abel's stories of
racial reconciliation and family heritage.

What then is a sociologist to make of Abel? Is he among the privi-
leged or the oppressed? Given his multiracial heritage and his deft linguistic movement across an array of racial categories, this question
proves most difficult to answer. Yet, as Abel interprets the Promise
Keepers' message on racial reconciliation, this question is moot. The
question to be asked is not one that gauges privilege or oppression,
but one that inquires, "Why can't we live together as brothers and sis-
ters in Christ?" And, to Abel at least, the answer is clear and compelling: "What is the real thing here? The real thing is that we"—whether
black, brown, white, or, as in Abel's case, all of the above—"are all
born of God." At the end of the day, race does not matter. God's history is not man's history.

Conclusion

It is intriguing that the Promise Keepers' call for
the eradication of racism and other social barriers rests largely on arguments about innate equality. Many in the movement talk of men as
"brothers" and characterize all persons as "God's children." Admirable
as these characterizations are, they do not readily lend themselves to
calls for social justice. When racial reconciliation is practiced at PK
conferences, it centers largely on admissions of each man's prejudi-
cial feelings. What's more, forgiveness in such venues is "a two-way
street." Yet, racial justice would require a search for social solutions
to the privileges conferred by whiteness in a racially stratified society. Why would a movement that puts racial reconciliation—and the
eradication of other social barriers—near the top of its agenda not call
for social justice? The answer to this question is found in the central
place that individualism and its counterpart, personal responsibility,
occupy in the cultural repertoire of American evangelicalism. Just as

men are saved one soul at a time, reconciliation supplants prejudice and trust replaces suspicion one man at a time.

Through conference activities and in accountability groups, men of different races are reconciled with their brothers from the "inside out"—that is, through a change of heart. What's more, such reconciliation is viewed as effecting change from the "bottom up"—that is, through personalized relationships formed at the grassroots level of social life. In the evangelical universe, heartfelt conversion is seen as more genuine and grassroots change is viewed as more authentic than "legislating" relationships from the "top down." Taking the men that I interviewed at their word, the Promise Keepers' engagement with the vexing issue of cultural difference has something to recommend it. In its best moments, evangelicalism fosters a recognition of the innate equality among "all God's children." Among this priesthood of all believers, claims to superiority—whether made on the grounds of race, class, denomination, or other social strata—indicate little more than the claimant's own lack of Christian humility and failure to understand God's will for his children. A biblical passage often cited by Promise Keepers discourages such hubris and urges each man instead "to act justly and to love mercy and to walk humbly with your God" (Micah 6:8).

Where the color line is concerned, the Promise Keepers have sought to underscore the importance of establishing personal relationships among men from different racial backgrounds. Here, the effort is to "put a face" on race by expanding one's friendship networks to include a racially diverse mix of men. Drawing from the confessional culture created at conferences and bolstered through accountability groups, these relationships provide men with a site for confessing and overcoming their racial animus. These close-knit interracial fellowships seem to alter men's perceptions of their brothers from different backgrounds by personalizing abstract categories like "race." In several instances, the Promise Keepers' emphasis on racial reconciliation has even contributed to broader forms of interracial contact, blurring the line between "black churches" and "white churches" through joint worship services and the forging of interdenominational fellowships in local communities. And, perhaps most notably, they remind Christians that the categories created in "man's history"—race, denomination, class, physical appearance—are products of social inequality rather than a reflection of God's will for his children.

Despite these emancipatory moments, the Promise Keepers' approach to racial reconciliation has its limits. Given its emphasis on changing hearts, this individualistic approach to eradicating inequality does not readily permit an interrogation of the social character of stratification. Social inequality is, in fact, social because it eclipses and encompasses the individual. It is not the product of any one person's caprice. Prejudice may be carried in the hearts of individuals. And discrimination may be most recognizable in small groups like friendship circles and Bible studies. Yet, stratification draws its force from *collectively* defined notions of color, character, and taste that are not reducible to their residues in the individual heart. Paradoxically, the Promise Keepers' personalized approach to eradicating social barriers changes hearts while forestalling an awareness of the structural privileges (better schooling, employment, and wage-earning opportunities) collectively conferred on some of God's children and not others. To be sure, racial stratification in America is not solely a matter of black and white. That is to say, American race relations are not reducible to black exclusion and white privilege. Nevertheless, "man's history" has created structural disparities that do more than merely obscure God's will for his children.

7 | Conclusion

Promise Keepers' Fate in a New Millennium

Remember the Promise Keepers? So began this volume. Given the few short years of fame enjoyed by the movement, one might reasonably ask what is worth remembering about the Promise Keepers. In this concluding chapter, I highlight the central insights to be gleaned from sustained reflection on PK in light of its quick rise to prominence and its equally dramatic fall from grace. I begin by identifying some of the Promise Keepers' key contributions to the cultural repertoire of American evangelicalism. I argue that, despite its short life course, the movement has shown evangelicals to be more culturally engaged than critics have often charged. In fact, the movement's selective appropriation of mainstream American culture (sport, gender, family, religion, and multiculturalism) gave the movement an air of flexibility that undoubtedly contributed to its broad appeal. Yet, given the ephemeral quality of contemporary American culture, paradox and flexibility within the movement likely contributed to its demise.

Paradoxes of Promise-Keeping: Social Engagement, Cultural Distinctiveness, and Evangelical Identity

In his seminal volume, *American Evangelicalism: Embattled and Thriving*, Christian Smith (Smith et al. 1998) offers a compelling rationale for the continued vitality of evangelical

Protestantism in contemporary America. Smith argues that the strength of evangelical Protestantism is found in the expansive cultural repertoire and flexible tools available within this religious subculture. In Smith's terms, the repertoire of American evangelicalism enables this subculture to establish a relationship of "distinctive engagement" with mainstream American culture. In other words, there are a number of tools within the evangelical cultural repertoire that enable those within this religious subculture to build bridges, albeit selectively, to the mainstream of American social life. The evangelical emphasis on personal conversion and the formation of grassroots religious networks resonate quite well with the American values of individualism, choice, and populism.

Despite these points of cultural convergence, however, evangelicals are careful to distinguish themselves from the mainstream of American social life. Evangelicals keep the cultural mainstream at arm's length by continuing to defend the infallibility of the Bible in the face of scientific rationality and the higher criticism of scripture that emerged in the wake of the Enlightenment. In contrast to benign or "tabula rasa" views of human nature, evangelicals underscore their subcultural distinctiveness by contending that human beings are inherently sinful. The evangelical counterbalance to human depravity is equally distinctive; salvation in this subculture is only possible through one's acceptance of Jesus Christ as one's "personal Lord and Savior."

Smith's subcultural identity perspective has much to recommend it, particularly when compared with earlier approaches. The secularization paradigm, at least in its neoclassical form (Berger 1967), predicted the ultimate demise of religion. From this vantage point, the pluralistic quality of modern culture tore asunder the "sacred canopy" under which religious believers previously were able to shield themselves. Religious accommodation and culture wars perspectives, though more contemporary, do not fare much better. Accommodationist theories suggest that evangelical commitment gradually erodes as modernity sweeps through the world of conservative Christianity (Hunter 1983, 1987). The culture wars thesis focuses on the retrenchment of evangelical Protestants in the wake of rapid social change and cultural upheaval (Hunter 1991). Culture wars theorists portray evangelical Protestants as the leading voice of "cultural orthodoxy" in America.

By contrast, Smith's theory highlights the dynamism of the evangelical subculture. Evangelical Protestantism continues to refashion its tool kit and expand its repertoire to meet the demands of a rapidly changing America. Rather than enlisting a teleological argument of religious decline (secularization) or a totalizing account of religious retrenchment (culture wars), subcultural identity theory invites an exploration of the uneasy tension between American evangelicalism and the broader milieu within which it is situated. Much beholden to Smith's perspective, I have characterized the Promise Keepers' relationship with American culture as one of paradox—an "approach-avoidance dance" with American culture, a "selective borrowing" from the secular mainstream.

Regardless of the language used, this case study of the Promise Keepers shows evangelical men to be thoughtful navigators of the tumultuous strait between theological orthodoxy and social engagement. My analysis of the rhetorical devices employed by the movement's leading authors (chapter 3) and the social practices undertaken at PK conferences (chapters 4 and 6) underscore the diverse uses to which cultural symbols and strategies have been put by the Promise Keepers. In her groundbreaking work on culture, Ann Swidler (1986) argues that cultural tools are not "social givens." Rather, they are capable of being used in many different ways by various social actors. Agency resides in the ability of social actors to use cultural tools in creative and unanticipated ways. Despite the persistence of unflattering stereotypes of American evangelicals as "dupes" or "foot soldiers," cultural creativity is clearly manifested within PK.

The Promise Keepers enlisted longstanding evangelical tools such as the Bible, Jesus Christ, personal conversion, advice manuals, and scripture study groups in their pursuit of godly manhood. Yet they have broadened the repertoire of American evangelicalism in the process. As illustrated in chapter 3, Promise Keeper authors utilize two key cultural strategies—the practice of discursive tacking and the deployment of gendered metaphors—to offer scriptural reinterpretations of godly manhood as the Rational Patriarch, Expressive Egalitarian, Tender Warrior, and Multicultural Man. These advice manuals do so by advancing various depictions of Jesus Christ, who is at once gendered (Rational Patriarch), ungendered (Expressive Egalitarian), transgendered (Tender Warrior), and raced (Multicultural Man). While these archetypes certainly influence the grassroots practices of Promise Keepers, cultural production within this movement has never been a top-down affair.

The populist character of American evangelicalism precludes the monopolization of cultural production by elite conservative Protestants. Innovative applications of cultural symbols and the creative enlistment of cultural strategies can be noted at PK's grassroots level as well. Such innovations emerged through the cultivation of meaningful account-ability partnerships between men, the performance of evangelized sports rituals at stadium conferences, the articulation of neopatriarchal terms like "servant-leadership" for PK husbands, and the initiation of interracial relationships in the pursuit of racial reconciliation.

To be sure, the Promise Keepers did not invent these cultural forms out of thin air. As demonstrated in chapter 2, many of the practices utilized in the movement have their history in religious revivalism, Muscular Christianity, or fraternal orders—all of which predate PK. Moreover, many of the strategies utilized within PK draw force from changes brought about by other social movements (feminism, men's movements, and gay rights advocacy) and current cultural trends (multiculturalism, consumerism, and changing gender relations). Thus, in enlisting the cultural strategies described here, the Promise Keep-ers draw boundaries around—and, at times, build bridges to—their fore-bears and cultural counterparts. Yet, through it all, one thing is clear. The symbolic repertoire of the Promise Keepers—the archetypes, mo-tifs, and advice genres discussed here—is robust. And this repertoire gives rise to an array of complex cultural strategies that provide evan-gelical Protestantism with the dexterity needed to stay current with the rapid pace of change in contemporary American society.

What, in the end, is to be made of the Promise Keepers' stunning success at attracting men to stadiums and the movement's apparent facility at bringing new believers into the evangelical fold? It is likely that the movement's variegated archetypes of godly manhood (chap-ter 3) and deft interweaving of sport, gender, family, spirituality, and cultural diversity at stadium conferences (chapters 4–6) are partly re-sponsible for its meteoric rise and its broad appeal. In its heyday, PK seemed capable of being all things to all people. Elements of hege-monic masculinity and traditional family relations maintained con-nections with old-guard evangelicals and hearkened back to a bygone era that seemed less confusing and less complicated than the contem-porary moment. Yet PK's integration of more contemporary perspec-tives—men's liberation, poeticized masculinity, and multiculturalism—helped the movement to counter charges of being backward, reaction-ary, and excessively nostalgic. And even as PK seemed to share some commonalities with these other men's movements (Messner 1997;

Schwalbe 1996), its distinctiveness was easily discerned by its explicit use of evangelical cultural tools to advance its vision(s) of godly manhood.

The paradoxes of promise-keeping presented here stand in bold contrast to critics who depict the Promise Keepers as an "essentialist retreat" from progressive social relations or as a reactionary third generation of the Christian Right. Not one but many images of godly manhood emerge from PK rhetoric and social practice. Traditionalist Promise Keepers define themselves against feminists and gay rights activists while, at the same time, taking pains to point out that the godly patriarch is a "tender-tough" man who eschews despotism. And men made uncomfortable by such neopatriarchal depictions could find support for their pursuit of emotional expressiveness and marital egalitarianism as well as a progressive approach to race relations. Such contradictions were amplified at Promise Keeper stadium conferences. Conferences let men get rowdy while inculcating gentility and respectability. Conventional understandings of gender and race are simultaneously criticized, parodied, and reinforced. Even where the issue of racial reconciliation alone is concerned, PK shows itself to be a forward-thinking multicultural movement in its attempt to break down the color line. Yet its "one man at a time" approach to racial reconciliation resonates with the current preference for "local" solutions to structural problems. PK is at once a champion of cultural diversity and an ally to those who wish to usher in America's "post–Civil Rights" era by dismantling Affirmative Action. In all of these ways, the Promise Keepers situate themselves in multiple locations on the terrain of contemporary cultural politics.

Of Ethnography and Sensate Religion: Recasting Subcultural Identity Theory

The series of paradoxes interrogated in this volume underscores the need for a notable recasting of subcultural identity theory. I have used the theory of boundary work and have introduced the concept of sensate religion in an attempt to do so. In the messy world in which we live, the negotiation of evangelical identity is never just a matter of redrawing religious boundaries. The cultural symbols and strategies that are used to craft religious identities simultaneously intersect with a dizzying array of social statuses—race, class, gender, age, sexuality, regionalism, and nationality—all of which figure into a religious movement like the Promise Keepers. It is heartening to see proponents of subcultural identity beginning to explore the ways in which religious identity intersects with some of these other social statuses—specifically, gender (Gallagher 2003) and race (Emerson and Smith 2000). However, more of this type of work needs to be done, and with additional attention to the complicated intersections between religion and still other forms of social cleavage (Ammerman 2004).

In addition, my exploration of the Promise Keepers has revealed something that is common knowledge among ethnographers of religious life but has yet to filter out beyond those circles. It is true enough that evangelical identities are rendered with the aid of cultural symbols—scripture, advice manuals, conference talks, logos, and the like. But the power of the Promise Keepers and evangelicalism more broadly is found not in nonmaterial cultural forms but in the material practices through which these symbols come alive. The extensive ethnographic accounts found throughout this book emerge from the realization that, in studying a social movement like PK, "walk" (ethnography) needs to take precedence over "talk" (interviews). To be sure, any analysis of the Promise Keepers would be incomplete without a careful examination of best-selling PK advice manuals and interview accounts drawn from men in the movement. Yet, as I conducted this research, I was told again and again by men with whom I interacted that the power of the movement in their lives was not something they could readily put into words. When I began frequenting accountability groups and attended a PK conference, I understood what they meant.

Evangelized sports rituals. Ear-splitting music. Sharing an embrace of racial reconciliation. How is someone raised outside the evangelical tradition to make sense of all this? Fieldwork invariably presents the researcher with conundrums. Yet the Promise Keepers taught me the importance of "being there"—the need to get out of my office and into the field as PK events unfolded and interactions among men in the movement ensued. There is a lesson here for scholars of religion, myself included. Qualitative accounts that overlook the *social practices* through which religious identities are accomplished and from which religious culture emerges are all missing something crucial.

Religious culture is created, in large part, through embodied practices—what I have here called the "sensate" dimension of religion. I have argued here that, among the Promise Keepers, such practices simultaneously reinforce and subvert social categories like gender, religion, and race. These are what I have called paradoxes of promise-keeping. Yet, on another level, these practices blur the distinction scholars have conventionally drawn between "material culture" and "nonmaterial culture." The account rendered in this volume is a product of this paradox manifesting itself to me. The vitality of evangelicalism is found in the "doing" of this religion. It is not insignificant that the panoply of unfolding religious experiences in an evangelical person's life are described as his or her "faith walk." This is an embodied metaphor, and one that underscores movement—literally, culture in action. As such, there is much more to be learned about this subculture by ethnographers of religion.

Warhol's Prophecy: Cultural Ephemerality and PK's Fifteen Minutes of Fame

By all estimates, the Promise Keepers' 1997 Stand in the Gap conference on the National Mall was the apex of the movement. In a metaphorical sense, Stand in the Gap could be viewed as the movement's triumphant "march into Jerusalem." How is it, then, that the Promise Keepers seem to be on the ropes, struggling to reinvent themselves, such a short time later? There are many possible causes. In a chapter published in 1999, Dane Claussen (editor of two anthologies on the Promise Keepers) highlights four reasons for the decline in conference attendance that began in 1997 (Claussen 1999). These explanations are worth considering when appraising the movement's broader fate as well.

First, PK leaders argued in reference to declining attendance that many men passed up attending regional events in 1997 because they were saving up the money and time needed to attend Stand in the Gap. This rationale fails to convince. If this explanation were accurate, conference attendance would have bounced back after Stand in the Gap. Yet, as outlined in chapter 1, both conference attendance and the visibility enjoyed by the movement have continued in a downward spiral. To his credit, Claussen too finds this explanation wanting.

A second explanation highlighted by Claussen concerns conference attendance fees. In 1997, PK adopted the policy of not charging for its stadium conferences as a means of making them more accessible to men who could not afford them. Claussen suggests that PK's decision to stop charging an admission fee might have been motivated by complaints about the $60 cost expressed by new or returning conference attendees. In other words, men stopped coming because the cost came to be seen as prohibitive, particularly among those who had

already been to a conference. This explanation is plausible. The movement has long attempted to secure conference-goer feedback, and it
might have noticed mounting opposition to the fee.

There is, of course, an alternative explanation related to this one.
An economic axiom suggests that consumers typically estimate the
value (that is, what they would perceive to be the inherent worth) of
a commodity by the price they are asked to pay for it. According to
this logic, if a consumer has to sacrifice to afford a good, the perceived
value of the commodity increases. Those who get something for nothing
do not value the item. In this sense, waiving the conference admission fee could have had the unintended consequence of devaluing conferences in the eyes of PK's consumer market. Rather than making
conferences more accessible, PK could have unwittingly recast "free"
conferences as events not "worth" attendees' time.

Third, Claussen cites McCartney's own commentary about the
resistance the movement has faced concerning racial reconciliation.
The 1996 conference series was called "Break Down the Walls," and
conference attendance began to fall off dramatically in 1997. By
McCartney's own account, flagging attendance is largely explained by
evangelical Protestants' reaction to the movement's effort to break down
walls. McCartney says that about four in ten complaints concerning
the 1996 conference series involved the racial reconciliation theme.
McCartney even surmises that much of the criticism leveled at PK from
other conservative Christian groups is actually racial animus cloaked
in more socially acceptable terms.

The last possible explanation, and the most compelling among
Claussen's four, is most easily summarized in four words: "Been there,
done that." Citing a "lack of new content" as a likely cause of flagging conference attendance, Claussen mentions a disaffected PK
conference-goer who explicitly expressed his displeasure with the lack
of novelty in PK conferences. This PK man had already attended two
conferences that seemed nearly identical to him. And he had no reason to believe that future PK conferences would feature new content.

One man I talked to after PK laid off their staff because of budget
problems offered a view that resonated with that of Claussen's infor-
mant. This central Texas Promise Keeper had attended the 1997 Stand
in the Gap conference. He said there was "nothing like it." This was
at once high praise and damning criticism, as the man making this
remark readily knew. He went on to explain to me that the Promise
Keepers should have "packed it in" after the march on the National

Mall. There was simply no way the movement could top Stand in the Gap. "Everything else they do will pale in comparison," he explained. This account raises, of course, another possible explanation for the Promise Keepers decline—namely, the image problem associated with the staff layoff and the cancellation of key events. Combined with the dramatic declines in conference attendance, a movement that managed its image so adroitly during its heyday suddenly seemed inept and disorganized. And, thanks to the media frenzy PK's public relations experts had generated, all the world was watching.

Even so, there is a larger process at work here than simply a lack of new content or a tarnished image. Consider the language that is so pervasive in our culture today. "Been there, done that." "What have you done for me lately?" "Here today, gone tomorrow." Better yet, consider the late artist Andy Warhol's prophetic reference to the fleeting "fifteen minutes of fame" that he predicted would characterize popularity in a rapidly changing society.[1] Whether taking the form of colloquial expressions or prophetic admonitions, all these idioms underscore the ephemeral character of American culture. In many respects, social life in twenty-first-century America is oceanic. It is vast, turbulent, and ever-changing; it is more liquid than solid. Zygmunt Bauman (2000) has astutely referred to the historical moment within which we live as "liquid modernity," thereby underscoring the rapidity with which today's novelties become yesterday's news. Bauman (2000: 2) reminds us that, much like the cultural ethos in which we live, fluids "cannot easily hold their shape"; liquids "neither fix space nor bind time." We thus find ourselves thrown into a world of "flexibility and expansiveness" (Bauman 2000: 9)

In a similar vein, Emily Martin (1994) has convincingly shown how notions of flexibility—in the worlds of science, business, health, and (I would add) gender and religion—have become the defining motif of American culture.[2] Interestingly, we are led to believe that freedom is found in a culture whose expansiveness does not bear down upon us so severely. But Bauman (2000: chap. 1) is quick to remind us that such freedom is a mixed blessing—and is not genuine emancipation at that. Indeed, for all of the allure that oceans hold (discovery, adventure, a seemingly limitless horizon), vast and turbulent seas lacking islands of refuge are as dangerous—and often deadly—as they are exciting. And so it was for the Promise Keepers.

Deep within the swirling ocean of American culture lies a genuinely sociological argument for the decline of the Promise Keepers. It is not sufficient to say that PK has simply maxed out on its ability to "wow" conference-goers, though that may be true enough. More important, I think, is the broader cultural context within which PK and their "target audience" have been situated. I have argued that the decision of the Promise Keepers to hold conferences in large stadiums and arenas is not simply a matter of finding a space where a revivalistic movement can fit 60,000 men. This space is replete with cultural significance—specifically, that of sport, gender, and race. Yet stadiums and arenas are cultured in another way as well. They are also venues for entertainment.

Thus, by diving headlong into the rough waters of American culture, the Promise Keepers invariably lend themselves to comparisons with the world of entertainment. And the consumers that rule the entertainment world are notorious for their fickle tastes and their insatiable appetites for ever more spectacular forms of excitement. The problem here is a cultural one—that of continually having to "up the ante." In many respects, PK conferences and the Promise Keepers movement writ large has run up against the same conundrum faced by other purveyors of culture in America, including musical groups that tour year after year and Hollywood producers trying to figure out how to make a sequel into a blockbuster. Artists and performers in each of these entertainment genres are ever confronted with expectations of significant improvements driving consumers' decisions about how to spend their entertainment dollars. How do they do it? They develop a new light show. They create more spectacular special effects. They make the violence more graphic and the sex more explicit. They give the dialogue a more poignant quality, or provide more clever innuendo. Of course, this is not to say that fickleness or an insatiable appetite for entertainment dictate Promise Keepers' reactions to conferences. The stated purpose is something different—changing hearts, winning souls. But, as the movement's signature event, Promise Keeper conferences were designed to be spectacles. They were intended to entertain as well as to edify. And the problem with a spectacle is that it needs to be outdone by something more spectacular and more stimulating the next time around.

The sociologist Pitirim Sorokin warned against as much when discussing the limits of sensate culture. Sorokin (1957: 697–698) argued that "overripe sensate culture creates a man . . . so 'wild' that he cannot—and does not want to—'tame himself.'" Ultimately, Sorokin argued, the "policeman of history" disciplines those who cannot bridle their passions. The untamed are ineluctably confronted with the consequences of their "folly." Now, this is not to say that the Promise Keepers are guilty of producing untamed, wild men. Quite the opposite has been shown here. Rather, the broader culture within which the Promise Keepers, and the rest of us, are situated is one governed primarily by a sensate mentality. In the Promise Keepers' efforts to meld aspects of sensate culture with evangelicalism (even selectively) through the spectacle of stadium conferences, flashy videos, and strategic media blitzes, they made a Faustian bargain. Afloat on the ocean of American culture for a time, they were eventually swallowed up by its turbulent tides. Like other men's movements before it, PK had its fifteen minutes of fame.

There is one more possibility that must be considered a leading contender among explanations for the demise of the Promise Keepers—namely, the revivalistic spirit of the movement. Although care should be taken when drawing generalizations from the dynamics manifested in one particular religious movement, the Promise Keepers' decline would seem to be connected with the movement's revivalistic character. American religion continues to be marked by dramatic change and innovation, a situation to which PK contributed and from which it profited during the 1990s. Congregations, denominations, and (for lack of a better word) "organized religion" continue to form the backbone of faith life in America. And when compared with organized religion, revivalistic movements are likely to exhibit a lack of staying power. Many studies have revealed that religious organizations need to be adaptable if they are to survive community change (Ammerman 1997; Bartkowski 2001a; Eiesland 2000; Warner and Wittner 1998), manage cultural conflict effectively (Becker 1999), and continue to attract new members (Stark and Finke 2000). Religious organizations that exhibit cultural dexterity are those that have enough tether to provide themselves with reasonable drift as the tides of American social life shift and swirl. Yet here is the key. Congregations, denominations, and "organized religion" can afford such drift because, unlike more ephemeral revivalistic movements, traditional religious organizations are blessed with an institutional base that serves as a stabilizing anchor (Ammerman 1997).

Thus, the fate of the Promise Keepers sheds important light on questions about the character of contemporary American culture and the keys to religious vitality in America at this time. Vital religious communities are those capable of combining a cultural tether that permits adaptability with a structural anchor that keeps a faith community from being swept away with the tide. The Promise Keepers' overabundance of tether and missing anchor was both boon and bane. These factors catapulted the movement to the forefront of American religious life for a time. Yet, the movement had trouble parlaying its fifteen minutes of fame into a more enduring place in the landscape of American religious and social life. The arrival of the new millennium has seen the dismemberment of the godly man, who now seems a mere shadow of his former self. Yet the death of the godly man is not the end of the story. The demise of the Promise Keepers contains within it precious insight into the ephemerality and sensate excesses of American culture. It is wise not to ask for whom the bell of American culture tolls. It tolls for us all.

Appendix:
Research Methodology

In this study, I have used several different data sources—texts, observational fieldnotes, and qualitative interviews. The methods used to collect and analyze these data are described briefly below.

Textual Analysis

The manuals chosen for the analysis in chapter 3 were selected through a multistage sampling technique. First, I sought to establish the general range of thematic variation in Promise Keeper gender discourse. After reading more than twenty advice manuals written by Promise Keeper conference speakers, sold on the PK website, and widely available in "men's sections" of Christian bookstores, I organized these manuals into various subgroups. The subgroups included manuals characterized by an overriding presence of the following themes: (1) gender traditionalism, (2) men's liberationism, (3) mythopoetic evangelicalism, and (4) multiculturalism. In the case of anthologies with multiple contributors, each of the chapters was analyzed and coded accordingly. All told, the advice of more than forty authors was analyzed. I was also careful to select and analyze manuals written by PK authors that were published over a span of time—including the writings of Promise Keeper speakers/authors published prior to the emergence of the movement. This sampling strategy allowed me to situate PK gender discourses on a temporal trajectory as a post–New

Christian Right evangelical movement while mapping PK's cultural engagement with other men's movements.

For this study, I intentionally selected one representative manual from each of these subgroups on which to focus my attention. Recognizing the inevitable trade-off between analytical breadth and depth, I adopted this approach to render an in-depth, nuanced analysis of PK gender discourse. General features of PK discourse have been treated in other works (Bartkowski 1997, 2001a; Bloch 2001; Donovan 1998; Lockhart 2001). My focused analysis of these texts was intended to provide unique insight into this pastoral literature. By opting against a "bird's-eye" analysis of a large textual sample, I produced an analysis more sensitized to the ways in which particular types of PK authors wrestle with the tensions and contradictions that surface in their advice manuals. These tensions, which tell us a great deal about the embattled state of social life (the "con-text," if you will), are never fully resolved. My particularistic focus enables me to dissect the rhetorical devices these authors deploy in attempting to bring about such a resolution.

Moreover, because PK members read these manuals as stand-alone commentaries (rather than through sampled groupings as contrived by scholars), my study is designed to present a more "readerly" analysis of these texts. This point is especially important. The men I spoke with who read such books did not read them in bunches, as would an academic looking to discover the defining elements of this "discourse." Men who made reference to such texts read them one at a time, either by themselves or in a men's group with which they were affiliated. Thus, I intentionally selected manuals that are situated in the various genres outlined above. And I have taken pains to present each manual selected in a way that might be consonant with their actual use among men who read them—thus, my reference to a readerly analysis. This is not to say that mine is the sole interpretation that can be generated from these texts. Rather, I aimed to understand how texts within each of these genres might resonate with those inside the movement, while laying bare the languages, argumentative logics, and layered ideologies across these genres. Those interested in a more traditional cumulative analysis of a large sample of evangelical texts of this sort should consult my previous work (Bartkowski 2001a).

Observational Fieldwork
and In-Depth Interviews:
An Ethnographic Perspective

I also conducted extensive ethnographic fieldwork to render the accounts provided in chapters 4–6. From 1996 to 1998, I attended a local men's gathering frequented by many Promise Keepers in the central Texas area, while also attending a variety of accountability groups held in either churches or other social venues (for example, restaurants). All told, I made fourteen of these field observations, each ranging from sixty to ninety minutes in duration.

In the summer of 1999, I attended the Choose This Day conference in San Antonio, Texas. That two-day conference, held in the San Antonio Alamodome, was attended by an estimated 50,000 men. The analysis of that conference was generated from fieldnotes rather than verbatim transcripts of audiotaped materials. Rest assured that I have made every effort to render accurate quotations of the words spoken there, whether of the public pronouncements of leaders on stage or of the private reflections of attendees in unstructured field interviews. Nevertheless, some allowance must be made for the fact that I recorded fieldnotes at this conference in written form rather than on audiotape.

During the summer of 1998, I conducted in-depth interviews with twenty local Promise Keepers; I recorded these interviews on audiotape. About one quarter of these interviews were conducted with men who were affiliated with an accountability group in which I had conducted observational research. The remainder of the men were contacted through a snowball sampling technique in which I asked those who had already agreed to participate if they knew of other men who might be willing to be interviewed for the study. The interviews were conducted in a semi-structured fashion, meaning that each respondent had the opportunity to answer every question. However, unanticipated topics that surfaced during the interview were pursued further through follow-up questions not originally included in the interview questionnaire. For that reason, I include the transcriptions of my own follow-up questions in several of the quotations that appear in this volume.

It is important to recognize that these men are not representative of "the men" affiliated with the Promise Keepers. Where possible, I have attempted to complicate such overly general categories. Thus, the men that I interviewed reflect a range of different standpoints and emanate from a variety of life circumstances. Where possible, I draw out connections between their life experiences and their standpoints as Promise Keepers. However, even here, care must be taken not to generalize without warrant. The perspectives that emerge from these interviews are not intended to be exhaustive of all possible perspectives of men in the movement. Such is not the goal of qualitative interviewing. Thus, although interview encounters present men with a set of themes commonly reflected on by PK men, my analysis intentionally opts for an idiographic (particularistic) analysis rather than a nomothetic (generalizing) approach. In short, I take care to explore the range of men's standpoints on the issues investigated, and I am primarily concerned with situating such standpoints in their proper social context rather than generalizing from these accounts.

Once recorded, the audiotaped interviews were transcribed. The interview transcripts were analyzed with a range of topics in mind, including: religious, gender, and racial identity; the means through which men first become exposed to and affiliated with the Promise Keepers; the meaning of key PK terms such as "accountability," "family leadership," and "racial reconciliation"; the promises that have been most rewarding and most difficult to keep; the nature and influence of conference-going experiences; and the effect of Promise Keeper affiliation on their primary social relationships with family, friends, and colleagues, among other topics explored. (These and other topics investigated are presented in the interview questionnaire reprinted at the end of this appendix.)

When analyzing the transcripts, I also paid attention to emergent themes (those that surfaced but which I had not anticipated). Because interviews are a site for organizing meaning through the practice of storytelling, I also identified the narratives men told me about their experiences in PK. And, of course, the data were analyzed with the theoretical concepts from chapter 2 in mind (namely, subcultural identity theory, boundary work, and ideational and sensate aspects of religion). I intentionally do not analyze interview responses in a question-by-question or issue-by-issue fashion. Such an approach would smack of compartmentalizing the lives and social experiences of interview subjects through an analytical grid. Consistent with ethnographic convention, my goal is to fold interview accounts together with those emerging from observational research to render rich, complex portraits of Promise Keepers and their social experiences. Thus, the analyses of these data succeed only to the extent that a dynamic "conversation" emerges from my effort to map out dialogical relationships between observational and interview data. Ethnography is undoubtedly a meaning-making endeavor, in that it tries to capture the texture and nuances of people's experiences rather than dryly "reporting" subjects' answers to interview questions. I reject a stimulus-response model of interview data analysis and instead embrace a more genuinely ethnographic approach.

Interview Sample Characteristics

Because men's standpoints are inflected by their social position, there is merit in knowing the types of men from whom these accounts are generated. The sample of men who participated in the audiotaped interview portion of this study was predominantly white (n = 15), though I was able to interview a few African American (n = 2) and Latino men (n = 3) as well. (Unstructured field interviews with men in accountability groups and at the conference I attended enabled me to correct for this sampling problem somewhat. Field interviews, however, were not audiotaped.) While I had difficulty securing in-depth interviews with black and Latino men, I sought sampling diversity in other ways. Interviewees were from a wide variety of religious denominations, including Assembly of God (n = 3), Baptist (n = 2), Church of Christ (n = 1), Evangelical Free (n = 2), and Methodist (n = 4). The remainder of the men in the sample were affiliated with nondenominational churches. These men were all members of a local church and attended worship services frequently. All but two attended church weekly; the two who did not attend weekly reported that they attended three times per week. All but one held one or more positions in their faith community, such as men's group leader, Sunday school teacher, choir member, treasurer, and the like.

The men that I interviewed covered a fairly wide age span, ranging from 30 to 57. The mean age of the men was 44.3. They were generally well educated, reporting an average of 16.3 years of schooling (range 12 to 19 years of formal education). (Sixteen years of schooling reflects the receipt of a bachelor's degree.) Only one of the men in my interview sample had no college experience; he had obtained his high school diploma. An appreciable number of the interviewees had completed schooling beyond their bachelor's degree.

All of the men I interviewed were employed. Taken together, they held jobs in a wide range of occupations—typically, in the service sector (for example, sales) or in a technical profession (for example, engineering). Two of the interviewees were full-time ministers, and one was a part-time pastor for ten hours per week. They worked for pay an average of 47.8 hours per week (range 40 to 60 weekly work hours). As a group, these men were employed in occupations that paid fairly well. The most commonly reported household income was over $100,000, with eight men reporting that the combined wage-earners in their home equaled or exceeded this amount. Despite this seemingly high level of economic privilege, the modal response for personal income (the wages earned by the particular men interviewed excluding other household wage-earners) clustered around two income categories provided on the survey—that of $30,000–39,999 (n = 4) and $40,000–49,999 (n = 3). The remainder of the men were spread across other income categories.

All of the men interviewed in this study were married at the time I interviewed them. Taken as a whole, they had been married to their current spouse for an average of 16.7 years. The length of current marriage ranged from 15 months to 35 years. All but five of the men were in their first marriage; four had been divorced and one was a widower. All of these men whose first marriage ended had remarried. All but one of the interviewees had children. Six of the men had two children, and five had three children. The remainder of the men had one child or more than three, though only two respondents fell in this latter category. The one man who did not have children was expecting his first child with his wife.

In-Depth Interview Questionnaire

1. To begin, tell me a bit about your personal religious beliefs and convictions. What are the religious beliefs that are most important to you?

Now, let's talk about the Promise Keepers (PKs) and your involvement with them.

2. How and why did you become involved in the PKs? What has been the extent of your involvement?

3a. What is it about the PKs that you have found most appealing?

3b. Are there any aspects of the PKs that have been unappealing or unsatisfying to you?

4a. Think about what you have learned from your association with the PKs. What do you think are the most important messages that the PKs offer to men today?

4b. Why do you think those messages are important?

Let's talk about some of the core concepts often identified with the Promise Keepers.

5a. The PKs stress that men should keep their word and honor their commitments. Is there any particular commitment you are most proud of honoring due to your involvement with the PKs?

5b. Some PK authors talk about particular commitments that they have had difficulty keeping and promises that they, at some point, have broken. What commitment has proven most difficult for you to keep, and how have you dealt with that challenge or that broken promise?

6. Some PKs talk about "godly manhood," or becoming "godly men."

6a. What does being a "godly man" mean to you?

6b. How, if at all, has this idea of "godly manhood" affected the way you view yourself?

7. One topic that is sometimes addressed by the PKs is family leadership.

7a. Have you heard this topic of family leadership addressed in your involvement with the PKs? If so, what has been said about family leadership?

7b. What do you personally think about what you have heard from the PKs concerning family leadership?

8. Many of the PKs talk about "racial reconciliation."

8a. What does this concept mean to you?

8b. Do you think the PKs have been successful in promoting racial reconciliation?

Let's discuss how your association with the Promise Keepers might have affected your relationships with people around you. How, if at all, has your affiliation with PKs impacted your relationship with:

9a. Your wife/fiancee/girlfriend or with a significant woman in your life? Other women in general?

9b. What is PK's central message on this topic? What has been its impact on you? How successful have you been in applying PK advice to this aspect of life?

10a. Other members of your immediate and extended family (esp. son[s], father, men in family)?

10b. What is PK's central message on this topic? What has been its impact on you? How successful have you been in applying PK advice to this aspect of life?

11a. Other significant men in your life (e.g., friends, colleagues, co-workers)?

11b. What is PK's central message on this topic? What has been its impact on you? How successful have you been in applying PK advice to this aspect of life?

12. How are the PKs viewed by pastors and members at your local church? By men in your church?

13. Finally, there is a great deal of discussion today about men's and women's roles in society and responsibilities in the family. What, if anything, do you think the PKs contribute to these discussions about gender roles and family relations in America today?

Notes

CHAPTER 1   THE RISE AND FALL OF THE CHRISTIAN MEN'S MOVEMENT

1. The article that begins with this question is Paulson 2000.
2. Everton (2001) and Quicke and Robinson (2000) provide excellent evaluations of charges that link PK with the New Christian Right. They find such explanations less than compelling, as I do. Still, the relationship between political movements and an identity movement like PK is a complicated one. Those opposed to abortion have been shown to be more supportive of the Promise Keepers (Johnson 2001). However, public rhetoric from the Promise Keepers often avoided abortion and other politically charged issues (Everton 2001; Diamond 1998). Thus, it is possible that PK is *interpreted* as a politically conservative group simply because of its orthodox theology.

    But what about the question of intent? Did PK use a form of "stealth politics" like that of the Christian Coalition? An examination of the group's religious roots suggest that this prospect is unlikely, or at least that it would have been most unwise. The Promise Keepers had early ties to the Vineyard Christian Fellowship, a Pentecostal wing of conservative Protestantism (Chrasta 2000; Longinow 2000). In his local "Middletown" study of support for PK, Stephen Johnson (2001) found that attendance at a Pentecostal/Holiness church or one with charismatic services was the best religious predictor of support for PK. For those not familiar with conservative Christianity, Pentecostals believe in speaking in tongues, modern-day revelation, and miraculous healing—controversial tenets even within conservative Protestantism (an umbrella group of evangelicals, fundamentalists, Pentecostals, and charismatics that together comprises 29 percent of the total American population—Smith 2000). Yet, Pentecostals are the smallest faction within conservative Protestantism, hardly the base from which one could imagine intentionally marshaling broad-based support for a political movement. Whereas evangelicals and fundamentalists comprise 11.2 percent and 12.8 percent of all Americans, respectively, Pentecostals represent a paltry 1.7 percent of the national population (Smith 2000: 16–18).

And yet, PK's initial linkages to Pentecostalism loosened as the movement grew. PK eventually adopted language that resonated with the more mainstream religious beliefs of evangelicalism found in such periodicals as *Christianity Today* (Everton 2001). However, this strategy was likely an effort to make the movement more religiously appealing rather than an attempt to exchange a religious focus for a political agenda. A 1995 survey of conference-going Promise Keepers in nine of fourteen conference sites (Morin 1997) revealed the success of this strategy. Nearly half (46 percent) of attendees surveyed self-identified as evangelical. Nearly a third (31 percent) claimed a fundamentalist affiliation, and 18 percent described themselves as charismatic (the conservative Protestant faction closest to Pentecostalism). Given the theological orthodoxy of PK, it is not surprising that a scant 5 percent described their church background as liberal.

3. Succinct scholarly analyses of Promise Keeper conferences and the group's engagement with sport, gender, and contemporary religion include Balmer 2000b; Beal 2000; Chrasta 2000; Deardorff 2000; Eidenmuller 2000; and Suk 2000.

4. Surprisingly little research has been conducted on PK accountability groups. See Healy 2000 for an intriguing analysis of small-group interaction among a "virtual community" of Promise Keepers online.

5. Additional work on the Promise Keepers' engagement with racial, denominational, and cultural diversity include Allen 2001; Diamond 1998; Hawkins 2000; Heath 2003; Jones and Lockhart 1999; Kimmel 1999; and Reynolds and Reynolds 2000.

CHAPTER 2 SITUATING THE PROMISE KEEPERS

1. Rational choice theory privileges human reason—the cognitive capacity to weigh costs and benefits while maximizing utility—in confronting the problem of religious identity and experience. In its otherwise laudable effort to reveal the rational properties of religious belief, this perspective generally overlooks the embodied dimensions of religious experience. Among cultural theories of religion, the record is not much better. America's culture wars have been conceptualized as being waged through the disembodied rhetoric of religious elites rather than in the actual spaces of home, church, and work through which embodied believers travel (see Bartkowski 2001b). And, despite its many merits, even subcultural identity theory privileges theological ideals and religious symbols as the primary tools through which religious identities are fashioned. From this vantage point, religious identities are negotiated through linguistic maneuvers and ideological work that, while thoughtful and eloquent, is bereft of physicality and potentially removed from lived experience. If culture indeed comprises both symbols and strategies, then cultural theories of religion that fail to account for the embodied character of religious experience overlook one important fact: action strategies require bodies!

It does bear mentioning that a handful of scholars have recently begun to investigate the embodied aspects of religion and spirituality (Adams 1998; Bartkowski 2000, 2001a, 2001b, 2002; Belzen 1999; McGuire 1990,

1996; Orta 1999). Moreover, several excellent explorations have examined the relationship between religion and the body in cross-cultural, historical, and theoretical perspective (Coakley 1997; Mellor and Shilling 1997; Turner 1996: chap. 3). These volumes explicitly seek to redress the "anti-body bias" (Scott and Morgan 1993) that has pervaded not only traditional social science in general, but research on religious history and culture, as well as sociological theory. I draw from these works in my explication of sensate religion. A handful of ethnographic investigations of non-mainstream religious groups (Belzen 1999; McGuire 1996; Orta 1999; Warner 1997) provide excellent explorations of the intersection of religious identity and embodiment. I seek to extend such work to the field of mainstream Christianity, namely, evangelicalism.

2. The same can be said about other dichotomies commonly used to make sense of culture, such as material versus nonmaterial culture (which I address in this volume's concluding chapter). Like sensate and ideational culture, the merits of such organizing frameworks are found primarily in the conceptual clarity they lend to cultural analysis. However, a dogmatic attachment to such dichotomies easily leads to rigidly categorical renderings of culture that miss its complexity and indeterminacy. Thus, my application of Sorokin's sensate/ideational framework should be viewed with an appreciation for both his insightfulness and the concepts' limitations.

3. Christianity does not have a corner on the deployment of symbolic representations of the body. For instance, some Zen koans liken superficial knowledge to the outer "flesh" and deeper wisdom to the inner "bone" (Reps 1994). Moreover, various Christian communities seize upon different aspects of embodiment to represent their distinct identities. Catholic Communion entails the congregation's collective consumption of the "body" and "blood" of Christ (both dispensed from a common vessel). Through the act of Catholic Communion, the individual is consumed (and subsumed) by the congregational body and the Church. Protestantism, however, reacts against this symbolic transformation and instead privileges salvation through biblical revelation. Thus, the metaphor of Protestantism is not that of the whole body being consumed by the community but rather that of the eye consuming the knowledge internalized through the careful study of scripture, specifically the Bible (Mellor and Schilling 1997).

CHAPTER 3 GODLY MASCULINITIES

1. The archetypal labels Rational Patriarch, Expressive Egalitarian, and Multicultural Man are etic terminology—that is, shorthand references I have coined during the course of my research. These particular terms are not used by Promise Keeper authors themselves. The use of these shorthand references enables me to identify the implicit masculine archetypes embedded within traditionalist, liberationist, and multicultural PK discourse. By contrast, the Tender Warrior archetype and racial reconciliation motif are emic terminology used by Promise Keeper writers themselves.

2. As pointed out by Lockhart (2001), much of the imagery used in Stu Weber's volumes is adapted from the mythopoetic framework articulated by Robert Moore and Douglas Gillette—amended by Weber to make it suitable for an evangelical audience.

3. For an incisive analysis of cultural notions concerning "the body of Christ" and other embodied visions of deity, see Moore 1996.

CHAPTER 4 REFORMING AMERICAN CULTURE

1. My goal in this chapter is to create, within the constraints of the written word, the conference-goer's sense of "being there." Thus, consistent with ethnographic convention, I use the present tense throughout much of this chapter and those that follow. For this same reason, my use of interview accounts in this chapter does not consist primarily of extensive quotations of interviews. Although I analyzed men's interview accounts of conference-going to develop the portrait presented here, the inclusion of direct retrospective quotes would disrupt the chapter's flow. Men's reflections on conference attendance are treated in chapters 5 and 6.

2. Following Cohan and Hark in *Screening the Male* (1993), I use the word "screening" intentionally here as a polysemous term. Consistent with common usage, live or filmed images of men are screened when they are broadcast through media such as television or cinema. But men are also screened for such media broadcasts inasmuch as these images provide a particular portrayal of "manhood"—often the result of strategic production decisions. As Cohan and Hark (1993: 3) argue, cinema "puts [the male] on screen, it hides him behind a screen, it uses him as a screen for its ideological agenda, and it screens out socially unacceptable and heterogeneous cultural constructions of masculinity."

3. Of course, given gender disparities in some marriages, a husband's act of service (for example, fixing a meal or washing the dishes) might be the wife's everyday responsibility. Thus, her performance of this chore might be defined as meeting a taken-for-granted obligation, whereas his relieving her of this responsibility from time to time might be viewed as a selfless act of service, one so unusual as to be worthy of praise. On the prospect for covert forms of power in evangelical marriages, see Bartkowski 1999, 2001.

4. To be sure, Protestantism in general and American evangelicalism in particular have long had an antiestablishment streak to them. The centuries-old Protestant notion of the "priesthood of all believers" runs counter to the pastor/congregant distinction. Yet, many contemporary Protestant (and even evangelical) churches are less structurally committed to a priesthood of all believers, as they now employ full-time, seminary-trained clergy (Finke 1994).

CHAPTER 5 THE ABCs OF PROMISE-KEEPING

1. Jesus Christ is a polysemous cultural resource for the Promise Keepers inasmuch as his core message is interpreted to mean many different things—for example, fearlessly fighting immorality (an ethic of authority) versus selflessly serving others (an ethic of compassion). Competing interpretations of the life of Christ lend themselves to PK support for traditional, liberated, poeticized, and racialized forms of masculinity politics (see chapter 3).

2. The word "brother" has long been used by religious communities to distinguish between insiders (members) and outsiders (nonmembers). Although PK invocations of the term "brother" conform to this usage, this term has multiple meanings. In the PK context, the term "brother" simul-

taneously establishes a man's organizational affiliation (PK member), his gender identity (masculine), and the quality of this affective relationship with other members (familial, brotherly love). My assessment of this term is rooted in poststructuralist theories of discourse, which encourage scholars to "let go ... of the notion that words have a meaning of their own, one pinned down for everyone alike in the system of language. ... [To the contrary,] words change their meaning ... and conflicting discourses develop even where there is supposedly a common language" (Macdonell 1986: 45).

3. Evangelicals generally consider masturbation to be a sexual sin. In some evangelical circles, the story of Onan (Genesis 38) is interpreted as a divine edict against masturbation. As the account goes, Onan "spilled his semen on the ground" and was struck dead by God for doing so. Interestingly, Onan was not actually masturbating when he "spilled" his semen. Rather, as commanded by God, he was having intercourse with his deceased brother's wife in order to produce progeny. Yet he refused to inseminate her by spilling his seed (withdrawal). Notwithstanding these specifics, this story is often interpreted as a prohibition against masturbation.

4. It is important to note that I do not use Jeff's narrative to suggest that PK men in general struggle with autoeroticism. (Indeed, Jeff himself overcame this struggle with the help of his accountability partner.) Rather, Jeff's narrative richly illustrates the processes of cathartic boundary work and the sequence of repentance (admission, contrition, absolution) in PK accountability groups. Nevertheless, it is interesting to note that a 1995 survey of select PK conference-goers revealed that six of ten PK conference attendees listed "sexual sin" as the single most significant sin they wished to confess (Morin 1997). Findings of surveys administered at mass gatherings such as PK conferences should be interpreted with some caution, however, because it is nearly impossible to obtain a genuinely random sample.

CHAPTER 6   MULTICULTURAL EVANGELICALISM

1. The phrase "the color line" was popularized by W.E.B. Du Bois, an African American sociologist who wrote prophetically in *The Souls of Black Folk* (1903: 283), "The problem of the twentieth century is the problem of the color line." It is noteworthy that this volume has been called "*the* African American book of the twentieth century" (Sundquist 1996: 97). In using this phrase, I retain the ambiguous meaning Du Bois initially intended it to have. Du Bois used the notion of the color line to refer "less [to] a boundary or legal barrier ... than a figure with temporal and geographical dimensionality, a figure that segregates and grounds at the same time" (Sundquist 1996: 7). Therefore, the color line operates differently, and is negotiated through variegated means, across distinctive cultural and historical contexts. Moreover, the color line is a site of racial paradox—it simultaneously unifies and divides, it is both productive and oppressive. The color line unifies in that it associates the person with a racialized community, and is productive (that is, constitutive) because it confers a group-specific racial identity upon the individual. Yet, at the same time, the color line naturalizes social divisions in the name of racial segregation and is oppressive because it is a tool for racial subjugation (typically, the marginalization of nonwhites). Du Bois was years ahead of his time

in pinpointing the way in which skin color becomes a socially constituted marker for racial identity and group affiliation, and in highlighting the ambiguity of this social construct.

2. It is noteworthy that, despite this effort at bilingualism, the PK catalog in question misspelled the word "libreia"—which should be "librero" or "libreria" (which could be loosely translated into English as "resource library" or "resource center").

3. This parody simultaneously destabilizes gender (male stoicism) and race (Mexican machismo). On the subversive nature of gender parodies, the work of Judith Butler (1990) is quite instructive. On the intersection of race and gender, see Glenn (1999).

4. The title of Steve's message, "By All Possible Means," lends itself to several different interpretations where race relations are concerned. Although this phrase—"by all possible means"—is used in the biblical passage cited by Steve, a similar appeal was invoked by Malcolm X ("by any means necessary") to press for the liberation of black Americans during the Civil Rights era. Thus, from our historical vantage point, race can be decoded from this message, though only with some interpretive effort.

5. One limitation of my study bears mentioning here. I was not able to track the development of interracial evangelical fellowships in central Texas beyond their emergence as described here. Because the Promise Keepers enjoy only a hint of the prominence they once had (see chapter 1 and the conclusion), their primary contribution to these efforts might have been simply to get them off the ground. Although the evidence presented here suggests that PK played a role in foregrounding racial divisions in churches and encouraging interracial fellowships, I do not wish to overstate the movement's influence on this front.

CHAPTER 7 CONCLUSION

1 In fact, Warhol predicted not only that fame in America would become more fleeting, but that everyone would enjoy it—a sort of populist, widely dispersed fame enjoyed for a scant fifteen minutes. The dispersion of fame is evidenced in the Promise Keepers and other grassroots social movements. Social movements, particularly those that mobilize under the banner of identity, can give "common people" a brief stint in the spotlight. Fame of a sort can come merely from being associated with a rabidly popular group. Yet, as Warhol's admonition suggests, fame in a society undergoing rapid change vanishes about as quickly as it appears.

2. On cultural flexibility in the domain of gender, see for example, Mary Rogers's (1999) study of Barbie dolls and their implications (what she characterizes as "plastic bodies" giving rise to "plastic selves"). On cultural flexibility in contemporary religion, faith, and spirituality, see David Lyon's (2000) delightful volume, *Jesus in Disneyland*. On the intersection of gender, evangelical religion, and cultural flexibility, see my earlier monograph (Bartkowski 2001a).

References

Abraham, Ken. 1997. *Who are the Promise Keepers? Understanding the Christian Men's Movement.* New York: Doubleday.

Adams, Nicholas. 1998. "Walter Benjamin on Liturgical Embodiment." *Telos* 113: 113–134.

Allen, L. Dean II. 2001. "Promise Keepers and Racism: Frame Resonance as an Indicator of Organizational Vitality." In *Promise Keepers and the New Masculinity: Private Lives and Public Morality,* ed. Rhys H. Williams, 55–72. Lanham, Md.: Lexington Books.

———. 2002. *Rise Up, O Men of God: The Men and Religion Forward Movement and the Promise Keepers.* Macon, Ga.: Mercer University Press.

Ammerman, Nancy T. 1997. *Congregation and Community.* New Brunswick, N.J.: Rutgers University Press.

———. 2003. "Religious Identities and Religious Institutions." In *Handbook of Sociology of Religion,* ed. Michele Dillon, forthcoming. New York: Cambridge University Press, 207–224.

Anderson, Terry. 2001. "Promise Keepers Brings Ministry to Kemper Arena." *Omaha World-Herald,* September 15.

Associated Press. 2000. "Promise Keepers Plan 18 Events in 2001, None in Colorado." December 27.

Balmer, Randall. 2000a. "Introduction." In *The Promise Keepers: Essays on Masculinity and Christianity,* ed. Dane S. Claussen, 1–7. Jefferson, N.C.: McFarland & Company, Inc.

———. 2000b. "Keep the Faith and Go the Distance: Promise Keepers, Feminism, and the World of Sports." In *The Promise Keepers: Essays on Masculinity and Christianity,* ed. Dane S. Claussen, 194–204. Jefferson, N.C.: McFarland & Company, Inc.

Baltimore Sun. 1998. "Promise Keepers to Stop Paying Its 345-Member Staff: Revenue Dips as Admission to Events Not Charged." February 20.

Bartkowski, John P. 1996. "Beyond Biblical Literalism and Inerrancy:

Conservative Protestants and the Hermeneutic Interpretation of Scripture." *Sociology of Religion* 57: 259–272.

———. 1997. "Debating Patriarchy: Discursive Disputes over Spousal Authority among Evangelical Family Commentators." *Journal for the Scientific Study of Religion* 36: 393–410.

———. 1998. "Changing of the Gods: The Gender and Family Discourse of American Evangelicalism in Historical Perspective." *The History of the Family* 3: 97–117.

———. 1999. "One Step Forward, One Step Back: 'Progressive Traditionalism' and the Negotiation of Domestic Labor within Evangelical Families." *Gender Issues* 17: 40–64.

———. 2000. "Breaking Walls, Raising Fences: Masculinity, Intimacy, and Accountability among the Promise Keepers." *Sociology of Religion* 61: 33–53.

———. 2001a. *Remaking the Godly Marriage: Gender Negotiation in Evangelical Families.* New Brunswick, N.J.: Rutgers University Press.

———. 2001b. "Faithfully Embodied: Religious Identity and the Body." Paper presented at the annual meetings of the Society for the Scientific Study of Religion, Columbus, Ohio.

———. 2002. "Godly Masculinities: Competing Discourses of Evangelical Manhood among the Promise Keepers." *Journal of Social Thought and Research* 24: 53–87.

Bartkowski, John P., and Helen A. Regis. 2003. *Charitable Choices: Religion, Race, and Poverty in the Post-Welfare Era.* New York: New York University Press.

Bauman, Zygmunt. 2000. *Liquid Modernity.* Cambridge: Polity Press.

Beal, Becky. 2000. "The Promise Keepers' Use of Sport in Defining 'Christlike' Masculinity." In *The Promise Keepers: Essays on Masculinity and Christianity,* ed. Dane S. Claussen, 153–164. Jefferson, N.C.: McFarland & Company, Inc.

Becker, Penny Edgell. 1997. "What Is Right? What Is Caring? Moral Logics in Local Religious Life." In *Contemporary American Religion: An Ethnographic Reader,* ed. Penny Edgell Becker and Nancy L. Eiesland, 121–145. Walnut Creek, Calif.: AltaMira Press.

———. 1999. *Congregations in Conflict: Cultural Models of Local Religious Life.* New York: Cambridge University Press.

Belzen, Jacob A. 1999. "Religion as Embodiment: Cultural-Psychological Concepts and Methods in the Study of Conversion among 'Bevindelijken.'" *Journal for the Scientific Study of Religion* 38: 236–253.

Berger, Peter. 1967. *The Sacred Canopy.* New York: Anchor.

Bloch, John P. 2001. "The New and Improved Clint Eastwood: Change and Persistence in Promise Keepers Self-Help Literature." In *Promise Keepers and the New Masculinity: Private Lives and Public Morality,* ed. Rhys H. Williams, 11–32. Lanham, Md.: Lexington Books.

Boston Globe. 1999. "Promise Keepers Canceling Rallies." April 2.

Brasher, Brenda. 1998. *Godly Women: Fundamentalism and Female Power.* New Brunswick, N.J.: Rutgers University Press.

Brickner, Bryan W. 1999. *Politics and Promises: The Promise Keepers.* Lanham, Md.: Rowman & Littlefield.

Burstyn, Varda. 1999. *The Rites of Men: Manhood, Politics, and the Culture of Sport.* Toronto: University of Toronto Press.

Butler, Judith. 1990. *Gender Trouble: Feminism and the Subversion of Identity.* New York: Routledge.

Cahn, Susan K. 1994. *Coming on Strong: Gender and Sexuality in Twentieth-Century Women's Sport*. Cambridge: Harvard University Press.

Chattanooga Times. 2001a. "Promise Keepers Still Draws." May 27.

———. 2001b. "Promise Keepers Rally Draws 14,000." May 27.

Chrasta, Michael J. 2000. "The Religious Roots of the Promise Keepers." In *The Promise Keepers: Essays on Masculinity and Christianity*, ed. Dane S. Claussen, 20–29. Jefferson, N.C.: McFarland & Company, Inc.

Clarke, Elizabeth. 2001. "Attack Seen as Chance to Win a War for Souls." *Washington Times*, November 5.

Claussen, Dane S. 1999. "What the Media Missed about the Promise Keepers." In *Standing on the Promises: The Promise Keepers and the Revival of Manhood*, ed. Dane S. Claussen, 17–34. Cleveland, Ohio: Pilgrim Press.

———. 2000. "'So Far, News Coverage of Promise Keepers Has Been More Like Advertising': The Strange Case of Christian Men and the Print Mass Media." In *The Promise Keepers: Essays on Masculinity and Christianity*, ed. Dane S. Claussen, 281–308. Jefferson, N.C.: McFarland & Company, Inc.

Coakley, Sarah, ed. 1997. *Religion and the Body*. New York: Cambridge University Press.

Cohan, Steven, and Ina Rae Hark, eds. 1993. *Screening the Male: Exploring Masculinities in Hollywood Cinema*. New York: Routledge.

Cole, Edwin Louis. 1982. *Maximized Manhood: A Guide to Family Survival*. Springdale, Pa.: Whitaker House.

Cole, Robert A. 2000. "Promising to Be a Man: Promise Keepers and the Organizational Constitution of Masculinity." In *The Promise Keepers: Essays on Masculinity and Christianity*, ed. Dane S. Claussen, 113–133. Jefferson, N.C.: McFarland & Company, Inc.

Columbus Dispatch. 1998. "Promise Keepers Needs Cash." February 20.

Connell, R. W. 1987. *Gender and Power: Society, the Person, and Sexual Politics*. Stanford, Calif.: Stanford University Press.

———. 1995. *Masculinities: Knowledge, Power, and Social Change*. Cambridge: Polity Press.

Culver, Virginia. 1997. "Promise Keepers Ends Fees for Events." *Denver Post*, October 22.

———. 1999a. "Promise Keepers Planning to Send Out Millennium Missives." *Denver Post*, November 11.

———. 1999b. "Promise on Minorities Not Kept: McCartney Laments Low Recruitment." *Denver Post*, July 17.

Deardorff, Don. 2000. "Sacred Male Space: The Promise Keepers as a Community of Resistance." In *The Promise Keepers: Essays on Masculinity and Christianity*, ed. Dane S. Claussen, 76–91. Jefferson, N.C.: McFarland & Company, Inc.

Diamond, Sara. 1998. *Not by Politics Alone: The Enduring Influence of the Christian Right*. New York: The Guilford Press.

Donovan, Brian. 1998. "Political Consequences of Private Authority: Promise Keepers and the Transformation of Hegemonic Masculinity." *Theory and Society* 27: 817–843.

Drew, Duchesne Paul. 2000. "Commitment Runs High at Conference of Promise Keepers: Even Though Crowd Numbers are Down, the Men in Attendance Find Inspiration." *Minneapolis Star Tribune*, October 1.

Du Bois, W.E.B. 1903. *The Souls of Black Folk*. Chicago: A. C. McClurg.

Dujardin, Richard C. 2001. "7,500 Men Seek Answers at Promise Keepers Rally." *Providence Journal–Bulletin*, July 29.

Dworkin, Shari L., and Michael A. Messner. 1999. "Just Do . . . What? Sport, Bodies, and Gender." In *Revisioning Gender*, ed. Myra Marx Ferree, Judith Lorber, and Beth B. Hess, 341–361. Thousand Oaks, Calif.: Sage Publications.

Eidenmuller, Michael E. 2000. "Promise Keepers and the Rhetoric of Recruitment: The Context, the Persona, and the Spectacle." In *The Promise Keepers: Essays on Masculinity and Christianity*, ed. Dane S. Claussen, 91–102. Jefferson, N.C.: McFarland & Company, Inc.

Eiesland, Nancy L. 2000. *A Particular Place: Urban Ecology and Religious Restructuring in a Southern Exurb*. New Brunswick, N.J.: Rutgers University Press.

Emerson, Michael O., and Christian Smith. 2000. *Divided by Faith: Evangelical Religion and the Problem of Race in America*. New York: Oxford University Press.

Emerson, Michael O., Christian Smith, and David Sikkink. 1999. "Equal in Christ, but Not in the World: White Conservative Protestants and Explanations of Black–White Inequality." *Social Problems* 46: 398–417.

Evans, Sarah M. 1997. *Born for Liberty: A History of Women in America*. 2d edition. New York: Free Press.

Evans, Tony. 1994. "Spiritual Purity." In *Seven Promises of a Promise Keeper*, 73–82. Colorado Springs, Colo.: Focus on the Family.

Everton, Sean F. 1999. "The Promise Keepers: Religious Renewal or Third Wave of the Religious Right?" Master's Thesis, San Jose State University.

———. 2001. "The Promise Keepers: Religious Renewal or Third Wave of the Religious Right?" *Review of Religious Research* 43: 51–69.

Farhat, Sally. 1999. "Promise Keepers Return to Some Smaller Crowds—Organizers Say Mission Remains Unchanged." *Seattle Times*, July 29.

Ferguson, Ann Arnett. 2000. *Bad Boys: Public Schools in the Making of Black Masculinity*. Ann Arbor: University of Michigan Press.

Finke, Roger. 1994. "The Quiet Transformation: Changes in Size and Leadership of Southern Baptist Churches." *Review of Religious Research* 36: 3–22.

Finnigan, David. 1998. "Christian Men's Group Widens Rally Invitation as Turnouts Dip." *Plain Dealer*, May 30.

Fong, Tillie. 1999. "Y2K among Promise Keepers' Worries Group Cancels Rallies on First Day of 2000." *Denver Rocky Mountain News*, April 2.

Gallagher, Sally K. 2003. *Evangelical Identity and Gendered Family Life*. New Brunswick, N.J.: Rutgers University Press.

Gallagher, Sally K., and Christian Smith. 1999. "Symbolic Traditionalism and Pragmatic Egalitarianism: Contemporary Evangelicals, Family, and Gender." *Gender & Society* 13: 211–233.

Glenn, Evelyn Nakano. 1999. "The Social Construction and Institutionalization of Gender and Race: An Integrative Framework." In *Revisioning Gender*, ed. Myra Marx Ferree, Judith Lorber, and Beth B. Hess, 3–43. Thousand Oaks, Calif.: Sage Publications.

Griffith, R. Marie. 1997. *God's Daughters: Evangelical Women and the Power of Submission*. Berkeley: University of California Press.

Hackstaff, Karla B. 1999. *Marriage in a Culture of Divorce*. Philadelphia: Temple University Press.

Hardisty, Jean. 1999. *Mobilizing Resentment: Conservative Resurgence from the John Birch Society to the Promise Keepers*. Boston: Beacon Press.

Hawkins, Billy. 2000. "Reading a Promise Keepers Event: The Intersection of Race and Religion." In *The Promise Keepers: Essays on Masculinity and Christianity*, ed. Dane S. Claussen, 182–194. Jefferson, N.C.: McFarland & Company, Inc.

Healey, Kevin. 2000. "The Irresolvable Tension: *Agape* and Masculinity in the Promise Keepers Movement." In *The Promise Keepers: Essays on Masculinity and Christianity*, ed. Dane S. Claussen, 215–226. Jefferson, N.C.: McFarland & Company, Inc.

Heath, Melanie. 2003. "Soft-Boiled Masculinity: Renegotiating Gender and Racial Ideologies in the Promise Keepers Movement." *Gender & Society* 17: 423–444.

Hetherly, M. 1997. "PK Publicity and Production: Between the Lines and Behind the Scenes." *The Humanist* 57: 14–18.

Hogan–Albach, Susan. 1998. "Fewer Signing Up for Keepers Rallies." *Minneapolis–St. Paul Star Tribune*, June 13.

Hunter, James Davison. 1983. *American Evangelicalism: Conservative Religion and the Quandary of Modernity*. New Brunswick, N.J.: Rutgers University Press.

———. 1987. *Evangelicals: The Coming Generation*. Chicago: University of Chicago Press.

———. 1991. *Culture Wars: The Struggle to Define America*. New York: Basic Books.

Ingersoll, Julie J. 1995. "Which Tradition, Which Values? 'Traditional Family Values' in American Protestant Fundamentalism." *Contention* 4: 91–103.

Ireland, Patricia. 1997. "Beware of 'Feel–Good' Male Supremacy." *Washington Post*, September 7.

Johnson, Stephen D. 2001. "Who Supports the Promise Keepers?" In *Promise Keepers and the New Masculinity: Private Lives and Public Morality*, ed. Rhys H. Williams, 93–105. Lanham, Md.: Lexington Books.

Jones, Steven L., and William H. Lockhart. 1999. "Race and Religion at the Million-Man March and the Promise Keepers' Stand in the Gap." In *Standing on the Promises: The Promise Keepers and the Revival of Manhood*, ed. Dane S. Claussen, 44–55. Jefferson, N.C.: McFarland & Company, Inc.

Juster, Susan. 1994. *Disorderly Women: Sexual Politics and Evangelicalism in Revolutionary New England*. Ithaca, N.Y.: Cornell University Press.

Kandiyoti, Deniz. 1988. "Bargaining with Patriarchy." *Gender & Society* 2: 274–290.

Kelley, Colleen E. 2000. "Silencing the Voice of God: Rhetorical Responses to the Promise Keepers." In *The Promise Keepers: Essays on Masculinity and Christianity*, ed. Dane S. Claussen, 226–238. Jefferson, N.C.: McFarland & Company, Inc.

Kenworthy, Tom. 1998. "Promise Keepers Group, Ailing Financially, to Quit Paying All 345 on Staff." *Washington Post*, February 20.

Kimmel, Michael S. 1996. *Manhood in America: A Cultural History*. New York: Free Press.

———. 1999. "Patriarchy's Second Coming as Masculine Renewal." In *Standing on the Promises: The Promise Keepers and the Revival of Manhood*, ed. Dane S. Claussen, 111–121. Cleveland, Ohio: The Pilgrim Press.

Ladd, Tony, and James A. Mathisen. 1999. *Muscular Christianity: Evangelical Protestants and the Development of American Sport*. Grand Rapids, Mich.: Baker Books.

Lamont, Michèle. 1992. *Money, Morals, and Manners: The Culture of the French and American Upper Middle Class*. Chicago: University of Chicago Press.

———. 2000. *The Dignity of Working Men: Morality and the Boundaries of Race, Class, and Immigration*. New York: Russell Sage Foundation.

Lamont, Michèle, and Marcel Fournier, eds. 1992. *Cultivating Differences:*

Symbolic Boundaries and the Making of Inequality. Chicago: University of Chicago Press.

Lemert, Charles. 2002. *Social Things*. 2d edition. Lanham, Md.: Rowman & Littlefield.

Lockhart, William H. 2001. "'We Are One Life,' but Not of One Gender Ideology: Unity, Ambiguity, and the Promise Keepers." In *Promise Keepers and the New Masculinity: Private Lives and Public Morality*, ed. Rhys H. Williams, 73–93. Lanham, Md.: Lexington Books.

Longinow, Michael A. 2000. "The Price of Admission? Promise Keepers' Roots in Revivalism and the Emergence of Middle-Class Language and Appeal in Men's Movements." In *The Promise Keepers: Essays on Masculinity and Christianity*, ed. Dane S. Claussen, 42–56. Jefferson, N.C.: McFarland & Company, Inc.

Lundskow, George N. 2002. *Awakening to an Uncertain Future*. New York: Peter Lang.

Lyon, David. 2000. *Jesus in Disneyland: Religion in Postmodern Times*. Cambridge: Polity.

Macdonell, Diane. 1986. *Theories of Discourse: An Introduction*. New York: Blackwell.

Mahoney, Dennis M. 2001. "Promise Keepers Rock Arena with Messages of God's Love." *Columbus Dispatch*, July 15.

Manning, Christel. 1999. *God Gave Us the Right: Conservative Catholic, Evangelical Protestant, and Orthodox Jewish Women Grapple with Feminism*. New Brunswick, N.J.: Rutgers University Press.

Maraghy, Mary. 2001. "Promise Keepers Brings Message Back to Duval Gathering: Smaller than '96 Session." *Florida Times–Union*, June 7.

Martin, Emily. 1994. *Flexible Bodies*. Boston: Beacon Press.

Mazer, Sharon. 1998. *Professional Wrestling: Sport and Spectacle*. Jackson: University Press of Mississippi.

McCartney, Bill. 1994. "A Call to Unity." In *Seven Promises of a Promise Keeper*, 157–168. Colorado Springs: Focus on the Family.

McCrimmon, Katie Kerwin. 1999. "Promise Keepers Encouraged to Celebrate Y2K with Jesus." *Denver Rocky Mountain News*, July 18.

McGuire, Meredith B. 1990. "Religion and the Body: Rematerializing the Human Body in the Social Sciences of Religion." *Journal for the Scientific Study of Religion* 29: 283–296.

———. 1996. "Religion and the Healing of Mind/Body/Self." *Social Compass* 43: 101–116.

Mellor, Philip A., and Chris Shilling. 1997. *Re–forming the Body: Religion, Community, and Modernity*. Thousand Oaks, Calif.: Sage.

Messner, Michael A. 1997. *Politics of Masculinities: Men in Movements*. Thousand Oaks, Calif.: Sage.

Moore, Stephen D. 1996. *God's Gym: Divine Male Bodies of the Bible*. New York: Routledge.

Morin, Richard. 1997. "Who Are the Promise Keepers?" *Washington Post*, September 29.

Moss, Khalid. 2001. "Rite of 'Passage': Promise Keepers Hopes to Help Teenage Males in Their Transition to Manhood." *Dayton Daily News*, December 15.

Murphy, Caryle. 1998. "Promise Keepers at Prayerful Crossroads: One Year after Mall Rally, Religious Group Grapples with Message, Money." *Washington Post*, October 7.

Niebuhr, Gustav. 1998. "Men's Group to Lay Off Entire Staff." *New York Times,* February 20.

———. 2001. "Promise Keepers Still Draws a Crowd." *New York Times,* May 21.

O'Driscoll, Patrick. 1998. "Promise Keepers to Lay Off Full–Time Staff." *USA Today,* February 19.

Oliver, Gary J. 1993. *Real Men Have Feelings Too.* Chicago: Moody Press.

Orta, Andrew. 1999. "Syncretic Subjects and Body Politics: Doubleness, Personhood, and Aymara Catechists." *American Ethnologist* 26: 864–889.

Paulson, Michael. 2000. "The Spiritual Life: Group Hopes for Comeback." *Boston Globe,* August 19.

Pevey, Carolyn, Christine L. Williams, and Christopher G. Ellison. 1996. "Male God Imagery and Female Submission: Lessons from a Southern Baptist Ladies' Bible Class." *Qualitative Sociology* 19: 173–193.

Quicke, Andrew, and Karen Robinson. 2000. "Keeping the Promise of the Moral Majority? A Historical/Critical Comparison of the Promise Keepers and the Christian Coalition, 1989–98." In *The Promise Keepers: Essays on Masculinity and Christianity,* ed. Dane S. Claussen, 7–20. Jefferson, N.C.: McFarland & Company, Inc.

Reps, Paul, ed. 1994. *Zen Flesh, Zen Bones.* Garden City, N.Y.: Anchor.

Reynolds, Lynn J., and Rodney A. Reynolds. 2000. "Ecumenical Promise Keepers: Oxymoron or Fidelity?" In *The Promise Keepers: Essays on Masculinity and Christianity,* ed. Dane S. Claussen, 175–182. Jefferson, N.C.: McFarland & Company, Inc.

Rich, Paul, and Guillermo de los Reyes. 2000. "Upstaging the Masons: The Promise Keepers and Fraternal Orders." In *The Promise Keepers: Essays on Masculinity and Christianity,* ed. Dane S. Claussen, 29–42. Jefferson, N.C.: McFarland & Company, Inc.

Risman, Barbara J. 1998. *Gender Vertigo: American Families in Transition.* New Haven, Conn.: Yale University Press.

Ritchie, Danielle. 2002. "Promise Keepers Open 16–City Tour at Sun Dome." *Tampa Tribune,* May 25.

Rivera, John. 2001. "Smaller, Wiser Promise Keepers: Men's Religious Group Survives Money Woes, Sets Modest Agenda." *Baltimore Sun,* June 15.

Rogers, Mary F. 1999. *Barbie Culture.* Thousand Oaks, Calif.: Corwin Press.

Rose, Susan D. 1987. "Women Warriors: The Negotiation of Gender in a Charismatic Community." *Sociological Analysis* 48: 245–258.

Rotundo, E. Anthony. 1993. *American Manhood: Transformations in Masculinity from the Revolution to the Modern Era.* New York: Basic Books.

Rubin, Lillian B. 1983. *Intimate Strangers.* New York: HarperPerennial.

Sargeant, Kimon Howland. 2000. *Seeker Churches: Promoting Traditional Religion in a Nontraditional Way.* New Brunswick, N.J.: Rutgers University Press.

Schwalbe, Michael. 1996. *Unlocking the Iron Cage: The Men's Movement, Gender Politics, and American Culture.* New York: Oxford University Press.

Scott, Sue, and David Morgan, eds. 1993. *Body Matters: Essays on the Sociology of the Body.* London: The Falmer Press.

Smalley, Gary. 1993. "Five Secrets of a Happy Marriage." In *Seven Promises of a Promise Keeper,* 105–114. Colorado Springs: Focus on the Family.

Smilde, David. 2003. "Skirting the Instrumental Paradox: Intentional Belief through Narrative in Latin American Pentecostalism." *Qualitative Sociology* 26:313–329.

Smith, Christian. 2000. *Christian America? What Evangelicals Really Want.* Berkeley: University of California Press.

Smith, Christian S., with Sally Gallagher, Michael Emerson, Paul Kennedy, and David Sikkink. 1998. *American Evangelicalism: Embattled and Thriving.* Chicago: University of Chicago Press.

Smith, Philip, ed. 1998. *The New American Cultural Sociology.* New York: Cambridge University Press.

Sorokin, Pitirim A. 1957. *Social and Cultural Dynamics.* New York: Transaction.

Spillman, Lyn, ed. 2001. *Cultural Sociology.* New York: Blackwell.

Stacey, Judith. 1990. *Brave New Families.* New York: Basic Books.

Stacey, Judith, and Susan E. Gerard. 1990. "'We Are Not Doormats': The Influence of Feminism on Contemporary Evangelicals in the United States." In *Uncertain Terms: Negotiating Gender in American Culture,* ed. Faye Ginsberg and Anna L. Tsing, 98–117. Boston: Beacon Press.

Stark, Rodney, and Roger Finke. 2000. *Acts of Faith: Explaining the Human Side of Religion.* Berkeley: University of California Press.

St. Louis Post–Dispatch. 1999. "Promise Keepers Drop New Year's Day Rallies." April 2.

Suk, John D. 2000. "Onward Broken Soldiers: A Rhetorical Analysis of the Atlanta Promise Keepers Clergy Conference." In *The Promise Keepers: Essays on Masculinity and Christianity,* ed. Dane S. Claussen, 164–175. Jefferson, N.C.: McFarland & Company, Inc.

Sundquist, Eric J. 1996. *The Oxford W.E.B. DuBois Reader.* New York: Oxford University Press.

Swidler, Ann. 1986. "Culture in Action: Symbols and Strategies." *American Sociological Review* 51: 273–286.

———. 2001. Talk of Love: How Culture Matters. Chicago: University of Chicago Press.

Tubbs, Sharon. 2002. "The Promise Keepers Ride Again." *St. Petersburg Times,* April 21.

Turner, Bryan S. 1996. *The Body and Society: Explorations in Social Theory.* London: Sage.

Vara, Richard. 1998. "Mother Teresa Tops '97 Stories." *Houston Chronicle,* December 27.

Wall, Lucas. 2000. "Promise Keepers Celebrate Their Faith." *Milwaukee Journal Sentinel,* August 13.

Warner, R. Stephen. 1991. *New Wine in Old Wineskins: Evangelicals and Liberals in a Small–Town Church.* Berkeley: University of California Press.

———. 1997. "Religion, Boundaries, and Bridges." *Sociology of Religion* 58: 217–238.

Warner, R. Stephen, and Judith G. Wittner, eds. 1998. *Gatherings in Diaspora: Religious Communities and the New Immigration.* Philadelphia: Temple University Press.

Waters, Ken. 2000. "Who Are These Guys? The Promise Keepers' Media Relations Strategy for 'Stand in the Gap.'" In *The Promise Keepers: Essays on Masculinity and Christianity,* ed. Dane S. Claussen, 255–269. Jefferson, N.C.: McFarland & Company, Inc.

Weber, Max. [1922] 1963. *The Sociology of Religion.* Boston: Beacon Press.

———. 1947. "The Social Psychology of the World Religions." In *From Max Weber: Essay in Sociology,* ed. H. H. Gerth and C. Wright Mills, 267–301. New York: Oxford University Press.

Weber, Stu. 1993. *Tender Warrior: God's Intention for a Man*. Sister, Ore.: Multnomah.

———. 1997. *Four Pillars of a Man's Heart: King, Warrior, Mentor, Friend*. Sister, Ore.: Multnomah.

White, Gayle. 2000. "18,000 Heading to Promise Keepers Meeting in Atlanta." *Atlanta Journal and Constitution*, October 21.

Williams, Christine L. 1995. *Still a Man's World*. Berkeley: University of California Press.

Williams, Rhys H. 2001. "Promise Keepers: A Comment on Religion and Social Movements." In *Promise Keepers and the New Masculinity: Private Lives and Public Morality*, ed. Rhys H. Williams, 1–10. Lanham, Md.: Lexington Books.

Index

About the Author

JOHN P. BARTKOWSKI is an associate professor of sociology at Mississippi State University. He is the author of *Remaking the Godly Marriage: Gender Negotiation in Evangelical Families* and *Charitable Choices: Religion, Race, and Poverty in the Post-Welfare Era.*